Exploring Diversity in Entrepreneurship

Series editors

Alan L. Carsrud, Åbo Akademi University, Turku, Finland
Malin E. Brännback, Åbo Akademi University, Turku, Finland

More information about this series at http://www.springer.com/series/13172

Leon Schjoedt • Malin E. Brännback
Alan L. Carsrud
Editors

Understanding Social Media and Entrepreneurship

The Business of Hashtags, Likes, Tweets and Stories

Springer

Editors
Leon Schjoedt
Babson College
Wellesley Hills, MA, USA

Malin E. Brännback
School of Business and Economics
Åbo Akademi University
Åbo, Turku, Finland

Alan L. Carsrud
School of Business and Economics
Åbo Akademi University
Turku, Finland

ISSN 2567-7357 ISSN 2567-7659 (electronic)
Exploring Diversity in Entrepreneurship
ISBN 978-3-030-43452-6 ISBN 978-3-030-43453-3 (eBook)
https://doi.org/10.1007/978-3-030-43453-3

This Springer imprint is published by the registered company Springer Nature Switzerland AG
The registered company address is: Gewerbestrasse 11, 6330 Cham, Switzerland

Acknowledgment

We greatly appreciate the contributions of our internationally based colleagues, graduate students, friends, and fellow authors to this volume. Without their contributions to a better understanding of social media in an entrepreneurship context, this volume would not have come into existence.

We also want to thank Nicholas Philipson and Nitza Jones-Sepulveda at Springer for their assistance, encouragement, and support throughout the process of developing the idea for the book.

Lastly, we want to thank our families for allowing us the over the 2-year period, from idea to publication, for this volume to come into existence. A special thank you to Krittaya Sangboon for planting the seed that grew into an idea for a book that has eventually become this volume. We appreciate their tolerance for us to endeavor into this project – this volume. Thank you.

Contents

List of Figures

List of Tables

About the Contributing Authors and Editors

Olivia Goncalves Adkins is the Deputy Director of Foundation Psychology at the University of Birmingham, Dubai. Prior to that, she was the Head of Foundation Studies at Curtin University, Dubai. She holds an MSc in Business Psychology and is a graduate member of the British Psychological Society. Her research interests include aspects of consumer behavior such as brand personality and entrepreneurship.

Christian V. Baccarella is an Assistant Professor at the Friedrich-Alexander-Universität Erlangen-Nürnberg (FAU), Germany. Moreover, he is a Visiting Lecturer at the Sofia University St. Kliment Ohridski, Bulgaria, CampusM21, Germany, and at the Universität zu Lübeck, Germany. After studying business administration in Germany and England, he received his PhD in the field of innovation management from FAU. His current research interests include social media, business model innovation, consumer behavior, creativity, new product development, and crowdsourcing.

Antonina (Tonya) Bauman teaches strategic management in the School of Business, Emporia State University, KS, USA. She completed her PhD at the University of Surrey, UK. She has lived, studied, and worked in three countries – Russia, the UK, and the USA. Her primary focus of research is online trust.

Bari Bendell is an Assistant Professor in Management and Entrepreneurship at the Sawyer Business School, Suffolk University, Boston, MA. Her research interests frequently revolve around entrepreneurship and innovation with a focus on understanding organization decisions as well as the individuals making them. Dr. Bendell's research endeavors to enhance the field's understanding of gender and environmental sustainability within entrepreneurship and innovation. Her latest research can be found in the *Journal of Business Ethics*, the *Journal of Business Research*, and the *Journal of Small Business Management*, among others.

Malin E. Brännback, DSc, BSc (Pharm) Chaired Professor in International Business at Åbo Akademi University, School of Business and Economics, Finland, where she received her Doctorate in Management Science in 1996. She has been Vice Rector of the university and Dean of the Faculty of Social Sciences, Business, and Economics and has been Visiting Professor in Entrepreneurship at Stockholm Business School, Stockholm University. She also holds a BSc in Pharmacy. Prior to her return to Åbo Akademi University in 2003, she served as Associate Professor in Information Systems at the University of Turku and Professor of Marketing at Turku School of Economics. She has published widely on entrepreneurship, biotechnology business, and knowledge management. She has coauthored with Alan Carsrud several books, including *Entrepreneurship* (2005, Greenleaf Publishing), *Understanding the Entrepreneurial Mind: Opening the Black Box* (2009, Springer-Verlag), *Understanding Family Businesses: Undiscovered Approaches, Unique Perspectives, and Neglected Topics* (2012), and *Revisiting the Entrepreneurial Mind: Inside the Black Box – An Expanded Edition* (2017, Springer-Verlag). She is on the review board of the *Journal of Small Business Management.* Her current research interests are in entrepreneurial intentionality, entrepreneurial cognition, and entrepreneurial growth and performance in technology entrepreneurship family business and social media.

Alan L. Carsrud completed his PhD and MA in Social Psychology from the University of New Hampshire, his EcD (hc) from Åbo Akademi University in Finland, and his postdoctoral studies at the University of Texas at Austin while his undergraduate degrees in Psychology and Sociology with honors from Texas Christian University. He has served on the graduate faculties of SUNY Brockport, Texas A&M University, The University of Texas at Austin, the University of Southern California, the University of California at Los Angeles, Bond University, the Australian Graduate School of Management, Florida International University, Ryerson University, and Abo Akademi University. He has published over 200 research papers and 12 books in psychology, management, entrepreneurship, and family business. He is now retired and living with his husband in Texas Hill Country.

Thomas M. Cooney is Professor of Entrepreneurship at the Technological University Dublin, Academic Director of the Institute for Minority Entrepreneurship, and Adjunct Professor at the University of Turku, Finland. He is a Former President of the International Council for Small Business (2012–2013) and of the European Council for Small Business (2009–2011) and was Chair of the ICSB 2014 World Entrepreneurship Conference. He is a Policy Advisor in governments, European Commission, OECD, and other international organizations. He is a Director of four enterprises and works in various capacities with a range of businesses. He has published nine books and presented widely on the topic, particularly in the area of entrepreneurship education and training. Further details of his work can be found at www.thomascooney.com.

Khyati Shetty Datta is the Head of Curtin Business and School of Arts of Curtin University, Dubai. Prior to that, she was an Assistant Professor at the Manipal Academy of Higher Education in Dubai. She holds an MBA degree in Marketing, Postgraduate Degree in Human Resource Management, and a PhD in Brand Personality Congruence. Her research interests include brand personality and entrepreneurship. She is a Fellow HEA and is also a Recipient of the Global Leadership Award 2017 and GCC Women Leaders Award 2018.

Felix Diehlmann is a Senior Consultant at the global management consulting firm Oliver Wyman. His current clients include leading companies in the manufacturing and heavy industry practice. Prior, he completed his Master of Science in Industrial Engineering at the Friedrich-Alexander-Universität Erlangen-Nürnberg (FAU), Germany. At the Baden-Wuerttemberg Cooperative State University (DHBW), he received his Bachelor of Engineering degree while working for the manufacturing company WITTENSTEIN SE.

Shainaz Firfiray is an Associate Professor in the organization and human resource management group in Warwick Business School, University of Warwick. She received her PhD in Management from IE Business School, Spain. Her research interests include social identity, work-life balance, diversity, and family firms.

Jason R. Fitzsimmons is the Chairperson at the School of Business at Manipal Academy of Higher Education in Dubai as well as Dean of Executive Education. Before moving to Dubai, he spent a number of years in Singapore and Malaysia, firstly at U21Global Graduate School in Singapore and then as Dean of the School of Business at GlobalNxt University, Kuala Lumpur, Malaysia. Prior to that, he was with the Brisbane Graduate School of Business at Queensland University of Technology in Brisbane, Australia. His research interests are in entrepreneurship, entrepreneurial motivations, entrepreneurial intentions, and entrepreneurial opportunities. He obtained his PhD and MBA from the Queensland University of Technology.

Luis R. Gomez-Mejia is Regent's University Professor of Management and holder of the Weatherup/Overby Chair at W.P. Carey School of Business, Arizona State University. He rejoined Arizona State University in 2016 after holding the Ray and Milann Siegfried Professor of Management Chair at the University of Notre Dame. Prior to that, he held the Benton Cocanougher Chair in Management at Texas A&M University, and before that, he was a Council of 100 distinguished scholar, Regent's Professor, and Horace Steel Professor of Management in the W. P. Carey School of Business at Arizona State University. He has served as Consultant to numerous organizations since then including such blue chip firms as IBM, DuPont, and Honeywell. Dr. Gomez-Mejia is an internationally renowned Scholar. He has published over 270 articles appearing in the most prestigious management journals including the *Academy of Management Journal*, *Academy of Management Review*, *Administrative Science Quarterly*, *Strategic Management Journal*, *Journal of*

International Business Studies, *Journal of Management*, *Journal of Management Studies*, and *Personnel Psychology*. His research has been cited approximately 36,500 times, making him in the top 1 % of most cited management professors for the past 8 consecutive years (as per Thomson Reuters Web of Science). He has also written and/or edited 20 management books published by Prentice Hall, McGraw-Hill, Southwestern Press, JAI Press, and Grid. His books *Managing Human Resources* and *Management: People, Performance, Change* are used in most of the business week's top 50 business schools.

Lauri Haapanen is an Assistant Professor of International Business at the Oulu Business School, Finland. He has more than 20 years of experience in international management – including CEO, COO, CFO, and board memberships – in fast-growing firms varying from start-ups to multinational firms. His main research interests reside in firm key functions. He has been studying how the interplay between R&D, sales and marketing, and top management influences SMEs' international expansion, cross-border mergers and acquisitions, and MNEs' performance at international markets.

Saara Holma has a Master of Science in International Business Management, Oulu Business School, Finland. During her studies in Oulu Business School, she focused her research on the success factors of digital business models and brand building in social media in internationalizing SMEs. She works as a Marketing Manager in a fast-growing recruitment marketing company Duunitori Oy. Through her work, she has a lot of hands-on experience in digital marketing and social media and building strong brands in SMEs.

Pia Hurmelinna is a Professor of Marketing, especially International Business, at the University of Oulu, Oulu Business School, and an Adjunct Professor in Knowledge Management at the Lappeenranta University of Technology, School of Business and Management. She has published about 70 refereed articles in journals such as *Journal of Product Innovation Management*, *Industrial and Corporate Change*, *Industrial Marketing Management*, *International Business Review*, *R&D Management*, and *Technovation*. She has contributed to book chapters, over 140 conference papers, and other scientific and managerial publications. Her research has involved innovation management and appropriability issues. The research covers varying contexts like internationalization and interorganizational collaboration.

Etain Kidney is Head of School of Marketing at TU Dublin, Ireland's first technological university. Etain's research interests are in digital marketing with a focus on social media and entrepreneurship.

Carol Lucy joined Emporia State University as an Assistant Professor of Management after completing her PhD from Southern Illinois University, Carbondale; her MBA from Saint Louis University; and her Bachelor of Science in Computer Science from Southeast Missouri State. Her research interests include entrepreneurship and small business. She began her career as a systems analyst and brings 30 years of industry and leadership experience to the classroom to assist students to learn the skills they will use every day in a practical and interactive classroom environment. She desires to provide students the opportunity to collaborate, innovate, and create ventures.

Atthaphon Mumi is a Lecturer of Management and Entrepreneurship at Mahasarakham Business School, Mahasarakham University, Thailand. He earned his PhD in Entrepreneurship from the University of Massachusetts Lowell, MA, USA. His research interests broadly include the entrepreneurial process, corporate entrepreneurship, digital entrepreneurship, organizational strategy, and social media. He serves as the Editorial Review Board Member of the journal *Small Business Economics* and *Journal of Entrepreneurship and Innovation in Emerging Economies*.

Shahrokh Nikou, DSc is Docent in Information Systems and a Senior Lecturer of Information Studies at the School of Business and Economics, Åbo Akademi University, Finland, where he received his PhD. He completed his MSc in Computer Networks from the Royal Institute of Technology, Stockholm, Sweden. His research interests relate to multidimensionality of literacies (e.g., digital and information) with the especial focus on the entrepreneurship and the generational differences. He has practical and academic experience in designing digital business models for global organizations and European SMEs. He is a Member of the editorial board *Telematics and Informatics*, *Electronic Markets*, *International Journal of Web Engineering and Technology* (*IJWET*), *Journal of Electronic Commerce in Organizations* (*JECO*), and *International Journal of Electronic Business Research* (*IJEBR*). He has over 55 articles in journals and conference proceedings in his area of expertise.

Thao Phuong Orrensalo is a PhD Candidate in Information Studies at the Åbo Akademi University. Her research interest relate to entrepreneurship and business start-ups and how digital transformation affects entrepreneurs. In particular, her research focuses on the impact of digital literacy and information literacy on new business creation.

Sona Sareen has the unusual claim of having achieved three master's degrees in three countries (MBA in India, MSc in Retail Management in Scotland, MSc in Digital Marketing in Ireland) and has received several distinctions and awards during her academic career. She also has over 14 years of industry experience as a Retail Management and Marketing Professional in the Hospitality and Retail sectors in multi-geographical locations.

Christian W. Scheiner is a Professor at the Universität zu Lübeck (Germany) where he is the Director of the Institute for Entrepreneurship and Business Development and the Head of the Start-up Consultancy. He is a Visiting Lecturer at the Sofia University St. Kliment Ohridski, Bulgaria, and has a second membership as Professor in the Faculty of Business Administration at the Christian-Albrechts-Universität zu Kiel (CAU), Germany. His research focus on the human side of entrepreneurial and innovative behavior. His recent interests tackle the issues around the intersection of social psychology and innovative/entrepreneurial behavior and the relationship between morality and innovation as well as entrepreneurship.

Leon Schjoedt, PhD is an Entrepreneurship Research Scholar at Babson College, USA. He earned his PhD from the award-winning doctoral program in Entrepreneurship at the University of Colorado Boulder. Beginning with his doctoral dissertation, his research continues to focus on entrepreneurial behavior – the intersection between entrepreneurship and organizational behavior. He has presented his research at numerous academic meetings, including the annual meeting for the Academy of Management and Babson College Entrepreneurship Research Conference. Leon has published more than 60 articles and book chapters, including *Entrepreneurship Theory and Practice*, *Journal of High Technology Management Research*, *International Journal of Entrepreneurial Behaviour & Research*, *Organizational Dynamics*, and *Small Business Economics*. In 2015, his research has been featured in *The Wall Street Journal*.

Diane M. Sullivan is an Associate Professor at the University of Dayton. She completed her PhD in 2006 at the University of Central Florida. Her research interests include early-stage entrepreneurial phenomena (e.g., networks, knowledge, and early growth), gender and entrepreneurship, and organizational creativity. She has published in journals such as the *Journal of Organizational Behavior*, *Journal of Management Studies*, *Entrepreneurship Theory and Practice*, *Journal of Business and Psychology*, *Journal of Small Business Management*, and *Journal of Managerial Psychology*. She has served as an Executive Officer (Secretary) for the Entrepreneurship Division of the Academy of Management from 2016 to 2022.

Gunilla Widén, DSc is Professor of Information Studies at Åbo Akademi University (ÅAU) and Adjunct Professor in Information Management at the University of Tampere, both in Finland. Her research interests are within two main areas, knowledge management and information behavior, with the aim to understand motives behind information and knowledge-sharing using, for example, information culture and social capital theory as well as to explore how social media affect information behavior among different groups in society. She has led several large research projects financed by the Academy of Finland, investigating key skills in information society as well as various aspects of social media, information behavior, and information literacy. She has recently been involved in European projects on youth information service development, has published widely in her areas of expertise, and has been appointed expert in several evaluation committees.

Part I
Social Media in Entrepreneurship Research: Where Are We?

Chapter 1
Social Media in an Entrepreneurship Context

Leon Schjoedt, Malin E. Brännback, and Alan L. Carsrud

Abstract In this introduction we set the stage for the chapters that make up this book. We have clustered the invited contributions in a manner that should facilitate reader's understanding of social media within an entrepreneurial context. This volume is not intended to be an exhaustive review of the literature on social media nor is it an extensive review of the role social media plays in entrepreneurial ventures. What it does explore are various aspects of how the social media in the twenty-first century has impacted entrepreneurial behaviors. We hope these chapters will stimulate future research on social media in an entrepreneurship context.

Keywords Context · Digital media · Entrepreneurship · Information · Social media

1.1 Introduction

One may argue that today's social media environment is merely a continuation of the communication revolutions that began with the development of language abilities in humans tens of thousands of years ago. It is merely the next step in the multimedia progression of smoke signals to the written word, movable type, telegraphs, radio, television, and now the Internet. That said, what makes social media today different is the ability to add content to the process as well as immediately respond to digitally presented information.

Online social media, like Facebook and YouTube, flourish in our global society, across organizations and countries, and among people. In fact, having access to

L. Schjoedt (✉)
Entrepreneurship Division, Babson College, Babson Park, MA, USA

M. E. Brännback (✉) · A. L. Carsrud
School of Business and Economics, Åbo Akademi University, Turku, Finland
e-mail: malin.brannback@abo.fi

L. Schjoedt et al. (eds.), *Understanding Social Media and Entrepreneurship*, Exploring Diversity in Entrepreneurship,
https://doi.org/10.1007/978-3-030-43453-3_1

social media is becoming an important prerequisite for being a digital citizen, even in societies that restrict such access. Social media are characterized as ubiquitous information systems (UIS) which means that they are available all the time everywhere to an ever increasing number of people regardless of economic status and political environment.

There is no denying that the use of social media is big and growing. Today, with a total worldwide population of 7.8 billion, there are an estimated 3.7 billion active social media users. The Internet which is less than 60 years old has 4.54 billion users (Smith, 2020a). For example, Facebook has 2.4 billion users and YouTube roughly 2 billion users with WhatsApp (1.6 billion) and WeChat (1 billion) trailing close behind. Facebook is adding 500,000 new users every day – or 6 new profiles every second. In the USA, Facebook is used by 69 percent and YouTube by 73 percent of the population (Clement, 2019; Perrin & Anderson, 2019). Social media use is not just a North American activity. In Finland, 63 percent of the population use Facebook, while in Denmark, 53 percent of Internet users used Facebook on a daily basis (Tankovska, 2019a, 2019b). While Facebook is largely missing from China (Zucchi, 2019), the domestic equivalent reportedly have millions of users.

India, USA, and Indonesia rank among the top three Facebook-using countries (with Thailand ranked number eight in the world) according to Leesa-Nguansuk (2018). In the USA, the use of social media varies depending on age according to a Pew Research Center survey conducted in February, 2019, with the pattern in social media use remaining similar in 2019 relative to 2018 (Perrin & Anderson, 2019).

While social media is used for personal and professional purposes, the choice of social media with respect to personal and professional use seems to vary widely. In the USA, younger users between 18 and 24 years of age tend to use Snapchat and Instagram and more experienced people (40+ years of age) tend to use Facebook and YouTube (Pew Research Center in Perrin & Anderson, 2019). Organizations appear to prefer Twitter, as do some political figures.

In spite thereof, Twitter only has 145 million daily users (Smith, 2020b), which is not a lot compared to the number of active daily Facebook users. Interestingly, 83 percent of Fortune 500 companies have a presence on Twitter (Bennett, 2014), whereas only 20 companies of these Fortune 500 companies actually engage with their customers on Facebook (Smith, 2020a). At the same time, 78 percent of people who complain to a brand via Twitter expect a response within an hour (Vaughan, 2014). There is a lot of money involved in social media. For example, in 2019, USD 90 billion was spent on social network advertising (Smith, 2020a). But social media is much more than just another virtual advertising billboard, abet one in which there is two-way, if not multiple way, communication.

Given these numbers, social media may be considered as a massive digital infrastructure that offers tremendous opportunities for companies and, certainly, for entrepreneurs. Before we go there let us take a step back to take a brief look at the rather short period of development and offer a definition of social media.

1.2 What Is Social Media?

We do not have to go all the way back to the dawn of civilization (although similar revolutions in communication have occurred such as the Guttenberg Bible ushering in moveable type) to appreciate the explosive evolution of social media. The current crop of digital natives, those who have grown up in the digital world, probably will argue that anything before the World Wide Web is prehistoric. We follow the convention that social media as we know it today was coined around 2003/2004 with the launch of Myspace and Facebook (Kaplan & Haenlein, 2010). Among IT professionals, the earliest version of social media was the creation of Usenet, which was a network community where mostly computer wizards and nerds hung out to exchange ideas and experiences. This was a government-funded project by the US Defense Advanced Research Projects Agency (DARPA) and largely limited to large research universities in the United States (Wikipedia "DARPA", 2020a).

The basis for social media of today is the launch of the World Wide Web (WWW) in 1989 and the user-friendly Mosaic browser. These two technological innovations were critical for the diffusion of the Internet and the web as a worldwide commodity and a commercial breakthrough. It became possible for private persons and companies to create a web presence via homepages. Most of these were rather simple and rather awful at first (Sterne, 1995, 1996). Around the mid-1990s there was an explosion in Internet volume with some companies catching on fast to the potential of the WWW while most companies did not quite appreciate the potential power of this global communication media. Most companies approached the Internet and the WWW with old school market and corporate communication strategies (Armstrong & Hagel III, 1996; Benjamin & Wigand, 1995; Brännback, 1997; Brännback & Puhakainen, 1998; Hoffman & Novak, 1996; McKenna, 1995; Rayport & Sviokla, 1994, 1995). Even worse, many firms had no Internet strategy at all. At the same time, a paradigm shift began to emerge in market communication from one-to-one communication to one-to-many communication or many-to-many communication (Hoffman & Novak, 1996). That is, it was technologically possible to employ multiple approaches to communication, but most companies were stuck on using the web as a one-to-one basis.

While the software technology for social media became increasingly available, the hardware was still hampered by lack of mobility of desktop computers and limited number of laptop computers among nonprofessional users. Early visionaries had proposed computers and other electronic devices would be portable and potentially the size of today's smartphones and tablet computers, also known as tablets (Weiser, 1991). By the mid-1990s, new social networking websites began to emerge with the "widely considered to be the very first social networking site" of GeoCities, appearing in November 1994, followed by Classmates in December 1995 and SixDegrees in May 1997 (Edosomwan, Prakasan, Kouame, Watson, & Seymour, 2011; Wikipedia "Social media", 2020c). These early entrepreneurial ventures recognized the potential inherent in social media and sought to exploit it. For social media to diffuse into an everyday global commodity, the introduction of mobile technology and high-speed Internet was absolutely critical. This imperative shift began to occur in the early 2000s with smartphones becoming widespread in use (Wikipedia "Smartphone", 2020b) and the introduction of the iPad in 2010, the first mass market tablet to achieve widespread market acceptance (Wikipedia "Social media", 2020c; Wikipedia "Tablet", 2020d).

Today, many of us can easily produce a list of social media platforms with which we, as users, are familiar. These may include Facebook, YouTube, Instagram, Twitter, WhatsApp, Tinder, Wikipedia, and many more. Today, the real challenge is to try and categorize social media in a meaningful way. In the academic literature, social media refers to "computer-mediated tools that make it possible for anyone to create, circulate, share, and exchange information in a variety of formats and with multiple communities" (Leonardi & Vaast, 2017, p. 150).

Another approach in considering social media is to rely on a few theories in the fields of media and social processes. Kaplan and Haenlein (2010), thus, arrive at two defining dimensions: social presence/media richness on one hand and self-presentation/self-disclosure on the other to posit that social media refers to "A group of Internet-based applications that build on the ideological and technological foundations of Web 2.0 and that allow the creation and exchange of user-generated content" (p. 61). Also in line with these two dimensions, Carr and Hayes (2015) define social media as "Internet-based channels that allow users to opportunistically interact and selectively self-present, either in real-time or asynchronously, with both broad and narrow audiences who derive value from user-generated content and the perception of interaction with others" (p. 50). This shows that the two dimensions allow a series of more or less comprehensive definitions of social media and for us to include a wider palette of different social media, blogs and microblogs, collaborative projects such as Wikipedia, social networking sites like Facebook and Instagram, content communities (e.g., YouTube), virtual social worlds, and virtual game worlds. The dimensions also allow for a short definition: *Social media refers to Internet-based applications that facilitate social networking and the creation and exchange of user generated content.*

1.3 Social Media, Businesses, and Entrepreneurship

Considering that a basic aspect of human behavior is to socialize, the volume of social media users, and the way social media has evolved in a relatively few years, it is no surprise that how we consume social media impacts our behavior and, in turn, organizations such as new ventures. There are, for example, significant differences in behavior between digital natives and digital immigrants (i.e., persons born or brought up before the widespread use of digital technology) as to how they use these ubiquitous information systems (Brännback, Nikou, & Bouwman, 2017; Nikou, Mezei, & Brännback, 2018; Vodanovich, Sundaram, & Myers, 2010).

The changes in our behavior impact institutions at all levels as social media changes how we learn, how we read, and, more generally, how we build relationships and interact. This is also evident in how social media changes consumers' buying and consumption behavior (Alalwan, Rana, Dwivedi, & Algharabat, 2017; Alves, Fernandes, & Raposo, 2016; Wang, Pauleen, & Zhang, 2016). In part, this is because social media impacts brand and image building (Agnihotri, Dingus, Hu, & Krush, 2016; Schivinski & Dabrowski, 2016), brand performances, and brand revenue generation (Singh & Sonnenburg, 2012) through its impact on marketing communication (Kozinets, De Valck, Wojnicki, & Wilner, 2010; Taiminen & Karjaluoto, 2015). Further, social media allows new ventures to have an international presence from the very start, a topic addressed in this volume by Hurmelinna-Laukkanen, Haapanen, and Holma (2020).

Thus, social media offers substantial potential for entrepreneurs, especially for start-ups, with limited resources to engage in market communication to build brand awareness at relatively low, or very low, costs (Parveen, Jaafar, & Ainin, 2016.) As such, social media is an external enabler for entrepreneurs, family businesses, SMEs, and large organizations (Leonardi & Vaast, 2017; von Briel, Davidsson, & Recker, 2018). That being said, everything that looks like gold may not actually be gold. This has led scholars to examine the dark side of social media (Baccarella, Wagner, Kietzmann, & McCarthy, 2018). Therefore, when we consider social media in an entrepreneurship context, we also need to consider the dark side of social media in entrepreneurship as is, for example, provided in this volume by Baccarella, Scheiner, and Diehlmann (2020).

As the preceding considerations show, knowledge about social media in existing businesses is still somewhat limited. It may be considered in its embryonic stage. However, this body of research on social media in a business context is more developed than the literature on social media in an entrepreneurship context. That the literature on social media in entrepreneurship is scant is shown by a couple of recent reviews of the literature (Olanrewaju, Hossain, Whiteside, & Mercieca, 2020; Secundo, Mele, Vecchio, & Degennaro, 2020). Even though the literature is limited, it is published in- and outside entrepreneurship-oriented outlets. In this volume Bauman and Lucy (2020) provide a review of the literature that is structured around important concepts in entrepreneurship like entrepreneurial opportunities.

Early research include works on using social media as platform for new venture creation and opportunity recognition (Khajeheian, 2013; Schjoedt, 2018), the challenges of small businesses in adopting social media tools (Durkin, McGowan, & McKeown, 2013; Michaelidou, Siamagka, & Christodoulides, 2011; Siamagka, Christodoulides, Michaelidou, & Valvi, 2015), the role of social media in entrepreneurial finance (Aggarwal, Gopal, Gupta, & Singh, 2012; Jin, Wu, & Hitt, 2017; Mumi, Obal, & Yang, 2019; Yang & Berger, 2017), and on specific social media platforms (e.g., Fischer & Reuber, 2014; Reuber & Fischer, 2011). Because of the potential for profound effects that social media may cause in an entrepreneurship context, and the fragmented nature of early research, this book presents an effort to integrate and structure the present body of literature on social media in an entrepreneurship context.

1.4 The Structure of This Volume

We now turn to integrate the chapters included in this volume in terms of the key foci and in an attempt to provide a context in which to view how the chapters relate to one another and in the context of published literature reviews (Olanrewaju et al., 2020; Secundo et al., 2020). Let us start with the recent reviews to set the stage. Olanrewaju et al. (2020) consider the literature in terms of critical theories and research methods used in the early research on social media and entrepreneurship. They find that most research investigates factors driving entrepreneurs' social media adoption and use and that entrepreneurs' use of social media has moved beyond marketing to business networking, information search, and crowdfunding to improve the innovation and new venture performance.

Secundo et al. (2020) find that the literature on social media in an entrepreneurship context is scant and fragmented and is dominated by unrelated research. Based on their content analysis, these scholars find four major research streams in the social media and entrepreneurship literature: (1) social media as technologies for entrepreneurial learning and self-employment, (2) entrepreneurs' use of social media for marketing purposes, (3) social media networking as enablers of end entrepreneurial ecosystems, and (4) entrepreneurs' use of social media to identify opportunities. Consistent with the review by Olanrewaju et al. (2020), Secundo et al. also observe that early research tend to focus on social media as a marketing tool while the more recent research considered in their study tend to be broader in scope by investigating entrepreneurial learning, network, ecosystems, and opportunity identification.

In this volume, Bauman and Lucy (2020) provide a review of the literature on social media as a basis for opportunities for entrepreneurs. Consistent with two other published reviews (Olanrewaju et al., 2020; Secundo et al., 2020), Bauman and Lucy note that social media was and continues to be mostly considered as a means of communication and as marketing tools. Focusing on opportunities social media present to entrepreneurs, they consider how social media impacts business models including the challenges entrepreneurs face with regard to social media. These challenges include the need to revise business models, technical knowledge, lack of appreciation of how social media impacts a business model in moving customers from passive to active influencers, and whether to launch a new venture based on a social media platform-based business model.

Further, based in the context of business models, Bauman and Lucy (2020) consider how social media presents opportunities to entrepreneurs in terms of opportunity recognition; resource acquisition and management, including knowledge sharing and management; institutional support for new ventures; and founding such as crowdfunding and virtual currencies. They place their considerations in the context of a model that originates with the effect opportunity recognition and exploitation have on the venture, knowledge, and surrounding institutions and how these relationships are mediated by the scope, scale, speed, and source of social media in the venture's digital business strategy.

In combination, these three reviews reveal that the literature on social media in an entrepreneurship context is emerging as a research topic. It also appears that the early research tends to be focused on more conventional topics in entrepreneurship, such as opportunity recognition, and the use of social media as a marketing tool. This more conventional approach may limit the potential for future research on social media in entrepreneurial contexts similarly to the narrowed focus on firm performance in the strategic management literature since inception and on opportunity recognition in the entrepreneurship literature during the 1990s and early 2000s. The reviews, combined, show there is a need to consider what we already know from the entrepreneurship literature in the context of social media. In this volume, this is done by the considerations of Sullivan and Bendell (2020) on gender; Mumi (2020) on effectuation; Sareen, Kidney, and Cooney (2020) on entrepreneurial teams; and Hurmelinna-Laukkanen et al. (2020) on international entrepreneurship.

The reviews also admonish us to avoid the literature on social media and entrepreneurship from becoming too focused and insular as additional research is conducted and published (George, Kotha, & Zheng, 2008). In this volume less conventional topics in entrepreneurship and social media research are included to stimulate new research to enlarge the entrepreneurship literature and research on social media in an entrepreneurship context. One such topic is information literacy. Nikou, Brännback, Orrensalo, and Widén (2020) investigate the role of information literacy and source selection in social media in entrepreneurship. They argue that information literacy is critical to locate, use, and evaluate information tools as well as information sources to solve a given problem. Just because a person owns a smartphone or a tablet does not make that person information literate. As such these scholars address an issue implicitly addressed in the review by Bauman and Lucy (2020), in this volume, on technical knowledge in the use of social media. Consistent with a substantial body of research on international entrepreneurship Hurmelinna-Laukkanen et al. (2020), in this volume, examine a sample of Western business ventures. To step away from the more conventional contexts of entrepreneurship and social media in Western societies, in this volume, Datta, Adkins, and Fitzsimmons (2020) examine a type of entrepreneur unique to social media, social media influencers. This type of entrepreneur is also addressed in this volume by Bauman and Lucy (2020) and by Sareen et al. (2020). Unlike other scholars, Datta, Adkins, and Fitzsimmons investigate social media influencers in an Islamic context, a context that has received limited attention in the literature on social media and entrepreneurship (Schjoedt, Fitzsimmons, Datta, & Sangboon, 2018).

Unlike the conventional approach to new topics in academic research that tend focus on the potential for betterment, in this volume, Baccarella et al. (2020) consider the dark side of entrepreneurs' use of social media to enrich our understanding and consideration of social media. Like other authors in this volume, Firfiray and Luis Gomez-Mejia (2020) consider the opportunities and challenges inherent in social media but unlike the other authors their considerations pertain to family businesses. While the family business literature has grown substantially, Firfiray and Luis Gomez-Mejia (2020) bring a new theory-driven perspective to this literature by using an affordance lens. While Sullivan and Bendell (2020), in this volume, use an affordance lens in the context of gender, Firfiray and Luis Gomez-Mejia (2020) use an affordance lens to illustrate how social media assist family businesses in their pursuit of socioemotional wealth.

As shown by our comments, research on social media in an entrepreneurship context holds substantial potential to further the entrepreneurship literature by extending our knowledge on established topics and to enlarge the literature by including new or little considered topics in entrepreneurship research. It is our hope that this volume will stimulate future research to generate a better and more nuanced understanding of social media in an entrepreneurship context.

References

Aggarwal, R., Gopal, R., Gupta, A., & Singh, H. (2012). Putting money where the mouths are: The relation between venture financing and electronic word-of-mouth. *Information Systems Research, 23*(3-part-2), 976–992.

Agnihotri, R., Dingus, R., Hu, M. Y., & Krush, M. T. (2016). Social media: Influencing customer satisfaction in B2B sales. *Industrial Marketing Management, 53*, 172–180.

Alalwan, A. A., Rana, N. P., Dwivedi, Y. K., & Algharabat, R. (2017). Social media in marketing: A review and analysis of the existing literature. *Telematics and Informatics, 34*(7), 1177–1190.

Alves, H., Fernandes, C. J., & Raposo, M. (2016). Social media marketing: A literature review and implications. *Psychology & Marketing, 33*(12), 1029–1038.

Armstrong, A., & Hagel III, J. (1996). The real value of online communities. *Harvard Business Review, 74*(3), 134–141.

Baccarella, C., Scheiner, C., & Diehlmann, F. (2020). Devil on the entrepreneur's shoulder – Analyzing the relationships between moral disengagement, founders' motives and unethical behavior of entrepreneurs on social media. In L. Schjoedt, M. E. Brännback, & A. L. Carsrud (Eds.), *Social media and entrepreneurship: The business of hashtags, likes, and tweets*. New York: Springer.

Baccarella, C. V., Wagner, T. F., Kietzmann, J. H., & McCarthy, I. P. (2018). Social media? It's serious! Understanding the dark side of social media. *European Management Journal, 36*(4), 431–438.

Bauman, A., & Lucy, C. (2020). Social media: Exploring entrepreneurial opportunities. In L. Schjoedt, M. E. Brännback, & A. L. Carsrud (Eds.), *Social media and entrepreneurship: The business of hashtags, likes, and tweets*. New York: Springer.

Benjamin, R., & Wigand, R. T. (1995). Electronic markets and virtual value chains on the Information Superhighway. *Sloan Management Review, 36*(2), 62–72.

Bennett, S. (2014). *83% of Fortune 500 companies have active Twitter profiles*. Retrieved from https://www.adweek.com/digital/fortune-500-twitter-2014/ on 25 January 2020.

Brännback, M. (1997). Is the internet changing the dominant logic of marketing? *European Management Journal, 15*(6), 698–707.

Brännback, M., Nikou, S., & Bouwman, H. (2017). Value Systems and Intentions to interact in social media: The digital natives. *Telematics and Informatics, 34*(4), 365–381.

Brännback, M., & Puhakainen, J. (1998). Web marketing: Has the distinction between products and services become obsolete? *Journal of Market-Focused Management, 3*(1), 47–58.

Carr, C. T., & Hayes, R. A. (2015). Social Media: Defining, developing, and divining. *Atlantic Journal of Communication, 23*(1), 46–65.

Clement, J. (2019). *Global social networks ranked by number of users 2019*. Retrieved from https://www.statista.com/statistics/272014/global-social-networks-ranked-by-number-of-users/ on 20 January 2020.

Datta, K. S., Adkins, O., & Fitzsimmons, J. R. (2020). Entrepreneurship and social media influencers in an Islamic context. In L. Schjoedt, M. E. Brännback, & A. L. Carsrud (Eds.), *Social media and entrepreneurship: The business of hashtags, likes, and tweets*. New York: Springer.

Durkin, M., McGowan, P., & McKeown, N. (2013). Exploring social media adoption in small to medium-sized enterprises in Ireland. *Journal of Small Business and Enterprise Development, 20*(4), 716–734.

Edosomwan, S. O., Prakasan, S. K., Kouame, D., Watson, J., & Seymour, T. (2011). The history of social media and its impact on business. *Journal of Applied Management and Entrepreneurship, 16*(3), 79–91.

Firfiray, S., & Luis Gomez-Mejia, L. (2020). In pursuit of socioemotional wealth: The affordances of social media in family firms. In L. Schjoedt, M. E. Brännback, & A. L. Carsrud (Eds.), *Social media and entrepreneurship: The business of hashtags, likes, and tweets*. New York: Springer.

Fischer, E., & Reuber, A. R. (2014). Online entrepreneurial communication: Mitigating uncertainty and increasing differentiation via Twitter. *Journal of Business Venturing, 29*(4), 565–583.

George, G., Kotha, R., & Zheng, Y. (2008). The puzzle of insular domains: A longitudinal study of knowledge structuration and innovation in biotechnology firms. *Journal of Management Studies, 45*, 1448–1474.

Hoffman, D. L., & Novak, T. P. (1996). Marketing in hypermedia computer-mediated environment: Conceptual foundations. *Journal of Marketing, 60*(3), 50–68.

Hurmelinna-Laukkanen, P., Haapanen, L., & Holma, S. (2020). Social media and small entrepreneurial firms' internationalization. In L. Schjoedt, M. E. Brännback, & A. L. Carsrud (Eds.), *Social media and entrepreneurship: The business of hashtags, likes, and tweets*. New York: Springer.

Jin, F., Wu, A., & Hitt, L. (2017). Social is the new financial: How startup social media activity influences funding outcomes. *Academy of Management Proceedings, 2017*.

Kaplan, A. M., & Haenlein, M. (2010). Users of the world, unite! The challenges and opportunities of Social Media. *Business Horizons, 53*(1), 59–68.

Khajeheian, D. (2013). New venture creation in social media platform: Towards a framework for media entrepreneurship. In M. Friedrichsen & W. Mühl-Benninghaus (Eds.), *Handbook of social media management* (pp. 125–142). Heidelberg, Germany: Springer.

Kozinets, R. V., De Valck, K., Wojnicki, A. C., & Wilner, S. J. S. (2010). Networked narratives: Understanding word-of-mouth marketing in online communities. *Journal of Marketing, 74*(2), 71–89.

Leesa-Nguansuk, S. (2018). *Thailand makes top 10 in social media use*. Retrieved from https://www.bangkokpost.com/tech/1420086/thailand-makes-top-10-in-social-media-use on 20 January 2020.

Leonardi, P. M., & Vaast, E. (2017). Social media and their affordances for organizing: A review and agenda for research. *Academy of Management Annals, 11*(1), 150–188.

McKenna, R. (1995). Real-time marketing. *Harvard Business Review, 73*(3), 87–95.

Michaelidou, N., Siamagka, N. T., & Christodoulides, G. (2011). Usage, barriers and measurement of social media marketing: An exploratory investigation of small and medium B2B brands. *Industrial Marketing Management, 40*, 1153–1159.

Mumi, A. (2020). Effectual entrepreneur and the use of social media for opportunity recognition. In L. Schjoedt, M. E. Brännback, & A. L. Carsrud (Eds.), *Social media and entrepreneurship: The business of hashtags, likes, and tweets*. New York: Springer.

Mumi, A., Obal, M., & Yang, Y. (2019). Investigating social media as a firm's signaling strategy through an IPO. *Small Business Economics, 53*(3), 631–645.

Nikou, S., Brännback, E., Orrensalo, T. P., & Widén, G. (2020). Social media and entrepreneurship – The role of digital source selection and information literacy. In L. Schjoedt, M. E. Brännback, & A. L. Carsrud (Eds.), *Social media and entrepreneurship: The business of hashtags, likes, and tweets*. New York: Springer.

Nikou, S., Mezei, J., & Brännback, M. (2018). Digital natives' interactive behaviour on social media: Value systems and gender. *Telematics and Informatics, 35*(2), 421–435.

Olanrewaju, A.-S. T., Hossain, M. A., Whiteside, N., & Mercieca, P. (2020). Social media and entrepreneurship research: A literature review. *International Journal of Information Management, 50*, 90–110.

Parveen, F., Jaafar, N. I., & Ainin, S. (2016). Social media's impact on organizational performance and entrepreneurial orientation in organizations. *Management Decision, 54*(9), 2208–2234.

Perrin, A., & Anderson, M. (2019). *Share of U.S. adults using social media, including Facebook, is mostly unchanged since 2018.* Retrieved from https://www.pewresearch.org/fact-tank/2019/04/10/share-of-u-s-adults-using-social-media-including-facebook-is-mostly-unchanged-since-2018/ on 20 January 2020.

Rayport, J. F., & Sviokla, J. (1994). Managing in the marketspace. *Harvard Business Review, 72*(6), 141–150.

Rayport, J. F., & Sviokla, J. (1995). Exploiting the virtual value chain. *Harvard Business Review, 73*(6), 141–150.

Reuber, A. R., & Fischer, E. (2011). Social interaction via new social media: (How) can interactions on Twitter affect effectual thinking and behavior? *Journal of Business Venturing, 26*(1), 1–18.

Sareen, S., Kidney, E., & Cooney, T. M. (2020). How is social media adopted by entrepreneurial teams? In L. Schjoedt, M. E. Brännback, & A. L. Carsrud (Eds.), *Social media and entrepreneurship: The business of hashtags, likes, and tweets*. New York: Springer.

Schivinski, B., & Dabrowski, D. (2016). The effect of social media communication on consumer perceptions of brands. *Journal of Marketing Communications, 22*(2), 189–214.

Schjoedt, L. (2018). Social media on opportunity recognition: The effects of entrepreneurs' attachment and control beliefs. *Academy of Management Proceedings, 2018*.

Schjoedt, L., Fitzsimmons, J., Datta, K. S., & Sangboon, K. (2018). *Emirati women entrepreneurs: The effects of work and family on life satisfaction*. Presented at the 11th Diana International Research Conference, Bangkok, Thailand, July 31 – August 2, 2018.

Secundo, G., Mele, G., Vecchio, P. D., & Degennaro, G. (2020). *Social media for entrepreneurship: Myth or reality? A structured literature review and a future research agenda*. Working Paper.

Siamagka, N. T., Christodoulides, G., Michaelidou, N., & Valvi, A. (2015). Determinants of social media adoption by B2B organizations. *Industrial Marketing Management, 51*, 89–99.

Singh, S., & Sonnenburg, S. (2012). Brand performance in social media. *Journal of Interactive Marketing, 26*(4), 189–197.

Smith, K. (2020a). *126 amazing social media statistics and facts*. Retrieved from https://www.brandwatch.com/blog/amazing-social-media-statistics-and-facts/#section-2 on 25 January 2020.

Smith, K. (2020b). *60 incredible and interesting Twitter stats and statistics*. Retrieved from https://www.brandwatch.com/blog/twitter-stats-and-statistics/ on January 25, 2020.

Sterne, J. (1995). *World wide web marketing*. New York: Wiley.

Sterne, J. (1996). *Customer service on the internet: Building relationships, increasing loyalty and staying competitive*. New York: Wiley.

Sullivan, D. M., & Bendell, B. (2020). Exploring the gendered nature of digital social networks. In L. Schjoedt, M. E. Brännback, & A. L. Carsrud (Eds.), *Social media and entrepreneurship: The business of hashtags, likes, and tweets*. New York: Springer.

Taiminen, H. M., & Karjaluoto, H. (2015). The usage of digital marketing channels in SMEs. *Journal of Small Business and Enterprise Development, 22*(4), 633–651.

Tankovska, H. (2019a). *Facebook usage frequency in Finland 2019*. https://www.statista.com/statistics/871870/facebook-usage-frequency-in-finland/. Retrieved 20 January 2020.

Tankovska, H. (2019b). *In Daily social media usage in Denmark 2018, by social media site*. Retrieved from https://www.statista.com/statistics/577440/daily-social-media-usage-in-denmark-by-site/ on 20 Janaury 2020.

Vaughan, P. (2014). *72% of people who complain on Twitter expect a response within an hour*. Retrieved from https://blog.hubspot.com/marketing/twitter-response-time-data on 25 January 2020.

Vodanovich, S., Sundaram, D., & Myers, M. (2010). Digital natives and ubiquitous information systems. *Information Systems Research, 21*, 711–723.
von Briel, F., Davidsson, P., & Recker, J. (2018). Digital technologies as external enablers of new venture creation in the IT hardware sector. *Entrepreneurship Theory and Practice, 42*(1), 47–69.
Wang, W. Y. C., Pauleen, D. J., & Zhang, T. (2016). How social media applications affect B2B communication and improve business performance in SMEs. *Industrial Marketing Management, 54*, 4–14.
Weiser, M. (1991). The computer for the twenty-first century. *Scientific American, 265*(3), 94–104.
Wikipedia. (2020a). *DARPA*. Retrieved from https://en.wikipedia.org/wiki/DARPA on 25 January 2020.
Wikipedia. (2020b). *Smart phone*. Retrieved from https://en.wikipedia.org/wiki/Smartphone on 25 January 2020.
Wikipedia. (2020c). *Social media*. Retrieved from https://en.wikipedia.org/wiki/Social_media on 25 January 2020.
Wikipedia. (2020d). *Tablet computer*. Retrieved from https://en.wikipedia.org/wiki/Tablet_computer 25 January 2020.
Yang, S., & Berger, R. (2017). Relation between start-ups' online social media presence and fundraising. *Journal of Science and Technology Policy Management, 8*(2), 161–180.
Zucchi, K. (2019). *Why Facebook is banned in China & how to access it*. Retrieved from https://www.investopedia.com/articles/investing/042915/why-facebook-banned-china.asp on 25 January 2020.

Chapter 2
Social Media: Exploring Entrepreneurial Opportunities

Antonina Bauman and Carol Lucy

Abstract The main purpose of this chapter is to review entrepreneurial opportunities presented by the social media. Although it grew over time and became a part of a business strategy, social media is still used mostly for communication purposes. Other areas of business transactions can gain from the social media as well. Creating value for customers, changing business models, and the environment in which a company operates are among those areas that are being overlooked by entrepreneurs. Businesses might see only the most visible part of the social media – online presence and marketing communication. However, there is more to social media than just online communication.

Keywords Social media · Entrepreneurial opportunity · Digital entrepreneurship

2.1 Introduction

Originally the social media was developed for networking of friends, who wanted to share their interests. As a set of the Internet-based applications, the social media allowed users to share their experiences and memories by creating their own content accessible by others (Jones, Borgman, & Ulusoy, 2015).

Although it grew over time and became a part of a business strategy, social media is still used mostly for communication purposes as it helps to promote products, build brand awareness, and persuade customers to buy (Parveen, Jaafar, & Ainin, 2016; Shahizan, Norshuhada, Nor Laily, Sobihatun Nur, & Mohd Samsu, 2012). As shown in the previous chapters and extant literature on this topic, social media helps entrepreneurs to attract new customers with personal messages, generate traffic, and communicate with existing clients more efficiently (Schaupp & Bélanger, 2013; Taiminen & Karjaluoto, 2015).

A. Bauman (✉) · C. Lucy
Emporia State University, Emporia, KS, USA
e-mail: abauman@emporia.edu

L. Schjoedt et al. (eds.), *Understanding Social Media and Entrepreneurship*, Exploring Diversity in Entrepreneurship,
https://doi.org/10.1007/978-3-030-43453-3_2

Parveen et al. (2016) report that the company's use of social media for business purposes has a strong impact on that company's performance as it lowers costs and improves customer relationships and customers' access to information. Social media marketing is important for SME as it offers companies with small marketing budgets and opportunity to gain a community of potential customers and become more competitive (Jones et al., 2015; Toombs & Harlow, 2014). Hence previous research focused primarily on the impact of the social media on the marketing strategies, specifically advertising – creating awareness of the product, establishing positive public relations, and building consumer loyalty.

However, the impact of the social media on the business performance is multifaceted as, in addition to communicating value, it creates opportunities to develop that value (Amit & Zott, 2001) and change the environment in which a business operates. In the world dominated by digitalization, companies operate in an ecosystem that is characterized by interdependence of partners and communication across time zones, geographical distances, and business functions (Bharadwaj, El Sawy, Pavlou, & Venkatraman, 2013). To remain profitable, companies need to deliver value to customers in a manner that is different from competition not only in a type of products or technologies used but also through innovative business models (Schiavi & Behr, 2018). Business models reflect the functions performed by businesses in order to deliver value to customers. These functions include but not limited to obtaining resources, developing processes, establishing a network of partners, and creating a profit formula (Ruggieri, Savastano, Scalingi, Bala, & D'Ascenzo, 2018; Schiavi & Behr, 2018).

Using social media requires new approaches to a business strategy (Kaplan & Haenlein, 2010) as social media shifted creating messages and content from the environment controlled by a company to an uncontrolled environment created by a crowd. This change disrupted not only the marketing activities but also business transactions established by traditional business models. A move from the pipeline or chain business model to a platform-type impacts not only the company's infrastructure but the entire ecosystem in which a company operates as logistic is based on the network structure (Ruggieri et al., 2018).

With many benefits, social media presents challenges for entrepreneurs who might not fully understand the impact of social media on their businesses. They might see only the most visible part of it – online presence and marketing communication for building relations (Jones et al., 2015). However, there is more to social media than just online presence.

While small businesses recognize benefits of social media, some entrepreneurs experience challenges as they either are not technically savvy to use social media efficiently or they do not have time to be active online (Jones et al., 2015). Roy, Maxwell, and Carson (2014) showed that although small and medium enterprises (SMEs) appear to have understanding of the important role that social media plays in business, they do not use the social media to its maximum capacity. Posting pictures on the social media on a weekly basis is not sufficient. Multiple studies demonstrate a gap between a strategic potential and a real execution of social media strategy. Since social media is a very affordable strategic tool for small businesses with their limited resources (Schaupp & Bélanger, 2013), it is crucial to show SMEs how social media affects business performance.

2.2 Social Media

Over the last decade the Internet has evolved from one-way communication and retrieval of information into a two-way social media accommodating collaborative efforts of users around the world (Campbell, Pitt, Parent, & Berthon, 2011). Back in 2004, O'Reilly and Battelle coined the term "Web 2.0," which described this interactive nature of a new technology and referred to users' engagement as "harnessing collective intelligence" (O'Reilly & Battelle, 2009, p. 1). Among some of the unique characteristics of the Web 2.0 researchers identified a simple interface with sophisticated functionality, data-oriented collaboration, easy retrieval of the data, community building, and content co-creation (Bleicher, 2006; O'Reilly & Battelle, 2009; Soto-Acosta, Popa, & Palacios-Marqués, 2017). The nature of the Web 2.0 technologies gave birth to social media and social networking. Although sometimes these terms are used interchangeably, there is a difference. Social media is defined as the Internet-based applications or services that allow creation and exchange of the user-generated content (Boyd & Ellison, 2007; Kaplan & Haenlein, 2010) while social networking refers to the process of communicating by using social media tools. Thus, social media present spaces for publishing text, images, audio, and video files, but an act of watching, uploading, and sharing those files would be networking. The number of the social media users grows fast. When Pew Research Center (PRC) published its first report on social media adoption in 2005, only 5% of American adults used at least one social networking platform; in PRC's 2019 report, the number of social media users had risen to 72% (PRC, 2019).

Academic literature (Ainin, Parveen, Moghavvemi, Jaafar, & Mohd Shuib, 2015; Shahizan et al., 2012) shows that the use of social media has a positive impact on business transactions as it helps to promote existing products and communicate their benefits to customers and increase the number of product information requests, number of purchases, and sales volume. Previous research identified the most common business use of social media is to pursue marketing and communication goals. Utilizing interactive tools, companies engage customers and build product awareness and consumer loyalty which increase sales (Castronovo & Huang, 2012; Jones et al., 2015). Social networks allow businesses to communicate with customers in a more personal way, develop company's reputation, and create a particular image. However, the social media shifts the control over conversations from businesses to customers which presents a challenge for companies (Heller Baird & Parasnis, 2011) as it can have both positive and negative impact on a company (Becker, Nobre, & Kanabar, 2013). Consumer evaluations of a company's actions, product quality, and overall competence and company character are produced and distributed online (Etter, Ravasi, & Colleoni, 2019). As sharing of those evaluations is done through posting original messages on the networks and forwarding somebody else's posts, the role of a company's customer services is becoming crucial in building a company's reputation. The shift from the transactional to relational paradigm in business means emphasis on the customer relations, transparency, and public communication. Businesses need to find ways to communicate "with" rather than "to" a new generation of empowered online customers described by Jones, Temperley, and Lima (2009) as "consumanagers" as they can impact company's reputation and future.

Researchers agree that nobody can really determine the full scope of the potential impact of social media on businesses (Amit & Zott, 2001). However, we are beginning to recognize its importance on organizational performance and entrepreneurial orientation as literature shows that social media has a very strong impact on an organizations' performance, especially in terms of information accessibility, improved customer relations, and cost reduction (Parveen et al., 2016).

2.3 Entrepreneurship and Business Models

Entrepreneurship is understood as "the identification and exploitation of previously unexploited opportunities" (Hitt, Ireland, Camp, & Sexton, 2001, p. 480). This definition shows two aspects of entrepreneurial ventures – (1) recognizing and evaluating opportunities and (2) acting upon them. Those two aspects are separate as evaluating opportunities is a future-oriented activity while acting relates to present and sometimes immediate actions (Autio et al., 2013). Those actions include but are not limited to developing new products, entering new markets, creating new resources, or using available resources in an innovative way.

Together these two elements (recognizing opportunities and acting on them) present a foundation for a competitive advantage. A company has a competitive advantage when it pursues the value creating strategy that is not being implemented by any current or potential competitors and is difficult to imitate (Barney, 1991). A competitive advantage is achieved through a combination of a business model and a business strategy which allows to create, manage, and deliver value to customers (Amit & Zott, 2001; Wheelen, Hunger, Hoffman, & Bamford, 2015). A business model is understood as a set of business activities that describe how a company transacts with customers and partners (Standing & Mattsson, 2018; Teece, 2018) while a strategy is a plan that shows how to perform those activities differently from the rivals or how to choose different activities to remain sustainable and competitive (Porter, 1996; Wheelen et al., 2015).

Researchers conducted multiple studies of business models in an attempt to offer a system that would explain what determines success of a venture. For example, Chesbrough and Rosenbloom (2002) identified six functions of a business model: creating a value proposition, identifying a market segment, building a value chain, calculating the cost structure and profit potential, establishing the position of a company in a value network, and developing a competitive strategy. Osterwalder and Pigneur (2010) analyzed nine business model blocks: customer segment, value proposition, channels, customer relationships, revenue streams, key resources, key activities, key partnerships, and cost structure. El Sawy and Pereira (2013) focused on the digital environment and proposed the VISOR model – value proposition, interface, service platform, organizing model, and revenue.

A unifying element of any business model starts with the technical inputs and ends in economic outputs (Chesbrough & Rosenbloom, 2002). Success of a business model depends on how well a company can reshape its initial model and modify it around changes in the external environment in an attempt to take advantage of the social media. In fact, many current businesses (e.g., social influencers and crowdsourcing) did not exist prior to these advances in technology. Digital technologies impact how companies conduct business in general and specific business transactions. These changes alter business models used by entrepreneurs to create value, but the basic components of business models remain the same.

2.4 Opportunities for New Ventures

Social media created a push for business models' evolution from focusing on customers as passive participants to making them active contributors and co-creators of value as well as participants of business processes (Kao, Yang, Wu, & Cheng, 2016). Digital technologies gave a burst to new business models such as on-demand services, sharing extra capacities, and crowdsourcing (Suseno, Laurell, & Sick, 2018). New opportunities are still around for entrepreneurs, but what are those opportunities?

Opportunities arise when entrepreneurs see a situation that can develop into potential value and lead to profits by meeting customers' needs and market demands (Park, Sung, & Im, 2017). Usually this situation is created by the changes in the environment (technological, social and demographic, political, and regulatory) and might lead to favorable conditions for an individual (George, Parida, Lahti, & Wincent, 2016). As Shane and Venkataraman (2000) explained, in a traditional economy, entrepreneurial opportunities come in a variety of situations: new products, new materials, new information, alternative use of resources, and others. The scope of those categories is somewhat limited to the size of the traditional entrepreneurial network. However, new technological developments added a different perspective on a window of opportunities as they allow for global exploration within the virtual network. According to Davidson and Vaast (2010) digital economy presents opportunities for starting new ventures (business-related opportunities), learning new information about how to develop and expand (knowledge-related opportunities), and involving those actors that can help to break boundaries and support entrepreneurial activities (institution-related opportunities).

The first most noticeable trend from the impact of the social media is in the area of business-related opportunities: a shift from the pipe-type to platform-type business models. A traditional, or a pipe-type, model of delivering value shows a flow of business activities from inbound logistics to after-sales support services and was summarized by Michael Porter (1985) in his concept of the value chain. This model offers a clear separation of a business and its production activities from a customer purchasing and using a product (Ruggieri et al., 2018). If an intermediary (such as a retailer) is used, there is no need for producers to interact with customers, as this is what the third party does. Leveraging digital tools offered an opportunity to businesses and customers to engage and co-create value (Kao et al., 2016). Platform-type business models are designed for websites or mobile applications. Companies find and match producers to customers as their main assets are information and interactions (Ruggieri et al., 2018). They serve as intermediaries facilitating transactions between providers of products and users of those products. The goal of the platform business model is to get providers and customers to interact through the platform (Kumar, Lahiri, & Dogan, 2018). This shift presents an opportunity for businesses to adjust their current model in an attempt to find a niche in a new market.

As more and more businesses create value based on the new technologies, a concept of digital entrepreneurship has been introduced. Digital entrepreneurship emphasizes the use of technology not only in finding new ways of conducting business (Amit & Zott, 2001; Suseno et al., 2018) but also in evaluating opportunities, exploiting those opportunities, and making decisions about the entry in or exit the marketplace (Standing & Mattsson, 2018).

New technologies present another opportunity to grow by gaining knowledge of business practices. That knowledge serves as a source of a competitive advantage in a marketplace. On the one hand, knowledge is globally dispersed, but on the other, communication technologies erase borders and eliminate distances between sources of knowledge (Papa, Santoro, Tirabeni, & Monge, 2018).

Knowledge is needed to make decisions about distribution of resources and leverage the most value out of a combination of those resources which contributes to innovation (Darroch, 2005). Knowledge management refers to the process of acquiring knowledge, disseminating it, and responding to knowledge (Darroch, 2005). What makes social media platforms different is that they have features that engage a large size audience around the world from posting messages to creating content. As an interactive platform, social media offers tools for generating and acquiring knowledge, sharing it, and acting upon it (Crammond, Omeihe, Murray, & Ledger, 2018; Papa et al., 2018). Through social media, for example, companies monitor consumer feedback and analyze online consumer behavior (Kao et al., 2016) and consumer trends and expectations (Park et al., 2017). The data collected from social networks can be used to make strategic decisions and to increase a company's customer base and market share (Crammond et al., 2018; Jagongo & Kinyua, 2013).

Previous research shows that sharing knowledge via the social media is positively related to innovation in small businesses (Soto-Acosta et al., 2017). Crammond et al. (2018) state that innovation is achieved through six phases of knowledge management actions within the social media: research, concept, institutionalize, develop, target, and advance. Research refers to the collection of the market data. Developing a "big idea" happens in the concept phase which gets institutionalized (adopted by a company). During the development phase resources are allocated and relationships with partners are established. Forecasting of financial performance and identifying new markets is done at the target phase. The final step of evaluating performance helps to advance the "big idea" as this evaluative feedback shows what should be improved to be successful (Crammond et al., 2018).

The third area of opportunities relates to the institutions that support entrepreneurial activities (Davidson & Vaast, 2010). Developing a business model to create and deliver value to customers is important but having resources to implement that model is crucial. Social media impacted how entrepreneurs find and receive funds to start their businesses.

As many researchers found, the financial crisis of 2008–2009 and regulatory changes presented obstacles for entrepreneurs in obtaining initial capital for their start-ups. Banks introduced additional requirements to minimize risk of not collecting money on a loan (Block, Colombo, Cumming, & Vismara, 2018). However, technological developments, globalization, and creativity resulted in new ways of obtaining resources – crowdsourcing. While crowdsourcing refers to soliciting tangible and intangible resources over the Internet, crowdfunding describes a nontraditional way of raising capital by placing a request to support a venture on a website either in the form of donation or in exchange for monetary or nonmonetary rewards in the future after a specified period of time (Beier & Wagner, 2015; Belleflamme, Lambert, & Schwienbacher, 2013).

Although studies acknowledge that there are four main categories of investment (donation, lending or loan-based, equity-based, and reward-based), they can overlap based on the type of the business project (Mollick, 2014; Zhao, Harris, & Lam, 2019). Donation-based is a philanthropical type of investment for which there is no financial or tangible return. Lending is a traditional form of loaning money in return for interest-based repay. In the equity-based crowdfunding transaction, individuals invest directly into a company by buying shares or a part of the business. In a reward-based transaction, individuals donate money in return for a reward (either a free product or a gift) (Mollick, 2014; Zhao et al., 2019). The reward-based contribution was found to be the most commonly used (Zhao et al., 2019).

Virtual currencies (like Bitcoin) and blockchain technologies are changing the business models of the finance and banking industry. Digital currencies, digital wallets, and overall, digital methods of payment are becoming a part of the daily business routine. On the one hand, these technologies provide new ways to evaluate risk and make financial investments easier; on the other hand, they increase risk due to the "domino effect" that a small error can have due to a chain design of a transaction (Block et al., 2018).

The ease of use of social media and its global reach encouraged innovation on the one hand, but also opportunistic mischief on the other. The same online tools that entrepreneurs use to grow their ventures have a dark side as consumers complain about privacy invasions, stolen identities, and breaches of online bank accounts. The main feature of social media – sharing and collaboration – could lead to inappropriate activities when ideas and products are stolen and intellectual property rights are broken (Baccarella, Wagner, Kietzmann, & McCarthy, 2018). Although online communities value virtual relationships, whether those relationships are formal or informal, they would like to reveal identities only to the extent that individuals are willing to share and keep those identities private (Kietzmann, Hermkens, McCarthy, & Silvestre, 2011).

Digital technologies compelled governments, associations, and organizations to update laws and policies regarding a wide range of issues: data privacy and security, financing and trading, consumer rights, and intellectual property. US government laws range from the Business Opportunity Rule (2012) to Children's Online Privacy Protection Act (1998) and from the Disposal of Consumer Report Information and Records (2004) to Regulation Crowdfunding (2017) in an attempt to create a legal framework that, on the one hand, legitimizes business transactions, but, on the hand, penalizes those actions that might harm customers. Changes in legal regulations affected traditional and online business practices: traditional bank business loan applications and online crowdfunding, product design and development, marketing and sales, distribution, and human resources management.

A combination of these developments – platform-type business models, social media, changing consumer behavior, and evolving business environment – created a shared economy (Puschmann & Alt, 2016). Traditionally, consumers purchased and owned products; however, in the past a shift from owning to temporary using or renting products had been observed (Hamari, Sjöklint, & Ukkonen, 2016; Matzler, Veider, & Kathan, 2015). Common examples of activities within the shared economy are bike- and carsharing services as well as a broad range of activities from renting rooms to swapping clothes (Heinrichs, 2013). The four main elements of the shared economy are identified as access to products rather than ownership, use of online platforms, monetary rewards for sharing, and a large number of interdependent users (Breidbach & Brodie, 2017; Hamari et al., 2016).

The shared economy reflects the impact of the social media on all three areas noted earlier: business, knowledge, and institution-related (Davidson & Vaast, 2010). First, it changed the business model from "sell to own" to "give access to" (business-related). Entrepreneurs identified areas in which they did not have to own tangible products but rather develop an online platform and match demand for a temporary use to supply those products. Second, it allowed to gain market intelligence (knowledge-related). Learning not only about consumer preferences and needs but also about new technologies offered a competitive advantage. Lastly, it affected institutions within the entire business environment. Banks, manufacturing plants, warehouses, and third-party distributors had to develop their online presence and join virtual networks. Some can see the shared economy as a disruptive threat while others as a unique opportunity.

2.5 Evaluation Process

As noted in the earlier section on entrepreneurship, a novel venture is founded based on two elements: (1) recognizing and evaluating an opportunity and (2) acting upon it (Hitt et al., 2001). Thus, occurrence of an action depends on the result of the decision whether an opportunity might present a profitable venture (McMullen & Shepherd, 2006). The shorter the time period between evaluation of opportunities and actions undertaken to take advantage of those opportunities, the higher the chances that entrepreneurs would gain a competitive advantage over rivals.

Rastkhiz et al. (2019) conducted a systematic review of the extant literature published in 2000–2017 on the criteria used to evaluate opportunities. The result of the review presented the most commonly used factors: economic and financial factors, market and industry, product issues, desirability, feasibility, human capital, and environmental factors (Rastkhiz et al., 2019). However, all these factors could be further grouped into four evaluation criteria related specifically to a digital strategy proposed by Bharadwaj et al. (2013). These four elements are "(1) the scope of digital business strategy, (2) the scale of digital business strategy, (3) the speed of digital business strategy, and (4) the sources of business value creation and capture in digital business strategy" (Bharadwaj et al., 2013, p. 472).

Measuring success depends on the companies' goals. If the goal is to develop awareness of a product, then the analysis of web traffic and number of followers on the social media could serve as achievement indicators (Castronovo & Huang, 2012). To measure whether a company achieved its planned level of sales, the number of purchases, bounce rate, and account traffic might be helpful (Castronovo & Huang, 2012). If the goal is to build loyalty, then the company should review the number of repeat visitors and followers, time spent on the site, and recommendations, among others (Castronovo & Huang, 2012).

As was mentioned earlier, social media present opportunities for starting new ventures (business-related opportunities), learning new information about how to develop and expand (knowledge-related opportunities), and involving those actors that can help to break boundaries and support entrepreneurial activities (institution-related opportunities) (Davidson & Vaast, 2010). Thus, evaluating opportunities presented by the social media from the traditional two perspectives (one from the business owner and another from the customer) is not sufficient. As a business owner, an entrepreneur focuses on return on investment and potential to grow but has to recognize that the role of the social media is changing. A customer wants seamless online experience that offers instantaneous information, easy business transaction, tracking of an order, and safety and security of the personal record. However, focusing only on the business-related opportunities eliminates other possibilities: gaining knowledge and seeking support of institutional actors.

Figure 2.1 summarizes pathways for evaluating the impact of the social media on entrepreneurial ventures discussed in this chapter. Entrepreneurs review opportunities presented by the social media from the perspective of the scope, scale, speed, and sources of their business strategy and then evaluate the impact of those opportunities either on the business model, knowledge of the business venture, or a business environment in which they operate. Once those opportunities are recognized, the type of the action depends on the same factors – the scope, scale, speed, and sources of their business strategy.

This model supports Sorenson's (2018) findings about three types of the impact that social relationships have on entrepreneurs. It was observed that social

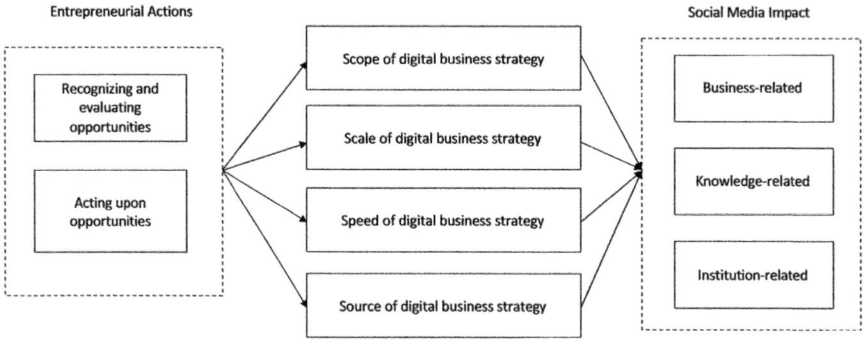

Fig. 2.1 Analyzing the impact of social media

relationships shape perceptions about entrepreneurship and help individuals to decide whether they should become entrepreneurs (Sorenson, 2018). Once individuals decide to start their businesses, social networks help to obtain funds, find suppliers, and attract and retain customers. Lastly, social relationships contribute to the satisfaction with life (Sorenson, 2018).

Although Sorenson's (2018) research focused on face-to-face social networks, it is applicable to the impact of social media. Recognizing an opportunity on a business level in the proposed model would correspond to the attractiveness of entrepreneurship perceived from others in the social network. This area determines not only what an individual could do to offer something of value to customers but also how to create that value. The model's level of knowledge supports Sorenson's (2018) aspect of knowing how to obtain funds, find suppliers, and attract customers. As was discussed earlier in the chapter, knowledge of the social media's tools and functions leads to a more effective use of crowdsourcing and implementation of marketing strategies. The model's last area of impact – institutional – could explain satisfaction with the lifestyle. If the environment is supportive of entrepreneurship, an entrepreneur feels content and satisfied with the business career. Government policies supporting and not limiting entrepreneurial activities contribute to success of the business operations.

The impact of social media on entrepreneurship is complex and it gets even more complicated as technology continues to develop. Although researchers agree that nobody can really determine the potential impact of social media on businesses (Amit & Zott, 2001), the model proposed in this chapter offers a framework for identifying potential areas of impact. Knowledge of the "big picture" will help entrepreneurs to find a niche supported by technology.

2.6 So What?

Although it started as a means of sharing personal information among friends, social media found its use in the business world. Social media can be both cost effective and efficient for small businesses as social networks reflect characteristics of small businesses – loose structure, informal relationships, interactive, and quick adaptation to the environment (Toombs & Harlow, 2014). Entrepreneurial innovation goes through two phases: developing a unique product or process and commercialization with a sustainable business model (Hsieh & Wu, 2019; Huizingh, 2011). Although these two activities require different resources, social media offers tools for both stages. Through social networks consumers can contribute to idea generation and product development. Social platforms assist with the sustainability of business models. For example, Facebook Store (https://www.facebook.com/store.tab/) offers a Facebook business page tab application that allows entrepreneurs to sell a product directly on their "Facebook Store." Amazon Web Services (https://aws.amazon.com) provides a variety of support services to businesses – from analytics to blockchain transactions.

As the business environment changes, so do businesses as they try to remain profitable. In order to sustain their competitive advantages, companies should keep a balance creating, delivering, and capturing value (Teece, 2018). This balance might be achieved by recognizing and realizing opportunities presented by the social media and new technology. Based on the previous research (Davidson & Vaast, 2010) that showed the impact of social media on entrepreneurship in three areas – business, knowledge, and institution – this chapter discussed and proposed a framework that assists both academics and practitioners with identifying and evaluating opportunities for new ventures.

Recognizing an opportunity leads to developing an initial business model which is more a proposal of how to deliver value while acting on it requires a strategy (Chesbrough & Rosenbloom, 2002). The use of social media helps entrepreneurs not only to design or adjust a business model and formulate a strategy but also ensure scalability of their business. Despite a dark side, social media present a business potential for exponential increase in return.

References

Ainin, S., Parveen, F., Moghavvemi, S., Jaafar, N. I., & Mohd Shuib, N. L. (2015). Factors influencing the use of social media by SMEs and its performance outcomes. *Industrial Management & Data Systems, 115*(3), 570–588.

Amit, R., & Zott, C. (2001). Value creation in e-business. *Strategic Management Journal, 22*(6–7), 493–520.

Autio, E., Dahlander, L., & Frederiksen, L. (2013). Information exposure, opportunity evaluation, and entrepreneurial action: An investigation of an online user community. *Academy of Management Journal, 56*(5), 1348–1371.

Baccarella, C. V., Wagner, T. F., Kietzmann, J. H., & McCarthy, I. P. (2018). Social media? It's serious! Understanding the dark side of social media. *European Management Journal, 36*(4), 431–438.

Barney, J. (1991). Firm resources and sustained competitive advantage. *Journal of Management, 17*(1), 99–120.

Becker, K., Nobre, H., & Kanabar, V. (2013). Monitoring and protecting company and brand reputation on social networks: When sites are not enough. *Global Business and Economics Review, 15*(2–3), 293–308.

Beier, M., & Wagner, K. (2015). Crowdfunding success: A perspective from social media and e-commerce. In *Proceedings of the 36th International Conference on Information Systems: Exploring the Information Frontier* (pp. 634–655). Association for Information Systems, Fort Worth, TX.

Belleflamme, P., Lambert, T., & Schwienbacher, A. (2013). Individual crowdfunding practices. *Venture Capital, 15*(4), 313–333.

Bharadwaj, A., El Sawy, O. A., Pavlou, P. A., & Venkatraman, N. (2013). Digital business strategy: Toward a next generation of insights. *MIS Quarterly, 37*, 471–482.

Bleicher, P. (2006). Web 2.0 revolution: Power to the people. *Applied Clinical Trials, 15*(8), 34–36.

Block, J. H., Colombo, M. G., Cumming, D. J., & Vismara, S. (2018). New players in entrepreneurial finance and why they are there. *Small Business Economics, 50*(2), 239–250.

Boyd, D. M., & Ellison, N. B. (2007). Social network sites: Definition, history, and scholarship. *Journal of Computer-Mediated Communication, 13*(1), 210–230.

Breidbach, C. F., & Brodie, R. J. (2017). Engagement platforms in the sharing economy: Conceptual foundations and research directions. *Journal of Service Theory and Practice, 27*(4), 761–777.

Campbell, C., Pitt, L. F., Parent, M., & Berthon, P. R. (2011). Understanding consumer conversations around ads in a Web 2.0 world. *Journal of Advertising, 40*(1), 87–102.

Castronovo, C., & Huang, L. (2012). Social media in an alternative marketing communication model. *Journal of M arketing Development and Competitiveness, 6*(1), 117–134.

Chesbrough, H., & Rosenbloom, R. S. (2002). The role of the business model in capturing value from innovation: Evidence from Xerox Corporation's technology spin-off companies. *Industrial and Corporate Change, 11*(3), 529–555.

Crammond, R., Omeihe, K. O., Murray, A., & Ledger, K. (2018). Managing knowledge through social media. *Baltic Journal of Management, 13*(3), 303–328.

Darroch, J. (2005). Knowledge management, innovation and firm performance. *Journal of Knowledge Management, 9*(3), 101–115.

Davidson, E., & Vaast, E. (2010, January). Digital entrepreneurship and its sociomaterial enactment. In *2010 43rd Hawaii International Conference on System Sciences* (pp. 1–10). IEEE.

El Sawy, O. A., & Pereira, F. (2013). VISOR: A unified framework for business modeling in the evolving digital space. In *Business modelling in the dynamic digital space. SpringerBriefs in Digital Spaces*. Berlin, Heidelberg, Germany: Springer.

Etter, M., Ravasi, D., & Colleoni, E. (2019). Social media and the formation of organizational reputation. *Academy of Management Review, 44*(1), 28–52.

George, N. M., Parida, V., Lahti, T., & Wincent, J. (2016). A systematic literature review of entrepreneurial opportunity recognition: Insights on influencing factors. *International Entrepreneurship and Management Journal, 12*(2), 309–350.

Hamari, J., Sjöklint, M., & Ukkonen, A. (2016). The sharing economy: Why people participate in collaborative consumption. *Journal of the Association for Information Science and Technology, 67*(9), 2047–2059.

Heinrichs, H. (2013). Sharing economy: A potential new pathway to sustainability. *GAIA-Ecological Perspectives for Science and Society, 22*(4), 228–231.

Heller Baird, C., & Parasnis, G. (2011). From social media to social customer relationship management. *Strategy & Leadership, 39*(5), 30–37.

Hitt, M. A., Ireland, R. D., Camp, S. M., & Sexton, D. L. (2001). Strategic entrepreneurship: Entrepreneurial strategies for wealth creation. *Strategic Management Journal, 22*(6–7), 479–491.

Hsieh, Y. J., & Wu, Y. J. (2019). Entrepreneurship through the platform strategy in the digital era: Insights and research opportunities. *Computers in Human Behavior, 95*, 315–323.

Huizingh, E. K. (2011). Open innovation: State of the art and future perspectives. *Technovation, 31*(1), 2–9.

Jagongo, A., & Kinyua, C. (2013). The social media and entrepreneurship growth. *International Journal of Humanities and Social Science, 3*(10), 213–227.

Jones, B., Temperley, J., & Lima, A. (2009). Corporate reputation in the era of Web 2.0: The case of Primark. *Journal of Marketing Management, 25*(9–10), 927–939.

Jones, N., Borgman, R., & Ulusoy, E. (2015). Impact of social media on small businesses. *Journal of Small Business and Enterprise Development, 22*(4), 611–632.

Kao, T. Y., Yang, M. H., Wu, J. T. B., & Cheng, Y. Y. (2016). Co-creating value with consumers through social media. *Journal of Services Marketing, 30*(2), 141–151.

Kaplan, A. M., & Haenlein, M. (2010). Users of the world, unite! The challenges and opportunities of social media. *Business Horizons, 53*(1), 59–68.

Kietzmann, J. H., Hermkens, K., McCarthy, I. P., & Silvestre, B. S. (2011). Social media? Get serious! Understanding the functional building blocks of social media. *Business Horizons, 54*(3), 241–251.

Kumar, V., Lahiri, A., & Dogan, O. B. (2018). A strategic framework for a profitable business model in the sharing economy. *Industrial Marketing Management, 69*, 147–160.

Matzler, K., Veider, V., & Kathan, W. (2015). Adapting to the sharing economy. *MIT Sloan Management Review, 56*(2), 71–77.

McMullen, J. S., & Shepherd, D. A. (2006). Entrepreneurial action and the role of uncertainty in the theory of the entrepreneur. *Academy of Management Review, 31*(1), 132–152.

Mollick, E. (2014). The dynamics of crowdfunding: An exploratory study. *Journal of Business Venturing, 29*(1), 1–16.

O'Reilly, T., & Battelle, J. (2009). *Web squared: Web 2.0 five years on* (Special Report). Retrieved from http://www.cs.cmu.edu/~jhm/Readings/web2009_websquared-whitepaper.pdf

Osterwalder, A., & Pigneur, Y. (2010). *Business model generation: A handbook for visionaries, game changers, and challengers*. Hoboken, NJ: John Wiley & Sons.

Papa, A., Santoro, G., Tirabeni, L., & Monge, F. (2018). Social media as tool for facilitating knowledge creation and innovation in small and medium enterprises. *Baltic Journal of Management, 13*(3), 329–344.

Park, J., Sung, C., & Im, I. (2017). Does social media use influence entrepreneurial opportunity? A review of its moderating role. *Sustainability, 9*(9), 1593. Retrieved from https://www.mdpi.com/2071-1050/9/9/1593. 4 June 2019.

Parveen, F., Jaafar, N. I., & Ainin, S. (2016). Social media's impact on organizational performance and entrepreneurial orientation in organizations. *Management Decision, 54*(9), 2208–2234.

Porter, M. E. (1985). *Competitive advantage: Creating and sustaining superior performance*. New York: The Free Press.

Porter, M. E. (1996). What is strategy? *Harvard Business Review, 74*(6), 61–78.

PRC (Pew Research Center). (2019, June 12). *Social media factsheet*. Retrieved from https://www.pewresearch.org/internet/fact-sheet/social-media/

Puschmann, T., & Alt, R. (2016). Sharing economy. *Business & Information Systems Engineering, 58*(1), 93–99.

Rastkhiz, S. E. A., Dehkordi, A. M., Farsi, J. Y., & Azar, A. (2019) A new approach to evaluating entrepreneurial opportunities. *Journal of Small Business and Enterprise Development, 26* (1), 67–84.

Roy, A., Maxwell, L., & Carson, M. (2014). How is social media being used by small and medium-sized enterprises? *Journal of Business and Behavior Sciences, 26*(2), 127–137.

Ruggieri, R., Savastano, M., Scalingi, A., Bala, D., & D'Ascenzo, F. (2018). The impact of Digital Platforms on Business Models: An empirical investigation on innovative start-ups. *Management & Marketing. Challenges for the Knowledge Society, 13*(4), 1210–1225.

Schaupp, L. C., & Bélanger, F. (2013). The value of social media for small businesses. *Journal of Information Systems, 28*(1), 187–207.

Schiavi, G. S., & Behr, A. (2018). Emerging technologies and new business models: A review on disruptive business models. *Innovation & Management Review, 15*(4), 338–355.

Shahizan, H., Norshuhada, S., Nor Laily, H., Sobihatun Nur, A. S., & Mohd Samsu, S. (2012). Social media for business: Knowledge gathering through focus group session with business owners. In *Proceedings of the Knowledge Management International Conference (KMICe)* (pp. 719–723).

Shane, S., & Venkataraman, S. (2000). The promise of entrepreneurship as a field of research. *Academy of Management Review, 25*(1), 217–226.

Sorenson, O. (2018). Social networks and the geography of entrepreneurship. *Small Business Economics, 51*(3), 527–537.

Soto-Acosta, P., Popa, S., & Palacios-Marqués, D. (2017). Social web knowledge sharing and innovation performance in knowledge-intensive manufacturing SMEs. *The Journal of Technology Transfer, 42*(2), 425–440.

Standing, C., & Mattsson, J. (2018). "Fake it until you make it": Business model conceptualization in digital entrepreneurship. *Journal of Strategic Marketing, 26*(5), 385–399.

Suseno, Y., Laurell, C., & Sick, N. (2018). Assessing value creation in digital innovation ecosystems: A Social Media Analytics approach. *The Journal of Strategic Information Systems, 27*(4), 335–349.

Taiminen, H. M., & Karjaluoto, H. (2015). The usage of digital marketing channels in SMEs. *Journal of Small Business and Enterprise Development, 22*(4), 633–651.

Teece, D. J. (2018). Business models and dynamic capabilities. *Long Range Planning, 51*(1), 40–49.

Toombs, L. A., & Harlow, R. M. (2014). More than just "like": An entrepreneurial approach to creating a social media ethos in small firms. *Academy of Marketing Studies Journal, 18*(2), 275–286.

Wheelen, T. L., Hunger, J. D., Hoffman, A. N., & Bamford, C. E. (2015). *Strategic management and business policy: Globalization, innovation and sustainability* (14th ed.). Boston: Pearson Education.

Zhao, Y., Harris, P., & Lam, W. (2019). Crowdfunding industry – history, development, policies, and potential issues. *Journal of Public Affairs, 19*(1), e1921. Available at https://onlinelibrary.wiley.com/doi/full/10.1002/pa.1921

Chapter 3
Social Media and Entrepreneurship: Exploring the Role of Digital Source Selection and Information Literacy

Shahrokh Nikou, Malin E. Brännback, Thao Phuong Orrensalo, and Gunilla Widén

Abstract Internet-based applications, such as social media, offer potentially effective and efficient vehicles to access, use, and distribute information as well as means to network with other actors. However, for realizing this potential, critical competencies are information and digital literacy. In this chapter we discuss the importance of information literacy (IL) in the context of social media. Information literacy is defined as cognitive skills necessary for using and evaluating information in an educated and effective way. IL is a necessary competence for entrepreneurs in general and specifically for entrepreneurs relying entirely or partially on social media in their entrepreneurial activities. We argue that access and use of information is an important way for entrepreneurs to reduce uncertainty in their entrepreneurial action. Information literacy and information source selection are important to practicing entrepreneurs as most need to access information in order to run their business, information from policy makers, financing institutions, tax authorities, and legal counsel, to name a few. This information is today inherently provided in digital format.

In this chapter our focus is on digital information and specifically digital source selection and information literacy. We have studied 145 Finnish entrepreneurs and analyzed their information literacy in relation to digital source selection. Results show that while information literacy impacts digital information source selection, that relationship is influenced by source accessibility and the task complexity. Interestingly, and somewhat unexpectedly, the study revealed that source selection is directly influenced by the opinions of peers or social norms.

Keywords Digital literacy · Digital transformation · Entrepreneurship · Information literacy

S. Nikou · M. E. Brännback (✉) · T. P. Orrensalo · G. Widén
School of Business and Economics, Åbo Akademi University, Turku, Finland
e-mail: malin.brannback@abo.fi

L. Schjoedt et al. (eds.), *Understanding Social Media and Entrepreneurship*, Exploring Diversity in Entrepreneurship,
https://doi.org/10.1007/978-3-030-43453-3_3

3.1 Introduction

Today, most information used in everyday life is digital. The use of ubiquitous information systems (UIS) such as Facebook, Twitter, and YouTube – social media – has become the norm for both personal and professional purposes (Vodanovich, Sundaram, & Myers, 2010). As Kaplan and Haenlein (2010, p. 67) stated: "In today's digital economy, everything is about social media and firms will be out of the cyberspace if they do not participate in social media platforms." Consequently, entrepreneurs are increasingly in cyberspace using information sources such as social media platforms to obtain information, to support their business growth, creating new networks among peers or customers or creating new business ventures (Kuhn & Galloway, 2015; Nambisan, 2017; von Briel, Davidsson, & Recker, 2018). UIS share a common characteristic that they are available everywhere and all the time.

Thus, in the context of social media, activities, and entrepreneurial activities especially, are less bounded and predefined. Social media due to this defining characteristic thus transforms the nature of uncertainty in entrepreneurial processes and outcomes and also how entrepreneurs deal with uncertainty (Nambisan, 2017). While social media has transformed our everyday lives for almost two decades, social media (and other digital technologies) and its role in shaping entrepreneurial opportunities, decisions, actions, and outcomes has been mostly neglected (Nambisan, 2017). Although digital technologies have indeed been subject to studies in entrepreneurship, these have primarily been treated as contexts of empirical work along with other forms of technology entrepreneurship. Only recently have digital technologies been considered as inherent to entrepreneurial processes and outcomes (Nambisan, 2017; von Briel et al., 2018).

Social media has been subject to scholarly inquiry that has occurred within other disciplines, e.g., information systems, marketing, and communications. Previous research show that firms use social media to communicate with customers, tap on customer preferences, build company reputation and image, build product awareness for the purpose of increasing sales, and enhance business performance (Jones, Borgman, & Ulusoy, 2015; Kaplan & Haenlein, 2010).

Popular press has since the dawn of Facebook and Twitter written extensively of social media entrepreneurs and the use of social media to drive business growth. An indication that this area is indeed novel comes from variance in defining social media within entrepreneurship: is it a platform, is it an ecosystem, or is it just infrastructure for communication and digital distribution? Nambisan (2017) defines social media as digital infrastructure and as an important external enabler of venture creation (Davidsson, 2015; von Briel et al., 2018). While we concur with this definition it is to our minds even more important to understand is that social media is an information system. This means that accessing and using information becomes an important skill and competence to leverage the full potential of social media as an external enabler of venture development. That very competence is known as information literacy.

In a world which is filled with information overflow and increasingly fake fact, fake news, fabrication, and disinformation, information literacy skills and capabilities become paramount. Traditionally, a person with the basic ability to read and write was referred to a literate person; however due to digitalization of work and business processes, the traditional definition of literacy is no longer relevant. In today's digital world, a person is required to have a profound set of skills and knowledge to efficiently find, locate information sources, and use information to solve an information need (Ciftci & Knautz, 2016).

Recent research has considered digital technologies as external enablers of entrepreneurial activities (von Briel et al., 2018; Nambisan, 2017). Against this, social media is understood as an external actor-independent enabler in new venture creation. However, we argue that the full potential of social media cannot be realized without an actor-dependent internal enabler, i.e., information literacy. Moreover, just because a person owns a smart phone and a laptop computer and has a Facebook, an Instagram, or a Twitter account does not make that person automatically information literate.

In this chapter we theorize on the importance of information literacy and specifically its relationship to digital source selection and how these become internal enablers in terms of necessary competences of entrepreneurs in digital entrepreneurial activities. Closely related to information literacy is the concept of digital citizenship, which is having literacy skills to navigate efficiently and safely in a digital environment (Sussaen & Acs, 2017). Hence, information literacy is a prerequisite to become a digital citizen.

Information literacy is defined as a set of cognitive skills which are used to evaluate information in an educated and effective way (Eshet-Alalai, 2004). Information source selection is a significant part of information-seeking behavior (Julien & Michels, 2013). Intelligent and efficient access to relevant information sources are critical factors necessary for completing complex tasks – such as venture creation by an entrepreneur (Smeltzer, Van Hook, & Hutt, 1991). Purposeful information-seeking begins with the selection of information sources (Bronstein, 2010). Information source selection is according to the extant literature determined by information literacy, information accessibility, information quality, and the complexity of the task to be performed (Bronstein, 2010; Lee, Paik, & Joo, 2012; Durodolu, 2016; Gross & Latham, 2009; Nikou, Brännback, & Widén, 2018). Moreover, previous studies have found that social norms have a direct impact on source selection as well as the usage of digital sources (Apuke & Iyendo, 2018; Constantinides & Holleschovsky, 2016; Schon, Ristic, & Manning, 2015). Thus, this chapter specifically looks at what factors influence entrepreneur's digital information source selection and what is the role of information literacy. Moreover, this analysis is conducted among a sample of entrepreneurs and how they use digital technology and what drives their selection of digital and online information sources to support their entrepreneurial activities. Before we consider information literacy and information source selection, we will briefly review the development of social media and the digital context that started with the emergence of what was known as electronic commerce that took the practice of entrepreneurship by storm in the

1990s. As a consequence, information is everywhere, and private citizens and businesses alike had to learn to deal with this avalanche of information in an informed way.

3.2 Social Media and Entrepreneurship

By the third quarter of 2019 Facebook had 2.45 billion and Instagram 1 billion monthly active users (www.statista.com), 1.6 billion users were accessing the WhatsApp messenger on a monthly basis, and Twitter averaged 330 million monthly active users. While Facebook, Instagram, and WhatsApp show no sign of decline, Twitter showed a decline from its all-time high of 336 million in the first quarter of 2018. The average daily time spent using social media was the highest in the Philippines, with 4 hours per day. This is twice the time spent in the USA of approximately 2 hours, which in turn is twice the time spent using social media in Finland. Social media is indeed big within the digital economy, and it should be of great interest to companies large and small.

Although social media as a term was coined around 2003 and 2004 when MySpace and Facebook were created, companies have in general been slow to include social media into their operations. One reason is that firms have been quite uncomfortable with information about them being freely available (Kaplan & Haenlein, 2010) and continuously modified beyond their control. On the other hand, social media offers businesses efficient means by which consumers can be included into firm's development processes and therein become contributors and co-creators of value (Kao, Yang, Wu, & Cheng, 2016). Social media impact firm performance as it allows firms – even small start-up firms – to engage in timely and direct end-consumer contact at relatively low cost and higher levels of efficiency compared to more traditional communication tools (Parveen, et al., 2016). On an individual basis social media offer means by which a person can identify and enact entrepreneurial opportunities.

Entrepreneurship scholars have in the same vein been slow in applying a digital technology perspective to entrepreneurship, where social media would be seen as a key enabler or a platform or an ecosystem (Nambisan, 2017; von Briel et al., 2018). Yet, the numbers speak of volumes that should have caught the mandated attention also in entrepreneurship research. One would rightfully assume this would be the case especially since the field of electronic commerce, propelled by the introduction of the World Wide Web (WWW), had been an entrepreneurial Eldorado during the 1990s. The dot.com industry went from boom to bust in just a few years at the turn of the millennium (Kaplan, 2002; Lindstedt, 2001). Electronic commerce created an unprecedented excitement in business over the endless possibilities of creating new business models that the world had seen nothing of before (Tapscott, 1996). Business was learning the basics of Internet marketing, to build customer relationships and create value in cyberspace (Brännback, 1997; Sterne, 1996). A massive number of firms were created without necessarily viable business models or in particular revenue models (Drucker, 2002) – and it all did not end well. While new digital technology enabled all this entrepreneurial activity, it did not change one basic requirement – the need for any firm to be profitable, which a lot of start-up dot.com firms had to learn the hard way.

During the 1990s existing businesses, large and small, participated in the dot.com boom by creating an Internet presence through a webpage (Brännback, 1997; Sterne, 1996). However, very few firms had a very good understanding of what to do with an Internet presence or how to manage such a presence. The webpages contained information about the firm, its products, and sometimes even contact information such as street addresses and phone numbers (!) but not always an e-mail address (Sterne, 1995). Most webpages were quite terrible in terms of user-interface design and usability. Not only was the technology to use in order to build a web presence in its infancy, so were the skills by the users. But, since everybody – private persons and businesses – were rushing to create an Internet presence, the web soon became quite crowded with available information of varying quality. It became important to be able to find information and to verify information sources and the accuracy of information.

A few years after the dot.com boom ended in a crash, the digital economy continued to evolve and social media developed from a platform called Web 2.0. In Web 2.0 content and applications were no longer created and published by individuals (as when creating an Internet presence). Instead they were continuously modified by multiple users in multiple ways, also known as user-generated content. Kaplan and Haenlein (2010, p. 61) define social media as: "a group of Internet-based applications that build on the ideological and technological foundation of Web 2.0, and that allow for the creation and exchange of User Generated Content." Wikipedia is an excellent example of a virtual encyclopedia, which is constantly modified. Sometimes the information is very accurate but often it is not and therefore Wikipedia is not, for example, accepted by many universities as a viable information source for academic theses work. Social media evolved as a result of the combination of technological (available hardware), economic (available tools that enabled UGC), and social (primarily young people with technical knowledge and skills to engage online) drivers.

While social media at first seemed to engage primarily digital natives (young people who were born into the digital world) (Tapscott, 1998), it soon proliferated across generations to include digital immigrants (those who were not born into the digital world) (Brännback, Nikou, & Bouwman, 2017; Nikou, Mezei, & Brännback, 2018; Vodanovich et al., 2010). Digital natives were usually highly skilled in using social media and other digital tools contrary to digital immigrants who were late adopters of social media and frequently struggled with using digital technologies. However, as pointed out in the introduction, being a skilled user of these technologies does not automatically imply the possession of skills to access, use, and evaluate the information these technologies contain. That is, it does not mean that the person is information literate. In a world which is filled with information overflow where the quality of the information can be challenged, information literacy skills and capabilities have become equally important with being a skilled user of technology.

Access to high-quality, accurate, and timely information is vital for any business survival and growth (Capella, 2012; Constantinides & Holleschovsky, 2016; Machado, 2016; Mir, 2014; Najat, 2017; Nguyen, 2018; Popovič, Hackney, Tassabehji, & Castelli, 2018). This is certainly the case also for practicing entrepreneurs. It includes information relevant for developing business strategy, processes and operations, market data and customer information, product information, legal information, and information on policy concerning taxation, to mention a few. Policy information is seen as critical for entrepreneurial success especially for start-up entrepreneurs (Akinso, 2018; Capella, 2012). Start-up entrepreneurs in particular are interested in finding information concerning governmental support mechanisms and information that can influence their choice of location. In most countries, governmental agencies offer a myriad of relevant and necessary information (e.g., business registration procedures) online, and the task for entrepreneurs is to find the right information (Li & Herd, 2017).

3.3 Information Literacy

Information literacy (IL) is a set of cognitive skills and competences to efficiently locate, use, and evaluate information tools as well as information sources to solve a given problem in an educated and effective way (Ciftci & Knautz, 2016; Eshet-Alalai, 2004). These skills are not restricted to digital contexts but all information. The point here is that information literacy becomes particularly important in the digital economy where the volume of digital information is massive and constantly increasing. In the digital context, IL includes critical thinking and the capability to efficiently search, identify, and evaluate web-based data (Ng, 2012). IL is the ability in recognizing the need for information, accordingly identifying, locating, accessing, evaluating, and employing the information responsibly to work-related performance, such as problem-solving and decision-making (Kirton & Barham, 2005; Ranaweera, 2008). Information literacy has proven its significance for the organizational and entrepreneurial success as it ensures and enhances the performance of the organization's information collecting process (Adeleke & Emeahara, 2016; Kim & Sin, 2011; Kirton & Barham, 2005; Oman, 2001). Information literacy helps the individual to develop critical awareness, which enables them to interpret and make knowledgeable judgments about an information source regarding its accessibility and quality. However, with a lack of efficient quality assurance mechanisms this may in some cases lead to a reluctancy to use digital information sources.

Previous research has found that IL is dependent on digital information source selection (Nicholas, Williams, Cole, & Martin, 2000; Odede & Nsibirwa, 2018; Singh, Ogbonnaya, & Ohakwe, 2011). Digital information source selection is impacted by how efficiently information seekers can access the needed information to perform a certain task or their ability to evaluate the relevance of the information sources based on the type of task at hand (Bawden, 2008; Hosier, 2015; Kim & Sin, 2011). This in turn is determined by the source characteristics. Low IL skills hinder the use of electronic sources (Lozanova-Belcheva, 2013) and have been shown to be one of the reasons for not engaging in online collaboration or, for example, using online government services (Kirui & Kemei, 2014).

Accessibility is a multidimensional characteristics of information sources. This includes the amount of effort required from the user and the amount of time it takes for the user to find necessary information, which in turn is determined by availability (24/7), convenience, comprehensiveness, easy to use, familiarity, understandability, and whether it is free to access or not (Agarwal, 2011; Bronstein, 2010; Case, 2012; Haase & Franco, 2011; Popoola & Okiki, 2013; Woudstra, Hooff, & Schouten, 2016). Most people tend to use an information source that require the least effort and risk-taking for them and that are impersonal. For example, Susanto and Aljoza (2015) found that perceived ease of use (easy navigation, quick response, fit interface, and accessible anywhere anytime) and perceived usefulness (information completeness, reducing cost, saving energy, saving time, and useful information) are the most critical to an individual's decision to use online government service.

The quality of information sources is one of the decisive criteria for selecting the digital information sources (Bronstein, 2010; Kim & Sin, 2011; Marton & Choo, 2002; Zhang, 2013). Quality of an information source is determined by the relevance, reliability, credibility, consistency, trustworthiness, and authoritativeness (Babalhavaeji & Farhadpoor, 2013; Pierce, 2008; Zhang, 2013). Some studies indicate that the quality of the information source is more important than accessibility (Bronstein, 2010; Kim & Sin, 2011).

Finally, the type of task will impact Xie and Joo (2010) information source selection. These can be complex or simple routine-like tasks such as information for product or company searches, government information, news information Bronstein (2010).

An interesting aspect of technology adoption in information seeking behavior and the use of social media is that it appears to be influenced by social norms (Brännback et al., 2017; Nikou, Mezei, & Brännback, 2018; Thompson, Higgins, & Howell, 1991). An individual's opinion and decision to use for example online government services is influenced by the expectations and recommendations of surrounding people, like co-worker, friends, and family (Gracia, Ariño, & Blanco, 2012). That is, users are highly influenced by their peers. That is, if peers access certain information sources online or use social media in their operations, this behavioral pattern seems to spread among peers (Kuhn & Galloway, 2015; Xie & Joo, 2010).

3.4 The Study

Based on the literature review above we developed a model (Fig. 3.1) to empirically explore the relationship of information literacy and digital source selection among entrepreneurs.

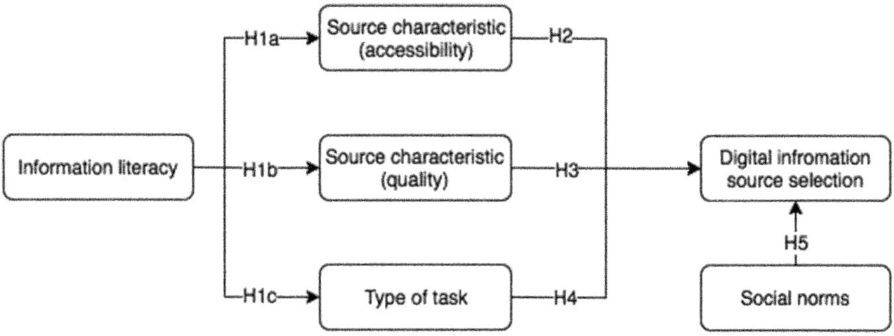

Fig. 3.1 The research model

The initial assumption is that there is a direct link between information literacy and digital information source selection (Hypothesis 1). However, a review of the literature reveals that two dimensions of source characteristics (accessibility and quality) as well as type of task may play a mediating role (Hypotheses 1a, 1b, 1c, 2, 3, 4). Moreover, previous research show that technology adoption and in particular decision to use social media is directly impacted by social norms (Brännback et al., 2017; Nikou, Mezei, & Brännback, 2018) and that peers impact entrepreneurial behavior in digital environments (Kuhn & Galloway, 2015). We therefore assume that social norms have a direct effect on digital source selection (Hypothesis 5). The following hypotheses were formed and tested:

H1: Information literacy skills of an entrepreneur have a positive effect on selecting digital information sources.

- H1a: Information literacy skills of an entrepreneur have a positive effect on the choice of digital information sources based on the accessibility of the sources.
- H1b: Information literacy skills of an entrepreneur have a positive effect on the choice of digital information sources based on the quality of the sources.
- H1c: Information literacy skills of an entrepreneur have a positive effect on the choice of digital information sources based on the type of task.

H2: Accessibility of the information sources has a positive effect on selecting digital information sources.

H3: Quality of the digital information sources has a positive effect on selecting digital information sources.

H4: Type of task has a positive effect on selecting digital information sources.

H5: Social norms have a positive effect on selecting digital information sources.

3.4.1 Survey Instrument and Data Collection

The main focus of our study is to explore whether the identified factors (i.e., information literacy, information sources' characteristics (accessibility and quality), type of tasks, and social norms) influence the entrepreneurs' digital information source selections. For data collection, a survey instrument was developed on the basis of established measures of constructs from different information behavior literature of social norms (Ayeh, Au, & Law, 2013; Gracia et al., 2012; Moghavvemi, Salleh, Zhao, & Mattila, 2012), information literacy (Kurbanoglu, Akkoyunlu, & Umay, 2006), source characteristics which include source accessibility and quality (Attuquayefio, Achampong, & Aryeetey, 2014; Bronstein, 2010; Xie & Joo, 2010), type of task (Bronstein, 2010), and, finally, the dependent variable information source selection (Ayeh et al., 2013; Kuma & Sampath, 2008; Lin & Lu, 2011). We slightly modified some of the items to make them contextually relevant for the analysis. A seven-point Likert scales were used to measure the items, where "1 indicates strongly disagree and 7 indicates strongly agree."

A questionnaire was distributed online among Finnish entrepreneurs in August 2019. Respondents were invited to provide their replies in the course of 4 weeks and a reminder was sent after 2 weeks.

The questionnaire consisted of questions on the participants' demographic background, their frequency, and self-reported proficiency in the use of digital tools and digital information sources. Out of 873 distributed questionnaires, we obtained 151 responses. After excluding incomplete responses, the final dataset consisted of 145 valid and usable responses.

To ensure that the dataset did not suffer from nonresponse bias and to determine whether there are significant differences between the two invitation waves, we performed a non-bias test (Henry, 1990). We compared those who responded within the first 15 days (early respondents) with those who responded during the last 2 weeks before the survey was closed (late respondents). Only three of the 69 items in the questionnaire had significant mean differences ($p < .001$); thus the data set did not contain nonresponse bias. We also performed a common method bias test to establish the validity of the research results. We used the Harman's one-factor test (via a principal component factor analysis) (Podsakoff & Organ, 1986). Results showed that no factor accounted for more than 50% (23.18%) of the variance; thus, common method bias was not an issue in the study.

3.4.2 Sample Characteristics

The total sample consisted of 145 entrepreneurs in Finland: 27% female and 73% male entrepreneurs. The average age was 40.35 years with the oldest born in 1952 and the youngest in 1998. The majority of the ventures were limited liability companies (79%) and 80% of the respondents were native Finnish citizens. A majority

(74%) hold at least a bachelor's or master's degree, 11% of the respondents have attended college but had not graduated, and only 7% hold a high school diploma or equivalent.

3.5 Results

Most respondents reported an extensive daily use of digital tools such as smart phones, laptops, and a constant online presence on the Internet. The most used digital information sources were search engines and social media; 80% used Google, Bing, or Yahoo several times a day, and 70% used social media (Facebook, Instagram, Twitter, LinkedIn, YouTube). However, only 3% reported using online governmental websites, i.e., the least used digital sources.

The result also showed that most of the respondents considered themselves as very proficient with Internet skills (mean = 7), including searching information through search engines, downloading/sending a file, opening an attachment, sharing and asking information on social media, and navigating information on websites. Respondents thus perceived themselves as very proficient in using search engines for finding and locating digital information (mean = 7); following by accessing organizational/institutional websites, online newspapers, and social media ($M = 6$); and online governmental websites and forum ($M = 5$). That is, based on their own perception of their skills they were information literate.

3.5.1 *Measurement Model*

We used confirmatory factor analysis (CFA) to examine the measurement model. The measurement model has been validated by performing the convergent validity and the discriminant validity tests. For examining the convergent validity, we adopted three criteria: Cronbach's alpha, composite reliability (CR), and average variance extracted (AVE) (Hair, Risher, Sarstedt, & Ringle, 2018). Cronbach's alpha is used for assessing the reliability of the measurement and the value is recommended to be and equal or greater than .70 (Cronbach, 1951; Hair et al., 2018). Composite reliability was assessed and all the CR values were above the recommended value of .70, ranging from .871 to .909 (Hair et al., 2018). Average variance extracted is a measure that reflects the convergence among a set of items in a latent construct. The value of AVE is recommended to be greater than .50 (Hair et al., 2018; Henseler, Ringle, & Sarstedt, 2015). Table 3.1 shows the results of composite reliability, AVE, the Cronbach's alphas, and item loadings were above the recommended level (>.70) in general and for both groups.

The square root of the AVE was measured for the discriminant validity assessment. Table 3.2 shows the square root of the AVE values for all constructs, indicating that the obtained values were greater than the correlations among them, thereby confirming discriminant validity (Hair et al., 2018).

Table 3.1 Construct reliability and validity

Constructs	Items	Loadings	α	CR	AVE
Information literacy	IL1	.88	.873	.904	.612
	IL2	.87			
	IL3	.79			
	IL4	.75			
	IL5	.76			
	IL6	.73			
Digital information source selection	DISS1	.85	.882	.909	.588
	DISS2	.71			
	DISS3	.70			
	DISS4	.71			
	DISS5	.79			
	DISS6	.82			
	DISS7	.77			
Source accessibility	SCA1	.77	.859	.905	.704
	SCA2	.89			
	SCA3	.86			
	SCA4	.80			
Source quality	SCQ1	.73	.819	.871	.576
	SCQ2	.79			
	SCQ3	.81			
	SCQ4	.78			
	SCQ5	.70			
Social norms	SN1	.87	.811	.888	.725
	SN2	.88			
	SN3	.81			
Type of task	TOT1	.87	.828	.887	.664
	TOT2	.73			
	TOT3	.90			
	TOT4	.75			

Note: *AVE* average variance extracted, *CR* composite reliability, *α* Cronbach's alpha

Table 3.2 Discriminant validity

Constructs	SCA	IL	SCQ	SN	DSS	TOT
Source accessibility	.839					
Information literacy	.579	.782				
Source quality	.616	.492	.759			
Social norms	.456	.472	.412	.851		
Digital source selection	.713	.541	.534	.561	.767	
Type of task	.680	.561	.592	.507	.709	.815

3.5.2 Structural Model

To assess the path coefficients, we used SmartPLS 3.0. The SEM results showed that the digital information source selection is explained by a variance of 69%, indicating that the predictors explained a large amount of variation. Type of task, sources' accessibility, and sources' quality were explained by variance values of 32%, 34%, and 24%, respectively.

Contrary to previous research results no direct link between information literacy and digital source selection was found (H1). Instead results showed that information literacy has a positive direct effect on both source characteristics, such that it has a significant effect on source accessibility (β = .58, t = 8.841, p = .001), as well as significant effect on source quality (β = .49, t = 7.176, p = .001). Thus, both H1a and H1b are supported by the model. Moreover, information literacy was found to have a positive significant effect on type of task (β = .56, t = 8.426, p = .001); thus H1c is also supported by the model. Results also showed that source accessibility has a direct relationship with digital information source selection (β = .32, t = 3.591, p = .001); thus H2 is supported by the model.

However, contrary to findings in previous studies source quality had no significant effect on digital information source selection; thus H3 was supported. The path relationship between type of task and digital information source selection was found to be significant (H4); in other words, type of task was positively associated with digital information source selection (β = .51, t = 5.524, p = .001). Finally, consistent with previous research findings, there is a positive and direct relationship between social norms and digital information source selection (β = .17, t = 2.404, p = .01); thus H5 was also supported by the model (see Fig. 3.2).

3.5.3 Mediation Test

As we did not find a direct path between information literacy and digital information source selection, we performed a mediation test. First, we assessed the results of total indirect effects and found significant indirect effects (β = .45, t = 8.193, p < .001). This result indicates that we also need to assess the specific indirect effects to see if there are any mediation effects and through which constructs. The results of specific indirect effects showed that the relationship between IL and digital information source selection is mediated through source accessibility (β = .18, t = 3.428, p < .001) and type of task (β = .29, t = 4.583, p < .001). However, source quality has no mediation role in this path relationships. Thus, we concluded that the path between IL and digital information source selection is partially mediated through source characteristics (i.e., accessibility) and type of task (see Table 3.3).

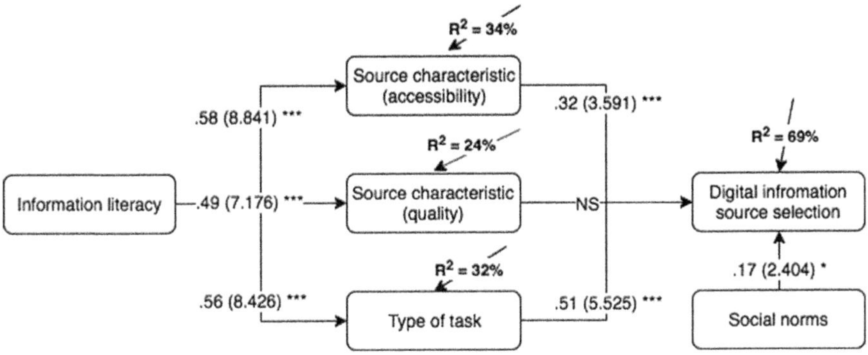

Fig. 3.2 Structural results

Table 3.3 Mediation test results

Relationship	Std beta	Std error	*t*-value	Significance
IL ➔ SCA ➔ DISS	.176	.051	3.428	.001
IL➔ SCQ ➔ DISS	−.013	.028	.487	.626
IL ➔ TOT➔ DISS	.287	.063	4.583	.001

Note: *DISS* digital information source selection, *IL* information literacy, *SCA* source characteristic (accessibility), *SCQ* source characteristic (quality), *TOT* type of task

3.6 Discussion

We have in this chapter taken the view that social media is a ubiquitous information system and a digital infrastructure. In contrast to traditional information systems social media is less predefined, less bounded, and less controllable (Kaplan & Haenlein, 2010; Nambisan, 2017; Vodanovich et al., 2010). These characteristics will impact entrepreneurial opportunities, decisions, actions, and outcomes. We have also said that social media transforms the nature of uncertainty in entrepreneurial processes and how entrepreneurs cope with uncertainty. Social media will impact the entire entrepreneurial process and offer an efficient means for creating a market orientation, supporting market access, innovation, and ultimately firm success (Renko, Carsrud, & Brännback, 2009).

But it is not only the digital technology which is important here. In this chapter our focus has been on an aspect, which refers to the ability to use technology and leverage the full potential benefits from such technology, namely, information literacy. The underlying argument here is that while social media offer a huge potential in saving costs related to managing a firm's customer base, which includes distribution and communication costs, those savings require specific skills and competences in the form of information literacy. Nambisan (2017) raises a number of interesting research questions with respect to creating a digital technology perspective within entrepreneurship research, which refer to digital infrastructure. One such question is: why does the use of social media by some entrepreneurs and not others lead to different cognitive and behavioral (entrepreneurial) outcomes? How does the collective characteristic of social media impact the collective nature of entrepreneurial agency and thereby the entrepreneurial processes and outcomes? Intuitively, we can say that information literacy certainly will be an element in providing an informed answer.

In this chapter we have restricted the discussion to information literacy only, as we are very much aware of the fact that literacy, which used to mean whether a person knew how to read and write, today has taken multiple forms. Along information literacy we also have media literacy and digital literacy, which could prove relevant in this context as well. However, we have deliberately chosen to restrict this discussion to information literacy only to underline the necessity to be able to access information, use information, and evaluate information. We have stated it multiple times that even if digital technology is available and individuals own smart phones, iPads, and laptops, it does not always mean that the same individual is information literate.

For example, information systems research distinguish between digital natives and digital immigrants, where the former are users who have grown up in a digital world and the latter started using systems at some stage in their adult life. While this categorization is somewhat rough and therefore has been criticized, there are clear differences between these groups of users that also should impact their use of social media as an external enabler and digital infrastructure of entrepreneurial activities. It is argued that digital natives are using technology differently and that they think and process information fundamentally differently from digital immigrants (Brännback et al., 2017; Nikou, Brännback, & Widén, 2018; Nikou, Mezei, & Brännback, 2018; Vodanovich et al., 2010). As educators and researchers in universities we can certainly agree to such an observation.

For the purpose of this chapter we conducted an exploratory study among Finnish entrepreneurs. While our analysis does not distinguish between the digital native entrepreneurs and the entrepreneurs who are digital immigrants, the reported age range 1952–1998 indicates that the sample would include both categories. Consequently, subsequent analysis would include potential gender differences and age differences – as we know from previous research that the use of information systems and social media is indeed gendered (Brännback et al., 2017; Nikou, Brännback, & Widén, 2018; Nikou, Mezei, & Brännback, 2018). The assumption would be that there will be differences in information literacy with respect to digital information source selection. Moreover, it is highly likely that the industry in which the entrepreneurs operate in will have an impact. The study was based on a survey where respondents conducted a self-assessment of their information literacy. This is of course problematic as this is a highly subjective measure and not surprisingly the respondents considered themselves highly information literate. This is consistent with self-reported assessments, where people in general tend to overestimate their competencies. However, there are some interesting deviations already in this small sample, which calls for additional analysis. For example, results revealed that the quality of the digital information source had no impact on digital information source selection (H3). Previous research show quite clearly that quality is far more important that accessibility (H2). In this study, that was not the case.

In subsequent studies specific measures of digital literacy and media literacy should be included. Different research methods would also be welcome, where, for example, log information of the user's actual use of social media or netnography (virtual ethnography). One of the arguments in this chapter has also been that information literacy is important for firm success especially where social media plays an important role. This, of course, calls for studies which include measures of firm performance both with respect to firm growth and profitability – in growth/decline of number of served customers, revenue growth, reduction of costs, and profitability.

References

Adeleke D. S., & Emeahara E. N. (2016). Relationship between information literacy and use of electronic information resources by postgraduate students of the University of Ibadan. *Library Philosophy and Practice (E-Journal)* 1381. Retrieved from: http://digitalcommons.unl.edu/libphilprac/1381.

Agarwal N. K. (2011). *Information source and its relationship with the context of information seeking behavior*. iConference.

Akinso A. (2018). *Successful strategies for the survival of business owners in Nigeria*. Walden Dissertations and Doctoral Studies Collection. Walden University.

Apuke, O., & Iyendo, J. T. (2018). University students' usage of the internet resources for research and learning: Forms of access and perceptions of utility. Computer science. Information science. *Heliyon, 4*(12), e01052.

Attuquayefio, S., Achampong, A., & Aryeetey, I. (2014). Extending TAM with social norm to model students' intentions to adopt ICT. *European Scientific Journal, 10*(14), 435–446.

Ayeh, J. K., Au, N., & Law, R. (2013). Predicting the intention to use consumer-generated media for travel planning. *Tourism Management, 35*, 132–143.

Babalhavaeji, F., & Farhadpoor, M. R. (2013). Information source characteristics and environmental scanning by academic library managers. *Information Research, 18*(1). paper 568. [Available at http://InformationR.net/ir/18-1/paper568.html].

Bawden, D. (2008). Digital literacies: Concepts, policies and practices. In C. Lankshear & M. Knobel (Eds.), *Origins and concepts* (pp. 17–32). New York: Peter Lang.

Brännback, M. (1997). Is the internet changing the dominant logic of marketing? *European Management Journal, 15*(6), 698–707.

Brännback, M., Nikou, S., & Bouwman, H. (2017). Value systems and intentions to interact in social media: The digital natives. *Telematics and Informatics, 34*(4), 365–381.

Bronstein, J. (2010). Selecting and using information sources: Source preferences and information pathways of Israeli library and information science students. *Information Research: An International Electronic Journal, 15*(4), 1–15.

Capella A. (2012). *Translating ideas into action: The policy entrepreneur role at the public policy process*. Madrid: XXII world congress of political science – "reordering power, shifting boundaries". International Political Science Association.

Case, O. D. (2012). *Looking for information: A survey of research on information seeking, needs and behavior* (3rd ed.). Bingley, UK: Emerald.

Ciftci, T., & Knautz, K. (2016). Information Facebook users. In K. Knautz & K. S. Baran (Eds.), *Facets of Facebooks: Use and users* (pp. 115–145). Berlin, Germany: De Gruyter.

Constantinides, E., & Holleschovsky, N. (2016). Impact of online product reviews on purchasing decisions. In *Proceedings of the 12th international conference on web information systems and technologies* (Vol. 1, pp. 271–278).

Cronbach, L. J. (1951). Coefficient alpha and the internal structure of tests. *Psychometrika, 16*(3), 297–334.
Davidsson, P. (2015). Entrepreneurial opportunities and the entrepreneurship nexus: A re-conceptualization. *Journal of Business Venturing, 30*(5), 674–695.
Drucker, P. F. (2002). *Managing in the next society*. New York: Truman Talley.
Durodolu, O. (2016). Technology Acceptance Model as a predictor of using information system' to acquire information literacy skills. *Library Philosophy and Practice (e-journal)*, 1450 1–27. Retrieved from: http://digitalcommons.unl.edu/libphilprac/1450.
Eshet-Alalai, Y. (2004). Digital literacy: A conceptual framework for survival skills in the digital era. *Journal of Educational Multimedia and Hypermedia, 13*(1), 93–106.
Gracia, D., Ariño, L., & Blanco, C. (2012). Understanding the influence of social information sources on e-government adoption. *Information Research, 17*(3) paper 531. [Available at http://InformationR.net/ir/17-3/paper531.html].
Gross, M., & Latham, D. (2009). *Undergraduate perceptions of information literacy: Defining, attaining, and self-assessing skills*. Florida State University Libraries.
Haase, H., & Franco, M. (2011). Information sources for environmental scanning: Do industry and firm size matter? *Management Decision, 49*(10), 1642–1657.
Hair, J. F., Risher, J. J., Sarstedt, M., & Ringle, C. (2018). When to use and how to report the results of PLS-SEM. *European Business Review, 31*(1), 2–24.
Henry, G. T. (1990). *Practical sampling. Applied social research methods series*. Newburry Park, CA: Page.
Henseler, J., Ringle, C. M., & Sarstedt, M. (2015). A new criterion for assessing discriminant validity in variance-based structural equation modelling. *Journal of the Academy of Marketing Science, 43*(1), 115–135.
Hosier, A. (2015). Teaching information literacy through "un-research". *Communications in Information Literacy, 9*(2), 162–135.
Jones, N., Borgman, R., & Ulusoy, E. (2015). Impact of social media on small businesses. *Journal of Small Business and Enterprise Development, 22*(4), 611–632.
Julien, H., & Michels, D. (2013). Source selection among information seekers: Ideals and realities. In *Proceedings of the annual conference of CAIS/Actes du congrès annuel de l'ACSI*.
Kao, T. Y., Yang, M. H., Wu, J. T. B., & Cheng, Y. Y. (2016). Co-creating value with consumers through social media. *Journal of Service Marketing, 30*(2), 141–151.
Kaplan, A. M., & Haenlein, M. (2010). Users of the world, unite! The challenges and opportunities of Social Media. *Business Horizons, 53*(1), 59–68.
Kaplan, P. J. (2002). *F'd Companies, spectacular dot-com flameouts*. New York: Simon & Schuster.
Kim, K., & Sin, S. J. (2011). Selecting quality sources: Bridging the gap between the perception and use of information sources. *Journal of Information Science, 20*(10), 1–12.
Kirton, J., & Barham, L. (2005). Information literacy in the workplace. *The Australian Library Journal, 54*(4), 365–376.
Kirui, E., & Kemei, P. (2014). Usability of E-government services in developing countries. *International Journal of Computer Trends and Technology (IJCTT), 15*(3), 102–107.
Kuhn, K. M., & Galloway, T. L. (2015). With a little help from my competitors: Peer networking among artisan entrepreneurs. *Entrepreneurship Theory and Practice., 39*(3), 571–600.
Kuma, G. T., & Sampath, B. T. (2008). *Use of electronic information sources by the academic community: a comparative study*. Proceedings of the 6th international Caliber 2008, from automaton to transformation, University of Allahabad, Allahabad, February 28–29, INFLIBNET, Ahmedabad, 529–40.
Kurbanoglu, S. S., Akkoyunlu, B., & Umay, A. (2006). Developing the information literacy self-efficacy scale. *Journal of Documentation, 62*(6), 730–743.
Lee, J., Paik, W., & Joo, S. (2012). Information resource selection of undergraduate students in academic search tasks. *Information Research, 17*(1), 1–19.

Li, J., & Herd, M. A. (2017). Shifting practices in digital workplace learning: An integrated approach to learning, knowledge management, and knowledge sharing. *Human Resource Development International, 20*(3), 185–193.

Lin, K. Y., & Lu, H. P. (2011). Intention to continue using Facebook fan pages from the perspective of social capital theory. *Cyberpsychology, Behaviour and Social Networking, 14*(10), 565–570.

Lindstedt, G. (2001). Boo.com och IT-bubblan som sprack (in Swedish: Boo.com and the IT-bubble which burst), Bokförlaget DN, Stockholm.

Lozanova-Belcheva, E. (2013). The impact of information literacy education for the use of E-government services: The role of the libraries. In S. Kurbanoğlu, E. Grassian, D. Mizrachi, R. Catts, & S. Špiranec (Eds.), *Worldwide commonalities and challenges in information literacy research and practice. ECIL 2013. Communications in computer and information science* (Vol. 397). Springer.

Machado, H. (2016). Growth of small businesses: A literature review and perspectives of studies. *Gestão & Produção São Carlos, 23*(2), 419–432.

Marton, C., & Choo, C. W. (2002). *A question of quality: the effect of source quality on information seeking by women in IT professions*. Proceedings of the ASIST annual meeting, 65, 140–151.

Mir, A. A. (2014). Effects of pre-purchase search motivation on user attitudes toward online social network advertising: A case of university students. *Journal of Competitiveness, 6*(2), 42–55.

Moghavvemi, S., Salleh, M., Zhao, W., & Mattila, M. (2012). The entrepreneurs perception on information technology innovation adoption: An empirical analysis of the role of precipitating events on usage behaviour. *Innovation-Management Policy & Practice, 14*(2), 231–246.

Najat, B. (2017). Importance of customer knowledge in business organizations. *International Journal of Academic Research in Business and Social Sciences, 7*(11), 175–187.

Nambisan, S. (2017). Digital entrepreneurship: Towards a digital technology perspective of entrepreneurship. *Entrepreneurship Theory and Practice., 41*(6), 1029–1055.

Ng, W. (2012). Can we teach digital natives' digital literacy? *Computers & Education, 59*(3), 1065–1078.

Nguyen, N. N. (2018). *The role of government in the development of ethnic entrepreneurs: A qualitative study on Vietnamese ethnic entrepreneurs in Finland*. Turku School of Economics: Master Thesis in International Business.

Nicholas, D., Williams, P., Cole, P., & Martin, H. (2000). The impact of the internet on information seeking in the media. *ASLIB Proceedings, 52*(3), 98–114.

Nikou, S., Brännback, M., & Widén, G. (2018). The impact of multidimensionality of literacy on the use of digital technology: Digital immigrants and digital natives. In H. Li, Á. Pálsdóttir, R. Trill, R. Suomi, & Y. Amelina (Eds.), *Well-being in the information society. Fighting inequalities. WIS 2018. Communications in computer and information science* (Vol. 907). Springer.

Nikou, S., Mezei, J., & Brännback, M. (2018). Digital natives' interactive behaviour on social media: Value systems and gender. *Telematics and Informatics, 35*(2), 421–435.

Odede, I. R., & Nsibirwa Z. (2018). Information literacy skills in using electronic information resource, 1–17. *Library Philosophy and Practice (e-journal)*. 1947. 1–17. Retrieved from: http://digitalcommons.unl.edu/libphilprac/1947.

Oman, J. (2001). Information literacy in the workplace. *Information Outlook, 5*(6), 33–35.

Parveen, F., Jaafar, N. I., & Ainin, S. (2016). Social media's impact on organizational performance and entrepreneurial orientation in organizations. *Management Decision, 54*(9), 2208–2234.

Pierce, R. (2008). *Evaluating information: Validity, reliability, accuracy, triangulation. Research Methods in Politics*. Canada: SAGE Publication.

Podsakoff, P. M., & Organ, D. W. (1986). Self-reports in organizational research: Problems and pro- spects. *Journal of Management, 12*(4), 531–544.

Popoola, S. O., & Okiki, O. C. (2013). Information availability and utilization as determinants of creativity of managers in commercial banks in Nigeria. *Journal of Information and Knowledge Management, 3*(8), 22–34.

Popovič, A., Hackney, R., Tassabehji, R., & Castelli, M. (2018). The impact of big data analytics on firms' high value business performance. *Information Systems Frontiers, 20*(2), 209–222.
Ranaweera, P. (2008). *Importance of information literacy skills for an information literate society*. Colombo, Sri Lanka: NACLIS.
Renko, M., Carsrud, A., & Brännback, M. (2009). The effect of a market orientation, entrepreneurial orientation, and technological capability on innovativeness: A study of young biotechnology ventures in the US and in Scandinavia. *Journal of Small Business Management, 47*(3), 331–369.
Schon, J., Ristic, I., & Manning, J. (2015). When the internet becomes the doctor: Seeking health information online. In M. Brann (Ed.), *Contemporary case studies in health communication: Theoretical and applied approaches* (2nd ed., pp. 311–322). U.S.: Kendall Hunt Publishing Company.
Singh, D., Ogbonnaya, C. O., & Ohakwe, J. (2011). Factors affecting the use of informationservices by international students. *Malaysian Continental Journal of Applied Science, 6*(3), 8–18.
Smeltzer, L. R., Van Hook, B. L., & Hutt, R. W. (1991). Analysis of the use of advisors as information sources in venture start-ups. *Journal of Small Business Management, 29*(3), 10–20.
Sterne, J. (1995). *World wide web marketing*. New York: Wiley.
Sterne, J. (1996). *Customer service on the internet: Building relationships, increasing loyalty and staying competitive*. New York: Wiley.
Susanto, T., & Aljoza, M. (2015). Individual acceptance of e-government services in a developing country: Dimensions of perceived usefulness and perceived ease of use and the importance of trust and social influence. *Procedia Computer Science, 72*, 622–629.
Sussaen, F., & Acs, Z. J. (2017). The digital entrepreneurial ecosystem. *Small Bsuiness Economics, 49*(1), 55–73.
Tapscott, D. (1996). *The digital economy. Promise and peril in the age of networked intelligence*. New York: McGraw-Hill.
Tapscott, D. (1998). *Growing up digital. The rise of the net generation*. New York: McGraw-Hill.
Thompson, R. L., Higgins, C. A., & Howell, J. M. (1991). Personal computing: Toward a conceptual model of utilization. *MIS Quarterly, 15*(1), 125–143.
Vodanovich, S., Sundaram, D., & Myers, M. (2010). Digital natives and ubiquitous information systems. *Information System Research, 21*(4), 711–723.
von Briel, F., Davidsson, P., & Recker, J. (2018). Digital technologies as external enablers of new venture creation in the IT hardware sector. *Entrepreneurship Theory and Practice, 42*(1), 47–69.
Woudstra, L., Hooff, B., & Schouten, A. (2016). The quality versus accessibility debate revisited: A contingency perspective on human information source selection. *Journal of the Association for Information Science and Technology, 67*(9), 2060–2071.
Xie, I., & Joo, S. (2010). Selection of information sources: Accessibility of and familiarity with sources, and types of tasks. *Proceedings of the American Society for Information Science and Technology, 46*(1), 1–18.
Zhang, Y. (2013). The effects of preference for information on consumers' online health information search behaviour. *Journal of Medical Internet Research, 15*(11), 234.

Part II
Social Media in Entrepreneurship Research: Where Have We Been?

Chapter 4
Effectual Entrepreneur and the Use of Social Media for Opportunity Recognition

Atthaphon Mumi

Abstract Social media have been perceived as the variety of online communication platforms that stimulate interaction in virtual communities. Existing studies have been found in manifesting the benefits of using social media for business-related purposes. Despite the emerging acceptance of these online communication platforms, few studies have explored social media in the context of entrepreneurship. This chapter, therefore, aims at providing an extended discussion of an entrepreneur's use of social media, through the lens of the effectuation theory. We argue and propose that effectual entrepreneurs could benefit from using social media as it would influence the level of opportunity recognition. In addition, we discuss the contingent relationship between social media usage and various effectual attributes—affordable loss, entrepreneurial passion, and entrepreneurial self-efficacy—toward opportunity recognition. The conceptual framework from this chapter can be used as a foundation for future social media studies in the context of entrepreneurship.

Keywords Communication platforms · Effectuation · Social media · Opportunity recognition

4.1 Introduction

Social media have gained tremendous attention from research scholars as the online platforms have changed the way organizations communicate with the stakeholders (Bird, Schjoedt, & Robert Baum, 2012). Social media such as Facebook, Instagram,

A. Mumi (✉)
Mahasarakham Business School, Mahasarakham University, Maha Sarakham, Thailand
e-mail: atthaphon.m@mbs.msu.ac.th

L. Schjoedt et al. (eds.), *Understanding Social Media and Entrepreneurship*,
Exploring Diversity in Entrepreneurship,
https://doi.org/10.1007/978-3-030-43453-3_4

Twitter, and YouTube have stimulated information sharing among its users, which have led to new communication as well as new marketing strategies utilized by many organizations (Hanna, Rohm, & Crittenden, 2011). These online platforms bring together billions of users who actively engage in virtual communities (Smith, 2016) and begin to create, share, and exchange information among their network peers (Kaplan & Haenlein, 2010; Leonardi & Vaast, 2017). Due to the popularity of social media, prior studies have investigated the phenomena in the business domain. Various studies have emphasized social media as the effective communication tools that influence sales (Dewan & Ramaprasad, 2014; Gopinath, Chintagunta, & Venkataraman, 2013; Nam & Kannan, 2014; Rui, Liu, & Whinston, 2013; Yu, Duan, & Cao, 2013), customer relationships (Laroche, Habibi, & Richard, 2013), and brand perception (Naylor, Lamberton, & West, 2012). Furthermore, social media have been found to affect a firm's overall value, shown through stock performance (Jiang, Chen, Nunamaker, & Zimbra, 2014; Luo, Zhang, & Duan, 2013; Schniederjans, Cao, & Schniederjans, 2013).

Despite the increasing attention on social media research in a variety of business literature, few studies have been found in exploring the phenomena of social media for an entrepreneurial context (e.g., Fischer & Rebecca Reuber, 2011; Fischer & Rebecca Reuber, 2014; Mumi, Obal, & Yang, 2019). Though some findings can be applied, when interpreting entrepreneurs as social media users, existing literature still needs a deeper understanding of the use of social media for various entrepreneurial processes and new venture creation. Besides many entrepreneurship scholars have emphasized digital entrepreneurship as an emerging research stream (Nambisan, 2017; Sussan & Acs, 2017), still social media in entrepreneurship has received relatively less attention. This chapter, therefore, discusses related literature on both social media and entrepreneurship, as well as proposing relationships through the effectuation theoretical lens.

Drawing from the existing arguments by Fischer and Rebecca Reuber (2011), interaction on social media can influence an entrepreneur's effectual thinking and behavior. The effectual entrepreneurs—those who utilize the resources available in identifying opportunities (Sarasvathy, 2001)—were argued to have higher success than the causal entrepreneurs, who are specific goal oriented, when it comes to the business development in the early stages (Dew, Sarasvathy, Read, & Wiltbank, 2008; Sarasvathy, Simon, & Lave, 1998; Wiltbank, Dew, Read, & Sarasvathy, 2006). Although the existing framework by Fischer and Rebecca Reuber (2011) has emphasized the relationships between social media and effectual entrepreneurs, the literature still needs further discussion regarding the phenomena of social media in contingent with other entrepreneurial attributes that may influence the entrepreneurial process. This chapter mainly contributes to this stream of research by providing an extended discussion of the relationships between social media and effectuation for an entrepreneur. Specifically, we discuss and propose the conceptual framework that may enhance the further investigation of this research domain by focusing on the relationships between social media and various effectuation contructs toward opportunity recognition.

We begin our discussion by reviewing the literature on social media. Based on King, Racherla, and Bush (2014)'s framework, we categorize our discussion based on our review into four different quadrants: Q1, antecedents of individual participation on social media; Q2, consequences to individuals; Q3, antecedents of a firm's participation on social media; and Q4, consequences to firms. These quadrants will help to shed light on the better understanding of antecedences and consequences of social media for both individuals and firms. Furthermore, we discuss effectuation theory in the following section before proposing the relationships between social media and effectual constructs toward the entrepreneur's opportunity recognition. We then conclude and discuss the contributions of this framework in the last section of this chapter.

4.2 Social Media Research: An Overview

According to Kaplan and Haenlein (2010), social media have gained its popularity since the establishment of "Open Diary" by Bruce and Susan more than 20 years ago. The Open Diary was the first online platform that brought together a community of writers, making it the starting point of several other well-established social media platforms such as MySpace, Facebook, and Twitter (Loughane, 2005). The topic of social media as emphasized by the scholar community has received tremendous attention as there are more than four million results from article searches in Google Scholar. Notably, the article by Kaplan and Haenlein (2010) entitled *Users of the world, united! The challenges and opportunities of social media* has received more than 16,000 citations.

Although there are various definitions of social media given by scholars, the essence reflects technology and the using purposes as defined by Kaplan and Haenlein (2010) in saying that social media is a type of internet-based applications that enhance the exchange of contents generated by its users. In addition, social media have been focused as the platforms for social information sharing through online interaction (Schniederjans et al., 2013), and it is the new era of information technology resulted in innovative communication, collaboration, consumption, and creation within and outside firm boundaries (Aral, Dellarocas, & Godes, 2013). The contents generated by users on social media serve as the two-way communication between the organization and its customers (Hanna et al., 2011). Therefore, it is important for the scholar community to investigate the topic of social media further as it is one of the effective tools for business communication. From the review of social media literature in business-related journals, we found crucial insights regarding the antecedences and consequences of participation by both individuals and firms. Following King et al. (2014), we categorize our review into four different quadrants as displayed in Table 4.1.

Table 4.1 Social media framework of antecedents and consequences for individuals and firms

Q1: Antecedents of individual participation on social media	Q2: Consequences to individuals
Social connection Information processing Self-expression	Purchasing intention Perceived brand relationship Virtual satisfaction Knowledge acquisition
Q3: Antecedents of firm's participation on social media	**Q4: Consequences to firms**
Feedback-seeking Information diffusion Maintaining stakeholder relationship Reputation management Understanding market environment	Brand equity Sales Brand buzz Firm financial value Product development Negative consequences

4.2.1 Quadrant 1: Antecedents of Individual Participation on Social Media (Q1)

This section has examined how people are motivated to participate in social media. From the review, we identify various factors which are found to influence the decision to start using social media: social connection, information processing, and self-expression.

Social connection Social connection emphasizes how people are socially motivated to connect on social media as being an active member of a virtual society. Based on the virtual ethnographic research by Croft (2013), social media involve interpersonal relationships and thereby stimulate the ties between users. Furthermore, it was found that the reason behind social media connection is people's intrinsic utility (Toubia & Stephen, 2013), social engagement by others (Moe & Schweidel, 2012; Rollins, Nickell, & Wei, 2014), and acceptance seeking (Bateman, Gray, & Butler, 2011; Croft, 2013; Heinonen, 2011; Ngai, Tao, & Moon, 2015). Thus, we can argue that people are participating in social media for social connection purposes, such as maintaining their relationships with others or gaining intrinsic utility/social acceptance from virtual communities.

Information processing Many people are active on social media due to the accessibility of new knowledge, which comes from other people's experiences shared in the online community. The Internet contains a broad array of knowledge; however, the specific information shared by people with mutual interest that is available on social media would lead to better accessibility and trust for the interest information. Therefore, individuals may utilize social media to find out more information about unfamiliar products or brands (Croft, 2013; Naylor et al., 2012; Orlikowski & Scott, 2013; Zadeh & Sharda, 2014). Supported by a study by Heinonen (2011), it was found that consumers are motivated by the information available on social media.

Self-expression Social media are the platforms that allow people to express themselves through various activities such as sharing photos or experiences with the online community (Croft, 2013). People often perceive social media as their online venue to express and share whatever they want. One of the motivations behind self-expression is the image-related utility (Toubia & Stephen, 2013) as people express themselves in a way that may enhance how they are perceived by others. Also, the prior study argues that self-expression is one of the entertainment activities on social media (Heinonen, 2011) where people enjoy their times in promoting themselves. Not only creating better image-related perceptions, people may also use social media to criticize others. For example, they may use social media as the venue to complain about products or services (Croft, 2013).

4.2.2 Quadrant 2: Consequences to Individuals (Q2)

From the review of the articles that mainly emphasize individual level of analysis, we realize that individuals would benefit from using social media in at least four dimensions: purchasing intention, perceived brand relationship, virtual satisfaction, and knowledge acquisition.

Purchasing intention There are various studies that display how social media influence customer's decisions in purchasing products or services (Naylor et al., 2012; Phang, Zhang, & Sutanto, 2013). One of the unique features of social media is the online word-of-mouth diffusion of information that assists decision making. The study by Ngai et al. (2015) also argues that social media influence individuals' intentions and behaviors. Particularly, there is evidence of positive correlation between social media usage and customer purchase expenditure (Goh, Heng, & Lin, 2013). Thus, we found that purchasing decisions can be influenced by the information available on social media.

Perceived brand relationship In addition to the people's intentions and behavior, it is argued that people also develop a better relationship with brand/firms as having loyalty and trust (Laroche et al., 2013) since social media allow individuals to have closer connection with the brand through their feedback on the products or services (Dou, Niculescu, & Wu, 2013; Naylor et al., 2012). Therefore, social media can be one of the essential factors in developing a better relationship between individuals and brands.

Virtual satisfaction Individuals also utilize social media for entertainment purposes (Heinonen, 2011), such as enhancing their imagination through other people's online activities. They also use and engage in social media to visually consume luxurious goods, as it may be impossible for them to acquire such goods physically (Croft, 2013). Therefore, in coping with individual satisfaction, at least virtually, we have found that individuals would perceive better virtual satisfaction from social media uses.

Knowledge acquisition Social media also satisfy individual's curiosity and provide sources of information. Individuals may seek more knowledge that serve their interests. Although limited study in business discipline was found in linking the use of social media toward knowledge and learning, Rollins et al. (2014) provide an example of how salespeople could enhance their knowledge by writing blogs. The knowledge from expressing and sharing the know-how on social media would, in turn, help the information sender to further develop new ideas. Furthermore, they also use social media as tools for researching unfamiliar products or services (Croft, 2013).

4.2.3 Quadrant 3: Antecedents of Firm's Participation on Social Media (Q3)

For a firm's perspective, social media have been emphasized as new element of business process (Hanna et al., 2011). Firms see social media as an opportunity to stimulate customer trust through better communication. In this quadrant, we identify five factors as to answer why firms decide to participate on social media platforms: feedback-seeking, information diffusion, stakeholder relationship, reputation management, and understanding market environment.

Feedback-seeking Various studies support a firm's intention to acquire feedback from the customer using social media (Dou et al., 2013; Luo et al., 2013; Schweidel & Moe, 2014; Yu et al., 2013; Zadeh & Sharda, 2014). Input from customer was difficult to obtain in the past due to a lack of effective two-way communication; however, social media have changed the way firms analyze customer demand and encourage opinion sharing regarding satisfaction of products or services. Furthermore, firms also observe the conversation on social media, especially regarding the investment from various stakeholders (Jiang et al., 2014) and crowdsource new ideas from the massive social media users (Aral et al., 2013). The feedback firms receive can enhance the co-created collaboration between the firm and customer for new product and service development (Dou et al., 2013; Swani, Brown, & Milne, 2014).

Information diffusion Firms also rely on social media as the cost-effective marketing platforms in sharing the various information (Stieglitz & Dang-Xuan, 2013; Swani et al., 2014; Zadeh & Sharda, 2014). For example, firms may promote their niche products through social media (Phang et al., 2013) or reach out to new customers (Dou et al., 2013; Michaelidou, Siamagka, & Christodoulides, 2011; Schniederjans et al., 2013). Prior studies have revealed that firms may choose to participate in social media in order to diffuse or share the information for various purposes.

Maintaining stakeholder relationship The stakeholders in this case are customers, employees, or investors that play important roles in the success of a firm. Therefore, maintaining a relationship with stakeholders can be regarded as one of the firm's primary objectives. Existing studies support this notion and argue that firms would participate in social media to foster better engagement with stakeholders and build better relationships with them (Aral et al., 2013; Goh et al., 2013; Michaelidou et al., 2011; Perrigot, Kacker, Basset, & Cliquet, 2012; Swani et al., 2014). This statement is also consistent with the review study by Ngai et al. (2015) who also assert that the firm engages stakeholders, such as customers, through the utilization of social media.

Reputation management One of a firm's reasons to participate in social media is to reach out to a large number of potential customers because positive perception by the public could be crucial to firm's success (Cheliotis, 2009; Mumi et al., 2019). On the other hand, prior literature has also exhibited that negative information through word of mouth can impact the level of trust received from customers (Kotler, 2011). Thus, it is crucial for a firm to properly manage its reputation, especially the corporate image on social media (Rokka, Karlsson, & Tienari, 2014; Schniederjans et al., 2013). As everyone is connected through this new information-driven venue, firms' online reputation becomes even more crucial.

Understanding market environment It is also vital for firms to understand how the market behaves as well as the surrounding environments such as the demand of customers, the competition, as well as the emerging opportunities. Although firms may use various methods to analyze the market environment, social media can be one of the tools for understanding market structure, opportunities, and competitive environment (Nam & Kannan, 2014). For example, Nam and Kannan (2014) provide empirical evidence that social media can be utilized to predict sales. Therefore, it can be concluded that firms would also employ social media in order to understand the current market environment.

4.2.4 Quadrant 4: Consequences to Firms (Q4)

In social media research, especially for business activities, this quadrant (Q4) has received the most attention as it is the concrete way to see how companies can benefit from their efforts on social media. This quadrant identifies six outcomes that have been mentioned in the literature: brand equity, sales, brand buzz, firm financial value, product development, and the negative consequences.

Brand equity Brand equity has received much attention recently, especially in marketing research. Prior studies have explored how social media can leverage the value of firm's branding. For instance, Naylor et al. (2012) argue that the passive presence on social media can influence consumer's brand evaluations. Another study also manifests that the purchasing relationship shown on social media can influence the level of demand (Oestreicher-Singer & Sundararajan, 2012). It is also essential to consider customer's opinions toward brand. Kumar, Bhaskaran, Mirchandani, and Shah (2013) have investigated and shown that social media could be used to increase positive word of mouth. Engaging in multidimensional communicative stream on social media would enhance customer's perceived quality of the firm (Fischer & Rebecca Reuber, 2014). Prior studies have also revealed the pieces of evidence of social media that could enhance customer loyalty. For example, Laroche et al. (2013) have found that brand community on social media is positively related to customer and company relationship which in turn increase brand loyalty. This is in alignment with the study by Rapp, Beitelspacher, Grewal, and Hughes (2013) that supported the use of social media for consumer-retailer loyalty. Finally, a study by Rishika, Kumar, Janakiraman, and Bezawada (2013) also provides shreds of evidence that participation in social media can increase the frequency of customer visits.

Sales Many studies provide supporting evidence that firm's participation in social media could influence sales (Gopinath et al., 2013; Rui et al., 2013; Stephen & Galak, 2012). As these platforms allow word of mouth, customers can make decision faster and more reliably as to whether they will buy the products or services. The positive effects of social media in relating to sales can be seen in a study by Gopinath et al. (2013), which revealed the release day sales of 75 movies was impacted by prerelease blog volume. Moreover, Rui et al. (2013) have analyzed the effects of social media sentiments and showed that positive twitter word of mouth is associated with higher movie sales.

Brand buzz One of the features of social media that enhance the volume of information can also be used to generate brand buzz—social recognition toward a brand. For example, firms that use social media would result in a higher level of word-of-mouth communication by various online users (Kozinets, Wojnicki, Wilner, & De Valck, 2010; Swani et al., 2014). Furthermore, firms also receive the information generated by users (Miller & Tucker, 2013) that can be used for the improvement of their products and services. Social media also contribute to firm's traditional marketing activities. For example, firms' use of social media would influence the availability of related content in newspapers, magazine, or television (Bao & Chang, 2014; Stephen & Galak, 2012).

Firm financial value The relationship between social media and firm financial value has gained significant attention from many scholars. The information shared online reaches the public, which includes investors (Mumi et al., 2019). Extant research has shown that activities on social media lead to financial value generation. Specifically, many scholars have investigated how social media could be the source of stock performance prediction (Jiang et al., 2014; Luo et al., 2013) and influence financial performance (Schniederjans et al., 2013). Furthermore, the information on social media can be applied for enhancing firm's stock return (Luo & Zhang, 2013; Nam & Kannan, 2014; Yu et al., 2013) and IPO value (Mumi et al., 2019). Various activities on social media have been shown to influence firm's value, such as tagging behavior (Nam & Kannan, 2014) and consumer buzz (Luo & Zhang, 2013).

Product development As previously discussed, a firm decides to participate in social media in order to receive feedback. As consequence, the information or feedback through social media enables firms to develop better products or services. This argument is supported by the prior social media studies by Aral et al. (2013) and Schweidel and Moe (2014) articulating that social media influence new and existing product development. Furthermore, the firm's use of social media boosts the value of products and services (Dou et al., 2013). Thus, this argument leads to the belief that firms may be able to develop better products and services from the utilization of social media.

Negative consequences Although social media provide many benefits for firms, prior studies also find various adverse outcomes from the use of social media. For example, a study by Moe and Schweidel (2012) asserts that firms may lose control of their audiences; this may lead to a negative perception from their audiences. This is because social media encourage the firm to be transparent and empower their customers' expression, thereby making firms vulnerable (Rokka et al., 2014). Furthermore, an empirical study of the music industry by Dewan and Ramaprasad (2014) found that social media can also lead to a decrease in song sales. Thus, it is believed that social media may also generate negative outcomes for firms in various circumstances.

Overall, this is a review of research regarding the participation in social media by both individuals and firms. Mainly, this section manifests the antecedences and consequences of individuals' and firms' participation in social media from various studies in business literature. From the review, only a few studies were found in exploring social media in relation to an entrepreneurship context. Therefore, the following section attempts to provide further discussion of social media in entrepreneurship as well as discuss the framework that can be used for a better understanding of this phenomena on entrepreneurial process.

4.3 Social Media Research in Entrepreneurship

Despite evidence from several social media studies in various business literature mentioned above, few studies were found that investigated social media for an entrepreneurship context (e.g. Fischer & Rebecca Reuber, 2011; Fischer & Rebecca Reuber, 2014; Mumi et al., 2019). Although the majority of current findings can be applied to an entrepreneur as the sharing platform user, the existing literature lacks a thorough understanding of the entrepreneur's use of social media in the entrepreneurial process. The main intent of this chapter is to understand the phenomena of social media in relation to entrepreneurship research. However, it is rather surprising that despite the popularity of social media for practical uses, few research articles were found on how social media could be beneficial for entrepreneurial activities. We believe it is important to understand how social media have been extensively utilized by various entrepreneurs in escalating the growth of their businesses (Weiss, 2014). Not only for marketing, but entrepreneurship scholars also argue that social media could stimulate entrepreneur's effectual thinking and behavior (Fischer & Rebecca Reuber, 2011). According to the existing literature, these thinking and behavior may enhance the success of entrepreneurs in the early stages of their business's development (Dew et al., 2008; Sarasvathy et al., 1998; Wiltbank et al., 2006). It is interesting that entrepreneurship scholars have introduced the effects of social media in relation to the concept of effectuation—one of the emerging theories in entrepreneurship.

Although prior studies refer to the influences of social media uses on entrepreneurial activities, especially the effectual thinking and behaviors, they did not further conceptualize in details on what kind of activities on social media would lead to changes in the perceptions and actions of effectual entrepreneurs. Furthermore, we still lack a better understanding of if social media can enhance other entrepreneurial attributes toward the opportunities for a new venture. This chapter contributes to this stream of research by focusing on the details of social media activities together with the entrepreneurial attributes—based on the effectual framework—that may influence entrepreneurial opportunity. The next section discusses the effectuation theory and proposes a framework that incorporates social media construct that influences the opportunity recognition of an entrepreneur.

4.4 Effectuation Theory

The accentuation of entrepreneurship research has focused on how firms come into existence. Through various theoretical frameworks, in particular from the neoclassical economic perspective, prior studies have concluded that firms are created as the result of different competencies related to finding and exploiting opportunities and resources (Chandler & Jansen, 1992; Cooper, Javier Gimeno-Gascon, & Woo, 1994). Rooted in Drucker (1985), which states that opportunities are discoverable by the searching process, existing entrepreneurship literature has emphasized the rational decision-making model and goal-driven behaviors in identifying opportunities (e.g., Bird, 1989). Until recently, an emerging stream of research provides a different view on the opportunity identification process and argues that individuals may not depend on goal-driven decision making when it comes to entrepreneurial opportunities (e.g., Dew, Read, Sarasvathy, & Wiltbank, 2009; Sarasvathy, 2001; Sarasvathy et al., 1998). Rather, entrepreneurs begin with their general aspirations and pursue them by using the resources currently available to them, a process called *effectuation* (Sarasvathy, 2001). Effectuation has received considerable attention as an opposing perspective to "causation" that is largely based on rational decision-making models and goal-driven processes (Gumpert & Stevenson, 1985). The difference between effectuation and causation can be explained through the story of a chef using the two approaches to prepare a meal (Sarasvathy, 2001). In the causation approach, a chef is given a specific menu in advance and needs to acquire the necessary ingredients to prepare it; the effectuation approach, on the other hand, begins with ingredients but without a specific dish in mind. The chef will utilize whatever ingredients available to prepare the best possible meal.

4.4.1 Opportunity Recognition via Social Media

Opportunity recognition has long been emphasized in entrepreneurship research (Baron, 2006). Many scholars believe that one of the critical factors that influence the success of an entrepreneur is the ability to recognize opportunity (e.g., Chandler & Hanks, 1994; Hofer & Sandberg, 1987; Sambasivan, Abdul, & Yusop, 2009). Existing literature provides the understanding of how entrepreneurs should actively be engaged in the search of the opportunity (Gaglio & Katz, 2001; Kirzner, 1979, 1997) and also how opportunities emerge from the varying environments such as technological, economic, or political factors (Schumpeter, 1934; Shane, 2003). In addition, scholars are also interested in the source of information that drives an entrepreneurial cognitive ability to identify new opportunities (e.g., Ozgen & Baron, 2007; Sarasvathy et al., 1998; Shane, 2000). According to a study by Ozgen and Baron (2007), the authors provide supportive evidence that the information embedded in the entrepreneur's networks influence opportunity recognition.

Similarly, this argument is also in line with the theory of effectuation (Sarasvathy, 2001), which suggests that entrepreneurs identify achievable outcomes from their existing resources or means. Although the current literature predominantly investigates the active search and the changing of environments, the understanding of opportunity recognition from social networks seems to be relatively less understood (Ozgen & Baron, 2007; Singh, 2000). Therefore, in this chapter, we attempt to explore the social sources of opportunity derived from social media—the emerging online communication tools that become very popular, drawing from the effectuation theoretical lens. Particularly, the level of an entrepreneur's social media participation can be signaled by their attachment level. Drawing from the prior study on attachment theory, attachment to social media exhibits the level of attraction that involves interaction via social media (VanMeter, Grisaffe, & Chonko, 2015).

From the effectuation perspective, we believe that the level of an entrepreneur's attachment to social media can enhance the realization of means and increase resources—whom I know and what I know—and in turn, this would impact their level of opportunity recognition. In the social media context, the advantages of ease of accessibility and low cost will provide entrepreneurs with more substantial and broader informal networks so that they can receive more information from people with whom they interact (Johansson, 2000), which in turn may help entrepreneurs identify new opportunities (Ozgen & Baron, 2007). For example, Hills, Thomas Lumpkin, and Singh (1997) provide evidence that entrepreneurs with more extensive networks discover more opportunities, especially the weak ties (Granovetter, 1973), that lead to more information. Thus, we posit the following proposition for social media and entrepreneur's opportunity recognition:

Proposition 1 Attachment to social media will be positively related to opportunity recognition.

4.4.2 The Moderating Role of an Affordable Loss

Affordable loss has been argued to be an important concept impacting the likelihood of co-created opportunities (Arend, Sarooghi, & Burkemper, 2015). Affordable loss is the perceived estimate made by an individual in relation to risk and loss as consequences of his or her actions (Dew, Sarasathy, Read, & Wiltbank, 2009). The affordable loss reflects the psychological orientation toward an acceptable level of risk and has been mentioned in the entrepreneurship context when entrepreneurs make decisions. Entrepreneurship scholars explain the concept of affordable loss on the basis of behavioral theory, elaborating that the affordable loss represents the psychological and cognitive orientation of expert entrepreneurs (Dew, Sarasathy, et al., 2009). Although very few prior studies have empirically investigated the effects of affordable loss that were found (Read, Song, & Smit, 2009; Wiltbank, Read, Dew, & Sarasvathy, 2009), it is believed that affordable loss can influence entrepreneurial decisions (Wiltbank et al., 2009); namely, an entrepreneur's decision making may depend upon his or her level of affordable loss. For example, Sarasvathy and Dew (2008) support the idea that entrepreneurs will make an investment decision only if they can tolerate the loss incurred due to an unexpected outcome. Wiltbank et al. (2009), using a scenario survey method that analyzed angel investors as to their use of prediction-oriented (as opposed to control-oriented/affordable loss) strategies, find that angel investors who emphasized a control-oriented strategy such as one based on affordable loss experienced a lower number of investment failures.

Therefore, based on the effectuation theory that incorporates the concept of affordable loss into the entrepreneurial process (Sarasvathy, 2001), we argue that the relationship between attachment to social media and opportunity recognition will be stronger for entrepreneurs with higher affordable loss, because when entrepreneurs utilize social media for identifying opportunity, they also rely on a certain level of affordable loss in making the decision. Particularly, entrepreneurs tend to neglect the opportunity when they are unable to realize the potential gain or loss (Dew, Sarasathy, et al., 2009). As aforementioned, the affordable loss is one of the crucial components in driving entrepreneurial decision. Without affordable loss, entrepreneurs might have a lower level of opportunity recognition. We argue that higher levels of affordable loss may lead to higher levels of opportunity recognition through social media attachment. Therefore, the next proposition is as follows:

Proposition 2 The affordable loss will positively moderate the relationship between attachment to social media and opportunity recognition.

4.4.3 The Moderating Roles of Effectual Logic: Who I Am

According to the effectuation framework that highlights the importance of existing means and self-recognition of "who I am," "whom I know," and "what I know" (Sarasvathy, 2001), the framework suggests that entrepreneurs would derive the opportunity based on various types of means (Sarasvathy, 2001; Wiltbank et al., 2006). Thus, it is also possible to expect the complementary effects of those means. In extending our argument for the primary relationship between social media and opportunity recognition, we believe that the effectual logic relating to "who I am" would influence such relationship. Consider social media participation as the networking capitals or means; prior studies also found the network and opportunity relationship which can be moderated by related "who I am" such as individualism and collectivism (Li, Chen, Liu, & Peng, 2014; Ma, Huang, & Shenkar, 2011). Following this logic, we argue that "who I am" recognition representing various entrepreneurial identities may moderate the relationship between social media and opportunity recognition. Specifically, we focus on two important constructs—*entrepreneurial passion* and *entrepreneurial self-efficacy* – that reflect "who I am" recognition in the entrepreneurship context.

Entrepreneurial Passion Cardon, Wincent, Singh, and Drnovsek (2009) define entrepreneurial passion as a positive feeling related to entrepreneurship activities that represent meaningful and salient self-identity. The effectuation theory supports that entrepreneurial passion yields "who I am" recognition since it distinguishes individuals who are willing to interact in any entrepreneurial activities from those who are not. The existing literature divides entrepreneurial passion into three groups: passion for inventing new opportunities, passion for founding new firms, and passion for developing a business (Cardon et al., 2009).

Relatively, we argue that entrepreneurial passion as a factor in identity recognition influences entrepreneurial actions. Precisely, entrepreneurs who are more passionate about inventing opportunities, founding new firms, and developing the business would be orientated toward the entrepreneurial process. Entrepreneurs utilize social media as networking means or "whom I know" component in effectuation framework for identifying opportunities. In addition, effectuation theory also asserts that entrepreneurs depend on self-recognition of "who I am" as the knowledge and resources that are argued to influence opportunity recognition. We believe that when entrepreneurs rely on resources, information, or networking through social media for opportunity recognition, furthermore, the effectiveness will be higher for those who display more passion for entrepreneurial activities. More specifically, we argue that passionate entrepreneurs would be more effective in utilizing the existing means through social media for their opportunity recognition. Thus, we posit the next proposition as follows:

Proposition 3 The relationship between attachment to social media and opportunity recognition will be positively moderated by a) passion for inventing opportunities, b) passion for founding new firms, and c) passion for developing the business.

Entrepreneurial Self-Efficacy Drawing on results of prior studies, this study views entrepreneurial self-efficacy as an individual's confidence in his or her ability to successfully manage the roles related to entrepreneurship (Chen, Greene, & Crick, 1998; Zhao, Seibert, & Hills, 2005), and thus it can represent the effectual component of "who I am." Self-efficacy is an entrepreneurship-related task that has been viewed as a key element explaining various entrepreneurship behaviors (Wilson, Kickul, Marlino, Barbosa, & Griffiths, 2009). In parallel with entrepreneurial passion, entrepreneurs who are perceived to have higher self-efficacy related to entrepreneurship activities would more likely be efficient in identifying and pursuing optimal goals in the effectual process. That is, entrepreneurial self-efficacy would influence the relationship between attachment to social media and opportunity recognition. A study by Ma et al. (2011) showed that opportunity recognition, which networking activities influence, can also be moderated by individual attribute. Therefore, this study proposes that entrepreneurial self-efficacy as one of the entrepreneurial attributes can also moderate the relationship between social media and opportunity recognition. Thus, higher entrepreneurial self-efficacy would be associated with a stronger relationship between attachment to social media and opportunity recognition.

Proposition 4 Entrepreneurial self-efficacy will positively moderate the relationship between attachment to social media and opportunity recognition.

4.5 Discussions and Conclusions

This chapter mainly emphasizes and discusses the use of social media for effectual entrepreneurs. Particularly, we review the literature on social media to have a better understanding of the antecedences and consequences of social media for individuals and firms, depicted in four different quadrants. From the review, it was found that social media research in the entrepreneurship context has received relatively little attention. We, therefore, discuss and apply the effectuation framework to shed light on social media for entrepreneurship. Existing literature emphasizes effectual entrepreneurs as entrepreneurs who rely on available resources as well as the recognition of effectual attributes (Sarasvathy, 2001). This chapter, therefore, discusses in more detail of effectual attributes in contingent with the use of social media for entrepreneurs.

Particularly, the effectuation theory has been used in this chapter as an extension of a study by Fischer and Rebecca Reuber (2011), who argue that social media interaction could influence effectual thinking. Drawing upon the effectuation framework, we propose that the attachment to social media, as signifying entrepreneur's network or "whom I know" in effectuation theory, could influence one of the most important entrepreneurial processes—opportunity recognition. Furthermore, we argue that the social media and opportunity recognition relationship can be moderated by affordable loss, entrepreneurial passion, and entrepreneurial self-efficacy as reflecting one of the effectual attributes— "who I am" recognition. We believe that these relationships are crucial in understanding the effects of social media usage for entrepreneurship literature and encourage further empirical investigation.

This book chapter contributes to the existing literature. This chapter broadens the effectuation theory and generalizes its framework to a social media context. In particular, the authors respond to the recent call for more effectuation research (Perry, Chandler, & Markova, 2012) by investigating how social media may influence an entrepreneur's opportunity recognition. In this chapter, we attempt to show that an effectuation framework can be used as the theoretical foundation for realizing entrepreneurial activities, especially when identifying the sources of opportunity. In future studies, scholars may draw from the effectuation theory and propose other means that potentially serve as valuable sources for entrepreneurial opportunities (Arend et al., 2015).

In addition, the conceptual relationship proposed in this chapter could also benefit how education on entrepreneurship makes use of social media as the tools for entrepreneurial process. More specifically, the topic of social media can be taught in entrepreneurship classes as one of the influential factors of opportunity. However, various dimensions need to be further investigated as for providing a better understanding of how social media could uniquely affect entrepreneurial activities, other than the advantages that appear in the marketing literature, such as sales (e.g., Gopinath et al., 2013; Nam & Kannan, 2014) or customer relationships (Laroche et al., 2013). The discussion in this chapter provides an early emphasis on social media in an entrepreneurship context through the effectuation framework. Further discussion can focus on social media in entrepreneurship education, especially in relation to how students could recognize opportunities and behave entrepreneurially as a result of using social media.

References

Aral, S., Dellarocas, C., & Godes, D. (2013). Introduction to the special issue-social media and business transformation: A framework for research. *Information Systems Research, 24*(1), 3–13.

Arend, R., Sarooghi, H., & Burkemper, A. (2015). Effectuation as ineffectual? Applying the 3E theory-assessment framework to a proposed new theory of entrepreneurship. *Academy of Management Review*. amr. 2014.0455.

Bao, T., & Chang, T.-l. S. (2014). Why Amazon uses both the New York Times Best Seller List and customer reviews: An empirical study of multiplier effects on product sales from multiple earned media. *Decision Support Systems, 67*, 1–8.
Baron, R. A. (2006). Opportunity recognition as pattern recognition: How entrepreneurs "connect the dots" to identify new business opportunities. *The Academy of Management Perspectives, 20*(1), 104–119.
Bateman, P. J., Gray, P. H., & Butler, B. S. (2011). Research note-the impact of community commitment on participation in online communities. *Information Systems Research, 22*(4), 841–854.
Bird, B. J. (1989). *Entrepreneurial behavior*. Scott Foresman & Company. Glenview, IL. Taylor & Francis.
Bird, B., Schjoedt, L., & Robert Baum, J. (2012). Entrepreneurs' behavior: Elucidation and measurement introduction. *Entrepreneurship Theory and Practice, 36*(5), 889–913.
Cardon, M. S., Wincent, J., Singh, J., & Drnovsek, M. (2009). The nature and experience of entrepreneurial passion. *Academy of Management Review, 34*(3), 511–532.
Chandler, G. N., & Hanks, S. H. (1994). Founder competence, the environment, and venture performance. *Entrepreneurship: Theory and Practice, 18*(3), 77–90.
Chandler, G. N., & Jansen, E. (1992). The founder's self-assessed competence and venture performance. *Journal of Business Venturing, 7*(3), 223–236.
Cheliotis, G. (2009). From open source to open content: Organization, licensing and decision processes in open cultural production. *Decision Support Systems, 47*(3), 229–244.
Chen, C. C., Greene, P. G., & Crick, A. (1998). Does entrepreneurial self-efficacy distinguish entrepreneurs from managers? *Journal of Business Venturing, 13*(4), 295–316.
Cooper, A. C., Javier Gimeno-Gascon, F., & Woo, C. Y. (1994). Initial human and financial capital as predictors of new venture performance. *Journal of Business Venturing, 9*(5), 371–395.
Croft, R. (2013). Blessed are the geeks: An ethnographic study of consumer networks in social media, 2006–2012. *Journal of Marketing Management, 29*(5–6), 545–561.
Dew, N., Read, S., Sarasvathy, S. D., & Wiltbank, R. (2009). Effectual versus predictive logics in entrepreneurial decision-making: Differences between experts and novices. *Journal of Business Venturing, 24*(4), 287–309.
Dew, N., Sarasathy, S., Read, S., & Wiltbank, R. (2009). Affordable loss: Behavioral economic aspects of the plunge decision. *Strategic Entrepreneurship Journal, 3*(2), 105–126.
Dew, N., Sarasvathy, S. D., Read, S., & Wiltbank, R. (2008). Immortal firms in mortal markets? An entrepreneurial perspective on the "innovator's dilemma". *European Journal of Innovation Management, 11*(3), 313–329.
Dewan, S., & Ramaprasad, J. (2014). Social media, traditional media, and music sales. *MIS Quarterly, 38*(1), 101–121.
Dou, Y., Niculescu, M. F., & Wu, D. J. (2013). Engineering optimal network effects via social media features and seeding in markets for digital goods and services. *Information Systems Research, 24*(1), 164–185.
Drucker, P. F. (1985). The discipline of innovation. *Harvard Business Review, 63*(3), 67–72.
Fischer, E., & Rebecca Reuber, A. (2011). Social interaction via new social media:(how) can interactions on Twitter affect effectual thinking and behavior? *Journal of Business Venturing, 26*(1), 1–18.
Fischer, E., & Rebecca Reuber, A. (2014). Online entrepreneurial communication: Mitigating uncertainty and increasing differentiation via Twitter. *Journal of Business Venturing, 29*(4), 565–583.
Gaglio, C. M., & Katz, J. A. (2001). The psychological basis of opportunity identification: Entrepreneurial alertness. *Small Business Economics, 16*(2), 95–111.
Goh, K.-Y., Heng, C.-S., & Lin, Z. (2013). Social media brand community and consumer behavior: Quantifying the relative impact of user-and marketer-generated content. *Information Systems Research, 24*(1), 88–107.
Gopinath, S., Chintagunta, P. K., & Venkataraman, S. (2013). Blogs, advertising, and local-market movie box office performance. *Management Science, 59*(12), 2635–2654.

Granovetter, M. S. (1973). The strength of weak ties. *American Journal of Sociology, 78*, 1360–1380.

Gumpert, D. E., & Stevenson, H. H. (1985). The heart of entrepreneurship. *Harvard Business Review, 63*(2), 85–94.

Hanna, R., Rohm, A., & Crittenden, V. L. (2011). We're all connected: The power of the social media ecosystem. *Business Horizons, 54*(3), 265–273.

Heinonen, K. (2011). Consumer activity in social media: Managerial approaches to consumers' social media behavior. *Journal of Consumer Behaviour, 10*(6), 356–364.

Hills, G. E., Thomas Lumpkin, G., & Singh, R. P. (1997). Opportunity recognition: Perceptions and behaviors of entrepreneurs. *Frontiers of Entrepreneurship Research, 17*, 168–182.

Hofer, C. W., & Sandberg, W. R. (1987). Improving new venture performance: Some guidelines for success. *American Journal of Small Business, 12*(1), 11–25.

Jiang, S., Chen, H., Nunamaker, J. F., & Zimbra, D. (2014). Analyzing firm-specific social media and market: A stakeholder-based event analysis framework. *Decision Support Systems, 67*, 30–39.

Johansson, E. (2000). Self-employment and liquidity constraints: Evidence from Finland. *The Scandinavian Journal of Economics, 102*, 123–134.

Kaplan, A. M., & Haenlein, M. (2010). Users of the world, unite! The challenges and opportunities of Social Media. *Business Horizons, 53*(1), 59–68.

King, R. A., Racherla, P., & Bush, V. D. (2014). What we know and don't know about online word-of-mouth: A review and synthesis of the literature. *Journal of Interactive Marketing, 28*, 167–183.

Kirzner, I. M. (1979). *Perception, opportunity, and profit: Studies in the theory of entrepreneurship*. Chicago: University of Chicago Press.

Kirzner, I. M. (1997). Entrepreneurial discovery and the competitive market process: An Austrian approach. *Journal of Economic Literature, 35*(1), 60–85.

Kotler, P. (2011). Reinventing marketing to manage the environmental imperative. *Journal of Marketing, 75*(4), 132–135.

Kozinets, R., Wojnicki, A. C., Wilner, S. J. S., & De Valck, K. (2010). Networked narratives: Understanding word-of-mouth marketing in online communities. *Journal of Marketing, 74*, 71.

Kumar, V., Bhaskaran, V., Mirchandani, R., & Shah, M. (2013). Practice prize winner-creating a measurable social media marketing strategy: Increasing the value and ROI of intangibles and tangibles for hokey pokey. *Marketing Science, 32*(2), 194–212.

Laroche, M., Habibi, M. R., & Richard, M.-O. (2013). To be or not to be in social media: How brand loyalty is affected by social media? *International Journal of Information Management, 33*(1), 76–82.

Leonardi, P. M., & Vaast, E. (2017). Social media and their affordances for organizing: A review and agenda for research. *Academy of Management Annals, 11*(1), 150–188.

Li, Y., Chen, H., Liu, Y., & Peng, M. W. (2014). Managerial ties, organizational learning, and opportunity capture: A social capital perspective. *Asia Pacific Journal of Management, 31*(1), 271–291.

Loughane, E. (2005). Net Success Interviews: Lulu.com.

Luo, X., & Zhang, J. (2013). How do consumer buzz and traffic in social media marketing predict the value of the firm? *Journal of Management Information Systems, 30*(2), 213–238.

Luo, X., Zhang, J., & Duan, W. (2013). Social media and firm equity value. *Information Systems Research, 24*(1), 146–163.

Ma, R., Huang, Y.-C., & Shenkar, O. (2011). Social networks and opportunity recognition: A cultural comparison between Taiwan and the United States. *Strategic Management Journal, 32*(11), 1183–1205.

Michaelidou, N., Siamagka, N. T., & Christodoulides, G. (2011). Usage, barriers and measurement of social media marketing: An exploratory investigation of small and medium B2B brands. *Industrial Marketing Management, 40*(7), 1153–1159.

Miller, A. R., & Tucker, C. (2013). Active social media management: The case of health care. *Information Systems Research, 24*(1), 52–70.
Moe, W. W., & Schweidel, D. A. (2012). Online product opinions: Incidence, evaluation, and evolution. *Marketing Science, 31*(3), 372–386.
Mumi, A., Obal, M., & Yang, Y. (2019). Investigating social media as a firm's signaling strategy through an IPO. *Small Business Economics, 53*(3), 631–645.
Nam, H., & Kannan, P. K. (2014). The informational value of social tagging networks. *Journal of Marketing, 78*(4), 21–40.
Nambisan, S. (2017). Digital entrepreneurship: Toward a digital technology perspective of entrepreneurship. *Entrepreneurship Theory and Practice, 41*(6), 1029–1055.
Naylor, R. W., Lamberton, C. P., & West, P. M. (2012). Beyond the "like" button: The impact of mere virtual presence on brand evaluations and purchase intentions in social media settings. *Journal of Marketing, 76*(6), 105–120.
Ngai, E. W. T., Tao, S. S. C., & Moon, K. K. L. (2015). Social media research: Theories, constructs, and conceptual frameworks. *International Journal of Information Management, 35*(1), 33–44.
Oestreicher-Singer, G., & Sundararajan, A. (2012). The visible hand? Demand effects of recommendation networks in electronic markets. *Management Science, 58*(11), 1963–1981.
Orlikowski, W. J., & Scott, S. V. (2013). What happens when evaluation goes online? Exploring apparatuses of valuation in the travel sector. *Organization Science, 25*(3), 868–891.
Ozgen, E., & Baron, R. A. (2007). Social sources of information in opportunity recognition: Effects of mentors, industry networks, and professional forums. *Journal of Business Venturing, 22*(2), 174–192.
Perrigot, R., Kacker, M., Basset, G., & Cliquet, G. (2012). Antecedents of early adoption and use of social media networks for stakeholder communications: Evidence from franchising. *Journal of Small Business Management, 50*(4), 539–565.
Perry, J. T., Chandler, G. N., & Markova, G. (2012). Entrepreneurial effectuation: A review and suggestions for future research. *Entrepreneurship Theory and Practice, 36*(4), 837–861.
Phang, C. W., Zhang, C., & Sutanto, J. (2013). The influence of user interaction and participation in social media on the consumption intention of niche products. *Information & Management, 50*(8), 661–672.
Rapp, A., Beitelspacher, L. S., Grewal, D., & Hughes, D. E. (2013). Understanding social media effects across seller, retailer, and consumer interactions. *Journal of the Academy of Marketing Science, 41*(5), 547–566.
Read, S., Song, M., & Smit, W. (2009). A meta-analytic review of effectuation and venture performance. *Journal of Business Venturing, 24*(6), 573–587.
Rishika, R., Kumar, A., Janakiraman, R., & Bezawada, R. (2013). The effect of customers' social media participation on customer visit frequency and profitability: An empirical investigation. *Information Systems Research, 24*(1), 108–127.
Rokka, J., Karlsson, K., & Tienari, J. (2014). Balancing acts: Managing employees and reputation in social media. *Journal of Marketing Management, 30*(7–8), 802–827.
Rollins, M., Nickell, D., & Wei, J. (2014). Understanding salespeople's learning experiences through blogging: A social learning approach. *Industrial Marketing Management, 43*(6), 1063–1069.
Rui, H., Liu, Y., & Whinston, A. (2013). Whose and what chatter matters? The effect of tweets on movie sales. *Decision Support Systems, 55*(4), 863–870.
Sambasivan, M., Abdul, M., & Yusop, Y. (2009). Impact of personal qualities and management skills of entrepreneurs on venture performance in Malaysia: Opportunity recognition skills as a mediating factor. *Technovation, 29*(11), 798–805.
Sarasvathy, D. K., Simon, H. A., & Lave, L. (1998). Perceiving and managing business risks: Differences between entrepreneurs and bankers. *Journal of Economic Behavior & Organization, 33*(2), 207–225.
Sarasvathy, S. (2001). Causation and effectuation: Toward a theoretical shift from economic inevitability to entrepreneurial contingency. *Academy of Management Review, 26*(2), 243–263.

Sarasvathy, S., & Dew, N. (2008). Effectuation and Over-Trust: Debating Goel and Karri. *Entrepreneurship Theory and Practice, 32*(4), 727–737.
Schniederjans, D., Cao, E. S., & Schniederjans, M. (2013). Enhancing financial performance with social media: An impression management perspective. *Decision Support Systems, 55*(4), 911–918.
Schumpeter, J. A. (1934). *The theory of economic development: An inquiry into profits, capital, credit, interest, and the business cycle*. New Brunswick, NJ: Transaction Publishers.
Schweidel, D. A., & Moe, W. W. (2014). Listening in on social media: A joint model of sentiment and venue format choice. *Journal of Marketing Research, 51*(4), 387–402.
Shane, S. (2000). Prior knowledge and the discovery of entrepreneurial opportunities. *Organization Science, 11*(4), 448–469.
Shane, S. A. (2003). *A general theory of entrepreneurship: The individual-opportunity nexus*. Northampton, MA: Edward Elgar Publishing.
Singh, R. P. (2000). *Entrepreneurial opportunity recognition through social networks*. New York, NY: Routledge.
Smith, K. (2016). Marketing: 96 amazing social media statistics and facts for 2016, 2016. Available at https://www.brandwatch.com/2016/03/96-amazing-social-media-statistics-and-facts-for-2016/.
Stephen, A. T., & Galak, J. (2012). The effects of traditional and social earned media on sales: A study of a microlending marketplace. *Journal of Marketing Research, 49*(5), 624–639.
Stieglitz, S., & Dang-Xuan, L. (2013). Emotions and information diffusion in social media—Sentiment of microblogs and sharing behavior. *Journal of Management Information Systems, 29*(4), 217–248.
Sussan, F., & Acs, Z. J. (2017). The digital entrepreneurial ecosystem. *Small Business Economics, 49*(1), 55–73.
Swani, K., Brown, B. P., & Milne, G. R. (2014). Should tweets differ for B2B and B2C? An analysis of Fortune 500 companies' Twitter communications. *Industrial Marketing Management, 43*(5), 873–881.
Toubia, O., & Stephen, A. T. (2013). Intrinsic vs. image-related utility in social media: Why do people contribute content to twitter? *Marketing Science, 32*(3), 368–392.
VanMeter, R. A., Grisaffe, D. B., & Chonko, L. B. (2015). Of "likes" and "pins": The effects of consumers' attachment to social media. *Journal of Interactive Marketing, 32*, 70–88.
Weiss, G. (2014). This is how small businesses are using social media. Available at https://www.entrepreneur.com/article/231515.
Wilson, F., Kickul, J., Marlino, D., Barbosa, S. D., & Griffiths, M. D. (2009). An analysis of the role of gender and self-efficacy in developing female entrepreneurial interest and behavior. *Journal of Developmental Entrepreneurship, 14*(02), 105–119.
Wiltbank, R., Dew, N., Read, S., & Sarasvathy, S. D. (2006). What to do next? The case for non-predictive strategy. *Strategic Management Journal, 27*(10), 981–998.
Wiltbank, R., Read, S., Dew, N., & Sarasvathy, S. D. (2009). Prediction and control under uncertainty: Outcomes in angel investing. *Journal of Business Venturing, 24*(2), 116–133.
Yu, Y., Duan, W., & Cao, Q. (2013). The impact of social and conventional media on firm equity value: A sentiment analysis approach. *Decision Support Systems, 55*(4), 919–926.
Zadeh, A. H., & Sharda, R. (2014). Modeling brand post popularity dynamics in online social networks. *Decision Support Systems, 65*, 59–68.
Zhao, H., Seibert, S. E., & Hills, G. E. (2005). The mediating role of self-efficacy in the development of entrepreneurial intentions. *Journal of Applied Psychology, 90*(6), 1265.

Chapter 5
Exploring the Gendered Nature of Digital Social Networks

Diane M. Sullivan and Bari Bendell

Abstract This chapter examines entrepreneurs' engagement with online social network sites (SNS) and the (positive and/or negative) roles they play relative to their networking. More specifically, given the widespread claims that the disembodiment of actors online creates a neutral meritocracy of opportunity, we explore how gender relates to entrepreneurs' use of and experiences with social media networking sites. By drawing on role congruity theory, the chapter considers whether proven offline differences in the (dis)advantages women and men entrepreneurs experience also carry over to the online entrepreneurial environment as well as whether they are likely to relate to the manner in which men and women entrepreneurs cultivate and/or engage with online network ties. Social media features and affordances are reviewed and proposals are developed related to how gender role norms might relate to an entrepreneurs SNS network. Specific social media features and affordances examined include SNS profiles, broadcasting communication behaviors, and social grooming. Additionally, the possibly more nefarious sides of SNS are considered. Specifically, the effects of context collapse and gendertrolling are examined relative to how their effects might impact women entrepreneurs as they work to cultivate and/or engage current or potential network partners through SNS.

Keywords Affordances · Entrepreneurial networking · Gender · Gendered · Network ties · Networks · Role congruence

---

D. M. Sullivan (✉)
University of Dayton, Management and Marketing Department, Dayton, OH, USA
e-mail: dsullivan1@udayton.edu

B. Bendell
Suffolk University, Management & Entrepreneurship Department, Boston, MA, USA
e-mail: bbendell@suffolk.edu

L. Schjoedt et al. (eds.), *Understanding Social Media and Entrepreneurship*, Exploring Diversity in Entrepreneurship,
https://doi.org/10.1007/978-3-030-43453-3_5

5.1 Introduction

As society increasingly employs online social media (e.g., LinkedIn, Twitter, Facebook, Instagram, TikTok, and Renren) to transmit broad messages and communicate directly with specific others, so too do entrepreneurs (Fischer & Reuber, 2011; Mumi, Obal, & Yang, 2019). Indeed, the proliferation of social media allows entrepreneurs to generate, disseminate, and exchange information about their products, venture, and fund-raising needs with multiple, though often, distinct online communities (e.g., customers, supporters, employees, and funders). As such, these communities can be considered as related to entrepreneurs' networks (Smith, Smith, & Shaw, 2017). Yet surprisingly, and perhaps due to the relatively recent emergence of social media, minimal research addresses how entrepreneurs' networks and networking activities may be associated with their social media use.

This chapter addresses this gap in the literature by examining online social network sites (SNS) and the (positive and/or negative) roles they play relative to entrepreneurs' networking.[1] More specifically, we explore how gender relates to entrepreneurs' use of and experiences with social media networking sites. Such an exploration is timely given the widespread claims that the disembodiment of (entrepreneurial) actors online (and on SNS, in particular) creates a neutral meritocracy of opportunity (Dy, Marlow, & Martin, 2017; Krishnan, 2015; Luckman, 2016). Challenging these claims, and drawing on role congruity theory (Eagly, 1987; Eagly & Wood, 2012), we consider whether some proven offline differences in the (dis) advantages women and men entrepreneurs experience (cf., Ahl, 2006; Bird & Brush, 2002) also carry over to online SNS.

We are motivated to explore gender relative to online SNS as research exploring gender has suggested that social constructions of gender prescribe acceptable norms for activities (e.g., actions, behaviors, decisions, career choices, etc.) that are perceived as congruent, or appropriate, for men and women (Fine, 2010, 2017). Traditionally, activities holding a more "masculine" character (e.g., entrepreneurship, engagement with technology, competitive behavior, etc.) are viewed as more gender congruent for men whereas behaviors holding a more "feminine" characteristic (e.g., communal and service-related activities such as family and social care taking, etc.) are thought to be more gender congruent for women (cf., Kidder & Parks, 2001). Deviations in relation to these norms are sometimes subject to sanctions or differing treatments and/or outcomes for individuals enacting them (Alsos, Hytti, & Ljunggren, 2016; Kidder & Parks, 2001). Building from this research, in the chapter, we describe how social constructions of gender might influence the ways in which men and women entrepreneurs use social media for networking and other entrepreneurial activities. In particular, we explain how men and women entrepreneurs might differentially utilize features of social media to impact

[1]Although the focus of the present chapter is social media, and SNS specifically, for entrepreneur's networking, other research would be well-advised to examine social media phenomena relative to other important outcomes and activities such as entrepreneurs' fundraising and marketing.

networking outcomes. In addition, we also explore how other phenomena related to social media—context collapse and trolling—may be subject to gender effects and we explain how these phenomena might relate to entrepreneurs' networking.

The remainder of the chapter proceeds as follows. First, we briefly introduce the types of social media our chapter emphasizes—social network sites—and provide a brief description of some of the primary social network sites entrepreneurs utilize for networking. We then provide a brief overview of research on gender differences relative to entrepreneurs' offline networks and provide a rationale for why gender differences related to entrepreneurs' networks and networking might also exist online. To begin explaining gender differences in entrepreneurs' online social networks, we highlight the important role of social media features and affordances (e.g., actions made available through social media). Accordingly, we discuss the importance of taking an affordance view when studying social media relative to networks and highlight three specific features or affordances that hold the greatest promise for explaining gender differences relative to entrepreneurs' social media networking activities. Fourth, we discuss the social media phenomenon of context collapse (i.e., when social media user's online social network is composed of network partners that come from different areas of the user's life like family, friends, coworkers, media, financiers, etc.). In our discussion of context collapse, we describe how men and women entrepreneurs might be required to approach "audience management" in different ways that could have important network effects. Fifth, we consider the more nefarious side of social media and discuss how trolling—or the intentional targeting of other users through derogatory behaviors online—relates to women entrepreneurs' social media presence and networking. Finally, we conclude the chapter by discussing promising areas for future research and highlight specific research questions related to gender and entrepreneurship, social media, and networking that future scholars might fruitfully pursue.

5.2 Social Media's Social Network Sites (SNS)

Although there are several forms of social media we focus on SNS, in the present chapter, because they are the most frequently used online social media platforms in terms of having the highest numbers of users. For that reason, we adopt the widely accepted definition of social network sites, as developed by Ellison and Boyd (2013), as follows:

> A social network site is a networked communication platform in which participants 1) have uniquely identifiable profiles that consist of user-supplied content, content provided by other users, and/or system-level data; 2) can publicly articulate connections that can be viewed and traversed by others; and 3) can consume, produce, and/or interact with streams of user-generated content provided by their connections on the site (2013, p. 158).

According to the Pew Research Center (2019), 72% of all Americans use some type of social media SNS (78% of women vs. 65% of men). Interestingly, a large number of these users engage on multiple social media platforms. For example, a significant majority of Twitter users also indicate that they use Facebook (90%) and Instagram (73%), with 54% of Twitter users on Snapchat and 50% on LinkedIn (Smith & Anderson, 2018). Consequently, there is conspicuous overlap between users of the various SNS platforms.

Four of the most common SNS sites, especially for entrepreneurs, include Twitter, Facebook, LinkedIn, and Instagram and each allows users to customize their free profile by adding their name and a short biography, a photo, and one or more website links (e.g., to their other social media accounts, personal, or work webpages). A brief description and notable highlights of these prominent platforms are below.

Twitter, launched in 2006, enables users to deploy 140 characters to quickly spread information and user updates. By the end of 2018, Twitter had 126 million daily users (Kastrenakes, 2019). These include a bevy of well-known entrepreneurs (e.g., @Oprah, @richardbranson, @toryburch, @BillGates, @Angie_Hicks, @ elonmusk, @CherWang), though several prominent female entrepreneurs are missing including Sara Blakely of SPANX and Bet365's Denise Coates. Twitter allows each user to curate their incoming and outgoing content (i.e., whose tweets they follow and who follows them) based on their interests and desire for privacy. Twenty-two percent of American adults use Twitter.

Facebook enables its 1.5 billion daily users (as of the end of 2018, Kastrenakes, 2019) to share pictures, stories, links, and other information with other Facebook members. A 2019 Pew Research Center survey found that 69% of American adults use Facebook, with about three-quarters of these users visiting the site once a day. The average number of friends among adult users is 338. Facebook, launched in 2004 (but only rolled out beyond Ivy League University users in 2006), requires users to list themselves by the name they use in real life to ensure accurate (and safe) connections in the social network (though there are some exceptions, for example, with German courts arguing the policy is illegal). Users have the ability to tailor their privacy settings so that only specific "friends" they added to their network are permitted to view their full profile description and online activity.

LinkedIn (2019) reports that over 190 million workers in the USA have profiles on the SNS. Launched in 2003, and acquired by Microsoft in 2016, LinkedIn enables users to network professionally with their network "connections." Users can list their professional skills, work experiences, and interests, as well as post and find jobs, message other users, and provide "endorsements" of other user's professional skills. Twenty-five percent of American adults use LinkedIn (Smith & Anderson, 2018).

Instagram is a social networking app for sharing photos and videos from a smartphone. Launched in 2010, Instagram has 500 million daily users (Kastrenakes, 2019). In using Instagram, users upload photos or videos to the SNS and share them with their followers (or a select subgroup). Instagram users are also permitted to view, comment on, and like posts shared by their friends on the platform. Thirty-five percent of American adults use Instagram (Smith & Anderson, 2018), which was acquired by Facebook in 2012.

5.3 The Scholarly Examination of SNS

Overall, due to their widespread adoption, SNS platforms have been proposed as representing a major change in the nature of human interactions (Papacharissi, 2010), thus requiring scholarly attention. Indeed, the use of such platforms is becoming ubiquitous among entrepreneurs. In determining a fruitful path forward for studying social media, researchers in the information sciences have highlighted certain attributes of SNS platforms that may be especially pertinent in understanding their use, principally in business domains. These include the development of *user profiles*, the capability to conduct *searches*, the ability to develop and manage *online relations*, and the ability to view others' networks (e.g., the *transparency* of online networks) (Kane, Alavi, Labianca, & Borgatti, 2014). These SNS features have also been emphasized as particularly relevant in the entrepreneurial domain (see Smith et al., 2017).

Broadly speaking, these SNS features (e.g., user profiles, searches, online relations, and transparency) have been suggested to provide what computer-mediated communication scholars call *affordances* (Baym, 2010). Affordances refer to the utility (e.g., actions/capabilities) users may exploit through their use of SNS technology attributes (Leonardi, 2014). For example, through a well-crafted user profile, entrepreneurs may be able to *signal* (an SNS affordance), or communicate, their legitimacy to other SNS users. User profiles also afford entrepreneurs the ability to *edit* (another SNS affordance) the content of their profiles to communicate competencies related to themselves and/or their ventures. According to Smith et al. (2017), affordances such as these (and others) may relate to networking outcomes entrepreneurs experience including increasing their network size and strengthening their network ties.

In the present chapter, we, too, believe entrepreneurs may realize network outcomes in association with their networking activities via engagement with the affordances and features of SNS. However, in line with research that has questioned the gender neutrality of digital entrepreneurship (cf., Duffy & Pruchniewska, 2017; Dy et al., 2017), we argue that gender differences likely exist in terms of how men and women entrepreneurs utilize SNS features and affordances as well as the outcomes entrepreneurs might realize through this engagement. For example, user profile content *signals* that might relay legitimacy and competence to SNS network partners may vary for men and women entrepreneurs and will likely result in varying SNS network outcomes (e.g., network size, speed of network growth differences, strength of tie differences, etc.). We explore the potential for gender differences related to SNS features, affordances, and networks below. To set the stage for our expectation of gender differences related to SNS affordances and networks, we first briefly review research that has examined gender differences in entrepreneurs' offline (i.e., "real world") networks.

5.4 Gender and Entrepreneurs' Offline Network Connections

Research on gender and entrepreneurship has broadly found that men and women entrepreneurs' networks and networking activities vary (Carsrud, Gaglio, Olm, & Churchill, 1987; Godwin, Stevens, & Brenner, 2006; Greve & Salaff, 2003; Orhan, 2001). For example, with respect to entrepreneurs' networks, some research suggests that women entrepreneurs emphasize networks that are composed more of individuals with whom they have a close relationship (e.g., spouse, family members, friends), whereas men are more likely to emphasize and rely on their networks of weaker, but broader, professional ties (Orhan, 2001). These differences in network composition are, perhaps, not surprising as they seem to conform to social constructions of gender that dictate norms of behavior where women emphasize the feminine role that focuses on communal behaviors, while men are expected to align with the masculine role that emphasizes assertiveness (Eagly & Wood, 2012).

In addition to network composition, it is curious that other research has found that men entrepreneur's networking activities enhance their expectations for venture growth whereas women entrepreneur's networking does not (Manolova, Carter, Manev, & Gyoshev, 2007). Yet, perhaps this is not surprising as men's emphasis on external, and professional, network ties may allow them to access more diverse information that can highlight growth opportunities as well as secure resources and assets to support their pursuit (Granovetter, 1973). On the other hand, women entrepreneurs' emphasis on developing networks of close connections primarily composed of family and friends might lead to information and resource access that is capable of supporting initial start-up activities. However, those network ties are likely to fall short of resources necessary to promote venture growth due to redundancies and resource restrictions (Uzzi, 1997). Overall, it seems that men and women's networks and networking activities appear to conform to norms as prescribed by their gender role.

This prior research examining men and women entrepreneurs' networks and networking has focused on examining networks utilizing traditional conceptual and operational treatments of networks (i.e., face-to-face or "offline" network ties) (cf., Carsrud et al., 1987). Given the increasing digitalization of business and entrepreneurial domains, we believe, to gain a fuller understanding of entrepreneur's networks, we need to examine characteristics and/or phenomena related to entrepreneurs' online, or social media, networks. For example, if online SNS provide a neutral meritocracy of opportunity (Krishnan, 2015; Luckman, 2016), then we might expect the SNS networking behaviors men and women entrepreneurs engage in, as well as the network tie relationships they realize, to be compositionally and qualitatively equivalent. However, as we will argue, much like men and women entrepreneurs' offline networks vary, we believe their online networks and networking will also vary. We develop this overarching proposition by drawing on research related to role congruity theory (Eagly, 1987; Eagly & Wood, 2012; Gupta, Goktan, & Gunay, 2014).

Broadly, research drawing on role congruity theory suggests that society holds connotations of what activities are viewed as appropriate or acceptable for men and women and these activities conform for masculine and feminine gender roles, respectively. For example, innovation is largely viewed as a masculine domain and therefore largely reserved for men (Alsos et al., 2016), whereas nursing is viewed as a feminine domain and largely reserved for women (Akerlof & Kranton, 2010). And, although men and women might be equally capable of and willing to enact both masculine and feminine activities (e.g., scholarship has found that men and women express similar attitudes about risk and a comparable level of risk propensity despite widely held perceptions that women are more risk averse than men), one's social environment largely prescribes which activities are viewed as more socially "appropriate" for men and women to enact (Fine, 2017). When deviations from these social norms occur, as might sometimes be the case when women engage in perceived masculine activities like entrepreneurship and/or the pursuit of innovation, the "rules" that apply to women and men entrepreneurs (i.e., qualifications required in order to gain access to entrepreneurial capital) might vary (cf., Aidis, 2016; Bijekić, Brink, Ettl, Kriwolusky, & Welter, 2016). Indeed, research has found that pitches given by female entrepreneurs are evaluated less favorably than identical ones given by their male counterparts (e.g., femininity precludes assertiveness), suggesting that gendered stereotypical behavior is not only socially constructed but also reinforced, even in entrepreneurial contexts (Bigelow, Lundmark, Parks, & Wuebker, 2014; Brooks, Huang, Kearney, & Murray, 2014; Kanze, Huang, Conley, & Higgins, 2018). Thus, men and women face strong pressures to exhibit socially constructed prescriptive gender stereotypes for masculinity and femininity, respectively. Building from this idea, we next consider how men and women entrepreneur's use of SNS features and affordances as well as their corresponding network outcomes might vary.

5.5 SNS Affordances

To further explore the intersection of gender, social media, and entrepreneurship, we draw upon the research conducted in the fields of new media and communication studies, human-computer interaction, and information science. Specifically, we focus on these fields' study of "affordances" (i.e., the potential for action) that new technologies such as SNS provide users (Gibson, 2014). Technology interfaces are typically structured to offer features that permit or limit particular actions, for example, creating an avatar animal in a video game with blue or purple fur, but not green. When users recognize that these features allow for some customization, the technology provides an affordance. Studying social media affordances is valuable because doing so offers an examination of different possibilities of action within a specific context (Gibson, 2000) at the intersection between the technology's features (especially those that enable the exhibition and management of information flow) and user goals (Leonardi & Vaast, 2017). Moreover, an affordance lens has the potential to help elucidate why, how, and when SNS and other social media diffuse across an organization or professional network and influence future behavior (Faraj & Azad, 2012). Thus, studying social media affordances is beneficial for theory building because affordances typically apply to all/most platforms which ensures that the research is more generalizable and can make a larger contribution than research that simply focuses on features of specific social media platforms (see Ellison & Vitak, 2015: p. 3). Interestingly, because the study of SNS affordances is at its infancy and SNS is a largely evolving technology, there is no finite list or strict definitions of SNS affordances, though some affordances have received more scholarly attention than others. Table 5.1 contains a list of SNS affordances that appear to be more commonly discussed in the literature, a corresponding affordance definition, and the relationship the affordance is, thus far, thought to have with SNS users' networks.

5.6 SNS Affordances and Entrepreneur Network Connections

Recent research has begun exploring the effects of SNS affordances on network connections generally and for entrepreneurs' network connections, specifically. For example, Ellison and Vitak (2015) suggested that specific SNS activities, such as communication behaviors afforded through SNS (e.g., *broadcasting* via timeline posts), can impact the social capital outcomes entrepreneurs might realize. Their reasoning is that certain SNS affordances communicate identity information to other SNS users that might relate to network outcomes, like growing the size of one's network and/or converting latent network ties into weak or strong ties (see also Ellison, Steinfield, & Lampe, 2010). Similarly, Smith et al. (2017) explored how certain SNS features and affordances might differentially relate to the broadening and deepening of entrepreneurial networks through certain network-affecting action mechanisms (e.g., updating one's *profile* to *signal* to other users that the entrepreneur is a relevant and appealing potential network partner). Broadly, this research suggests that through calculated uses of SNS features and affordances (e.g., signaling via profile content), entrepreneurs might be able to expand the size of their networks (e.g., broaden their networks) and/or increase the number of strong ties represented within their SNS online connections (e.g., deepen their networks). What is interesting about prior research on SNS use and networks is that the research uniformly suggests there is a connection between SNS use and varied network outcomes (see also Fischer & Reuber, 2011; Mumi et al., 2019). However impressive, notably absent from this research is a thorough examination of whether individual differences (e.g., gender, culture, etc.) might impact the nature of these relationships.

Table 5.1 Common SNS affordances

Affordance name	Definition	Key relationships to networks	Relevant citations
User profile[a]	Biographical information of the user that may be entered or featured on the SNS	If the content of one's profile allows other users to find commonality and/or identify with one another The profile can act as "social lubrication" that can help users expand their SNS network size	Ellison and Vitak (2015)
Broadcasting	Is a specific communication behavior on SNS whereby users have the ability to efficiently communicate with many users and, specifically, their entire network of connections (e.g., post information for the consumption of others)	Can increase network size Can increase access to bridging ties Can lead to network resource access	Ellison and Vitak (2015); Vitak and Ellison (2013)
Social grooming	Is a specific communication behavior on SNS whereby users target their posts or comments to specific other users (e.g., @name or tagging other users in a post)	Can increase network size Can increase access to bridging ties	Ellison and Vitak (2015)
Visibility	The ability to activate or deactivate posted information and/or allow others to view a user's network connections	Can increase network size Can increase the number of weak ties in a user's network	Smith et al. (2017); Treem and Leonardi (2012)
Association	The ability for others to see the relationship between users on SNS (e.g., who is a "friend" or "connection") and the relationship between users and the content they post (e.g., who posts what content)	Can increase network size Can increase the number of weak ties in a user's network Both size and weak ties are thought to accumulate due to the ability of users to access new connections from their "friend's" networks	Smith et al. (2017); Treem and Leonardi (2012)
Persistence	The ability to locate posted information over time (e.g., after original posting)	Can lead to network resource access (e.g., information from network ties)	Smith et al. (2017); Treem and Leonardi (2012)

[a]User profiles are sometimes considered an SNS feature/attribute versus an affordance

5.7 Gender Differences, SNS Affordances, and Entrepreneurs' Network Connections

Prior research examining SNS features and affordances has purported that use of SNS can result in varying social capital and network outcomes, particularly for entrepreneurs (cf., Smith et al., 2017). When it comes to entrepreneurs' use of SNS for networking, we assert that the ways men and women engage with and utilize the features of SNS for network change will vary. That is, in line with premises from role congruity theory, we believe that the masculine context of entrepreneurship (Ahl, 2006; Fine, 2017) will increase the likelihood that women entrepreneurs engage with SNS in socially ascribed, role congruent, ways that can impact SNS networking outcomes.

Role congruity theory suggests that men and women will not only enact behaviors in gender stereotypical ways, but that the context they find themselves in will provide cues for the behaviors that are viewed as socially appropriate and that one is expected to follow (Carr & Steele, 2010). Numerous scholars have noted that the entrepreneurial context is characterized as highly masculine. For example, Fine notes, "The successful entrepreneur doesn't just have the necessary skills, resources, and business connections; he is also a masculine hero…" (2017, p. 160). Additional entrepreneurial stereotypes include that entrepreneurs are aggressive, risk-taking, and highly autonomous. These characteristics contrast with the feminine role women are expected to enact, which emphasizes warmth and a gentle, communal, nature (Ahl, 2006; Baron, Markman, & Hirsa, 2001; Fine, 2017).

Because of the strong effects of the socialization men and women entrepreneurs experience over time in relation to their gender, they learn what are viewed as culturally appropriate norms and enact them accordingly. That is, men and women enact socially desirable behaviors congruent with their gender to avoid the possibility of negative outcomes, including backlash, that can occur if they were to engage in nonnormative behavior (Amanatullah & Morris, 2010; Bijekić et al., 2016; Eagly & Karau, 2002; Heilman, Wallen, Fuchs, & Tamkins, 2004; Rudman & Glick, 2001). In line with this idea, we believe that women and men entrepreneurs' use of SNS for networking will conform to gender roles of femininity and masculinity, respectively. As a result, we believe the network-based outcomes men and women entrepreneurs might realize will also vary. Below we consider this possibility as we explore entrepreneurs' use of SNS profiles, and the broadcasting and social grooming affordances, used in SNS networking.

5.7.1 SNS Profile

SNS profiles are highly controlled, with individuals generally presenting themselves in static and self-conscious ways. Not surprisingly, one's online identity presentation via their profile is limited in collaborative scope. Broadly, the research suggests that the content in one's profile can relate to networks in two ways: (1) by legitimizing the user in the eyes of the viewer (e.g., customer, potential friend, lender, investor, etc.) and/or (2) by providing signals of the user's identity that can act as the "social lubrication" to find common ground and establish a relationship (i.e., network effects that turn "latent ties" into actual ties, thus expanding one's network, etc.). As such, in order for the content of one's user profile to enable users to expand their network size, users must carefully craft, edit, and/or maintain profiles that communicate socially approved, identity-consistent, information.

Social constructions of gender have led to prescriptions of what constitutes socially approved attributes of an individual's identity based on their sex. In the context of entrepreneurs' SNS profiles, we believe men will likely craft SNS profiles that elucidate assertive, competitive, and agentic characteristics of themselves as entrepreneurs and their ventures as strongly viable firms. Alternatively, women, in embracing the feminine role, are likely to more strongly emphasize profile attributes that relay a gentler, friendly, and collectivist persona for themselves and their ventures. And, although women and men might include some gender role incongruent profile information, in line with role congruity we expect this should be the exception not the norm, and limited in scope, so as to avoid any potential backlash from other SNS users.

As a consequence of the varying information men and women entrepreneurs emphasize in their SNS profile, we expect the networking outcomes men and women realize in relation to their profiles are also likely to vary. SNS profile information is a primary SNS feature through which SNS users identify common ground or signal one's values and beliefs to others in an effort to expand their SNS network size (Ellison & Vitak, 2015; Smith et al., 2017). Given the gendered role signals communicated in men and women entrepreneurs' SNS profiles, we expect that SNS network growth experienced by men entrepreneurs will primarily consist of other men whereas women's SNS network growth will primarily consist of other women. Further, because of the relatively greater competitive emphases of men entrepreneurs' SNS profiles, their SNS networks are also likely to contain a greater number of instrumental contacts, such as investors, who might provide resources helpful for growing the venture. *Overall, we expect that due to society's pressure to conform to gender role norms, men and women entrepreneurs' SNS profile content and resulting SNS entrepreneurial network characteristics* (e.g., *gender representativeness and entrepreneurial resource providers) will vary in gender role congruent ways.*

As described, we believe that SNS user profiles relate to gender, SNS networking behaviors (profile content), and SNS network outcomes. Interestingly, user profiles sometimes hold a more static nature to them in that, although they are editable, they can also be more stable in their content and character (cf., Ellison & Boyd, 2013). However, other SNS affordances are more dynamic. For example, some affordances involve specific actions whereby SNS users communicate with others through the social media platform. Two such affordances that we believe hold additional promise for explaining gender differences in entrepreneurs' networks are *broadcasting* and *social grooming*. We turn to these affordances next.

5.7.2 Broadcasting

The broadcasting SNS affordance refers to social media users' ability to post messages that other users can see. Because others can see these posts, broadcasting is viewed as one of the "specific communication behaviors users perform" on an SNS (Ellison & Vitak, 2015, p. 11). Some research has suggested that broadcasting can have an effect on social capital outcomes, particularly in terms of accessing resources that reside within one's network and/or the networks of a user's SNS contact. In general, a SNS user can prepare a post that can be efficiently communicated to their entire network of SNS connections that can often lead to the access of needed resources like information or financial capital via current connections and/or to new network partners who could provide access (i.e., a contact a "friend" might recommend).

Social constructions of gender often lead to certain expectations in regard to the communication styles and appropriateness of requests within which men and women should engage. For example, men, in adhering to the masculine role, are expected to portray an agentic and dominant communication style. Women, on the other hand, are expected to communicate in a friendly, unselfish, and emotionally expressive manner (Eagly & Wood, 2012). In line with this, we believe that the content, tone, and topics represented in men and women entrepreneurs' SNS posts are likely to vary. For example, by directly and succinctly communicating venture resource requests, a male entrepreneur may receive more positive SNS network responses (e.g., a connection to a lender, investor, supplier, etc.) compared to a woman entrepreneur utilizing the same communication style. To realize a similar outcome (i.e., access to another user's network partners), women entrepreneurs might be expected to communicate in a softer, less direct, manner that frames the request in terms of communal benefits. Failure to remain sensitive to role expectancies might lead to network access restrictions. *Overall, we believe the SNS network effects realized (network size growth and network resource access) by men and women entrepreneurs will vary based on how congruent their broadcasting communication behaviors are with gender role expectations.*

5.7.3 Social Grooming

Social grooming is another specific communication behavior that SNS users can engage in on social media. The essence of social grooming involves how SNS users attend to the posts of other specific SNS users. This can occur through actions such as leaving comments on others' posts, making original wall posts on other user's social media pages, leaving @ or hashtag replies for other users, favoriting and/or liking another user's post, etc. Social grooming has been purported to relate to specific network effects, through activating access to bridging social capital that can help expand a user's network size and increase the number of weak tie partners within the SNS network. More specifically, through attending to specific other users and/or their posts, social grooming is thought to generate a norm of reciprocity when requests are made (i.e., providing access to one of your network contacts when another user is in need).

In line with social constructions of gender, we believe that what is viewed as socially appropriate (and therefore network effecting) social grooming behavior might vary for men and women entrepreneurs. For example, given the assertive quality of the masculine role, men are likely to be positively rewarded (e.g., through network benefits realized) when they engage in (1) more numerous social grooming behaviors and (2) when their social grooming activities involve more varied SNS network partners. That is, we believe, in line with role congruity theory that men entrepreneurs will be more favorably evaluated when their social grooming activities are far reaching and involve responding to posts of other SNS users, even those with whom they have a very weak connection (e.g., casual acquaintances) (cf., Carter, Brush, Greene, Gatewood, & Hart, 2003). These social grooming activities are likely to lead to men entrepreneurs activating bridging social capital, thus gaining access to additional network ties and expanding their set of weak tie network partners. However, such social grooming behaviors when enacted by women entrepreneurs are likely to result in fewer network changes. This is because the feminine role of women entrepreneurs precludes assertiveness (Brooks et al., 2014). Social grooming behaviors, particularly when they involve SNS users with whom the women entrepreneurs have a very weak relationship, are likely to be perceived as communication behaviors that are simply too forward and gender incongruent. Thus, *we expect that social grooming is likely to be a less effective SNS affordance for women entrepreneurs who are trying to expand the size of their SNS network and/or increase the number of weak tie network partners represented in their SNS networks.*

5.8 The Audience (and Context Collapse)

Social media offers entrepreneurs the opportunity to communicate directly with current and potential customers, employees, funders, traditional media, and other members of their entrepreneurial ecosystems. Business owners and aspiring entrepreneurs have embraced social media to varying extents by joining platforms such as LinkedIn, Twitter, Instagram, and Facebook and enacting an array of communication behaviors to develop their audience (i.e., network) and support for their entrepreneurial endeavors. For instance, SNS can be used for self-promotion and to post information on upcoming products, services, or events, as well as links to websites, videos, and interactions with news media (e.g., interviews or quotes). The audience (i.e., current or potential network partners) intended for each of these types of communication is often visualized by the individual in an effort to properly manage their self-presentation based on the latest social context and relevant technological affordances. Research shows that most SNS profile owners acknowledge having multiple audiences and that there is a need for variable self-presentation as they craft their communications specifically for one or more of their audiences (Ellison, Vitak, Gray, & Lampe, 2014).

SNS platforms are valuable in that they reduce spatial and temporal boundaries which allow users to easily reach a potentially unlimited audience and provide the opportunity to showcase both their personal and professional sides. However, entrepreneurs, like any user of social media, need to address the potential problems associated with the social media phenomena of context collapse (i.e., having many distinct social network members or audiences subsumed into one following). By bringing together multiple audiences into a single context (e.g., family members, potential funders, media, etc.) SNS platforms make it difficult for individuals to utilize the same techniques online that they employ to handle their multifaceted identity in face-to-face conversations. For example, the complexities of identity lead many people to only share certain stories with a specific audience (e.g., with co-workers, but not with family members or acquaintances) and to use the shared language, syntax, and styles that are unique to that audience. Indeed, context collapse makes it challenging for entrepreneurs to not only present themselves favorably and appropriately to each distinct audience, but to maximize the effectiveness of their communication across each audience (e.g., funders, employees, friends, and family) as they all receive the same "message" about "who" the entrepreneur is.

The increasing number of users online across multiple SNS platforms may make it more challenging to gain a sense of one's own audience for each technology-mediated conversation—leading users, especially entrepreneurs, who may be nervous about upsetting members of their network (e.g., funders, suppliers, employees, customers)—to only make posts that they believe the largest number of their current and future audiences will "get" and find non-offensive (Marwick & Boyd, 2011). Of course, SNS profile owners could navigate their multiple, intersecting audiences by strategically (and painstakingly) concealing information from specific audiences while targeting others in order to try to present an interesting, yet authentic and appropriate, self across each social context. This time-consuming process, however, may involve calibrating specific privacy settings on each SNS platform, using a single platform to engage with a specific audience to the exclusion of others, or creating multiple profiles on each SNS platform to speak to each audience, which is likely untenable in the long run.

Individuals concerned with context collapse must manage their impressions "by balancing personal/public information, avoiding certain topics, and maintaining authenticity" (Marwick & Boyd, 2011: p. 124). This is especially true for entrepreneurs seeking funding, as investors have been shown to make decisions based on their evaluation of both the "horse and the jockey" (i.e., the entrepreneur and the business opportunity) (Mitteness, Baucus, & Sudek, 2012). Thus, the process of strategically appealing to one's online social network reflects a careful calculation to develop a personal brand and commodify oneself (Hearn, 2008). However, consciously speaking to one's audience may be viewed by some members as inauthentic (Marwick & Boyd, 2011). Authenticity provides meaning and purpose to one's life (McCarthy, 2016) and facilitates trust building and information sharing behaviors necessary for developing and maintaining network relationships (both personal and professional) (Vannini & Williams, 2016).

In an effort to control their authenticity, many entrepreneurs may feel the need to engage strategies of communicating widely but consistently on SNS and differentiating between the personal and the private. Much like how politicians manage their political image (Lilleker & Jackson, 2011), entrepreneurs can create and manage their entrepreneurial image through selective disclosures about their private selves. The need to carefully create and manage one's entrepreneurial image on social media is likely to be more complex and important for women compared to men entrepreneurs.

Even though a greater examination of gender is taking place within the field of entrepreneurship currently, research still doesn't typically acknowledge, let alone account for, the ways in which gender shapes the theoretical approach taken, how data is collected, or how conclusions are drawn. Specifically, in the context of this chapter, the literature on entrepreneurs and social media has yet to fully engage with issues of gender. We posit that due to gender stereotypes, the disproportionately negative social pressures and conventions that women face (Carter & Steiner, 2004), and the "stalled revolution" (Walter, 2011, p. 9) of women's advancement toward parity, *women entrepreneurs may be more prone to experiencing the ill effects of context collapse through their online SNS.*

Women, particularly those in leadership positions, have long had to deal with navigating "acceptable" social and professional boundaries in ways that men have not (Jamieson, 1995). In business, women are frequently "measured by two yardsticks: how *as women* they carried out the sales or management role; and how *as managers* they lived up to images of womanhood" (Kanter, 2008, p. 214). Indeed, as Nichols (1993, p. 58) explains:

> "This double yardstick of gender appropriateness and managerial effectiveness often leaves women in an unbreakable, untenable double bind. Women who attempt to fit themselves into a managerial role by acting like men, are forced to behave in a sexually dissonant way. They risk being characterized as "too aggressive," or worse, just plain "bitchy." Yet women who act like ladies, speaking indirectly and showing concern for others, risk being seen as "ineffective," as someone skilled in the soft side of communications but unable to do the hard work of management."

Therefore, by claiming that women are naturally endowed with superior emotional and communication skills, society penalizes women who do not exhibit these qualities (Fine, 2010). Such "double binds" are frequently involved in response to women's communication style and language. For example, women, but not men, risk being perceived as behaving improperly when engaged in strong adversarial conduct as required by their professional role (Jamieson, 1995). Even a sense of humor places women in a double bind as they are expected to applaud the comedy of men without creating humor of their own or taking themselves too seriously (Mickes, Walker, Parris, Mankoff, & Christenfeld, 2012; Walker, 1988). Indeed, women operate in a constellation of double binds.

These "self-defeating traps" (Kanter, 2008) may be particularly salient when women entrepreneurs engage in social media use. In online social networks each post, tweet, and comment can be scrutinized by one's entire audience and revaluated in the future by the same network members or new ones. The permanence of online activities coupled with increased reports of harassment online in the form of attacks on a victim's physical appearance, gender, sexual orientation, race, and professional character have led to widespread concern among adult Americans about being bullied or harassed online (onlineharassmentdata.org, 2018). Such concerns may be particularly salient for women online as they are at a greater risk than men for not only generic harassment (57% vs. 42%, respectively) (onlineharassmentdata.org, 2018) but also sexual harassment (21% vs. 9%, respectively) (Duggan, 2017). Lastly, with 39% of the technology experts, scholars, government leaders, and corporate executives surveyed by Pew Research Center (Rainie, Anderson, & Albright, 2017) expecting an online future shaped more by negative activities than positive ones, *context collapse may become an even greater issue for women entrepreneurs online, thus limiting the networking benefits they might realize.*

5.9 Gender, Entrepreneur Networks, and Trolling on Social Media

Studies consistently show that women's online behavior is more frequently policed than men's and that women (especially those in positions of prominence or power like politicians or journalists) are judged more harshly for deviating from the stereotypical social norms (Amnesty International, 2019; Gardiner et al., 2016). Specifically, women are subjected to more "trolling" online (i.e., posting incendiary comments as a means of eliciting strong emotional reactions from the chosen target or their supporters) than men (Amnesty International, 2019). Mantilla (2013) argues that this aggressive, attention-seeking behavior aimed at women online is distinct from generic trolling and should be labeled "gendertrolling" because it is dramatically more destructive to its victims. Gendertrolling tends to involve a coordinated effort by numerous people to overwhelm the victim with gender-based insults that use vile and pejorative language designed to humiliate, insult, and even threaten women (and their supporters) over a sustained period of time (sometimes years) (Mantilla, 2013). This networked misogyny and virulent sexism often originates from somewhat privileged male members of a loose online network known as the *manosphere* (Marwick & Caplan, 2018; Phillips, 2015).

While generic trolling can be savagely cruel, the attacks often remain limited to one or two websites or social media platforms. By comparison, gendertrolls relentlessly pursue their victims across multiple online sites and even into actual life by: sending mail, packages, or food to the victims home; doxing (publishing the victim's personal private information—e.g., email address, home address, and phone number); and swatting (a criminal harassment tactic used to trick emergency service dispatchers into believing there is a violent situation involving an armed suspect at the victim's address) (Mantilla, 2013). Given that gendertrolling frequently occurs in response to women speaking out about misogyny or sexism (Mantilla, 2013), female SNS users are subjected to yet another digital double bind that might keep women from revealing their private selves, feeling comfortable in voicing their opinions online, occupying male-dominated space/networks, and participating fully online. Thus, in part:

> due to gendertrolling, cultivating one's online self-presentation may feel particularly like a careful art for women that compounds the complexities they might encounter when cultivating and/or engaging current or potential network partners.

5.10 Promising Areas for Future Research

One particularly promising direction for future research lies in studying gender and social media in relation to network characteristics and connection effects. First, scholars should examine and evaluate entrepreneur's online social networks in terms of how each of the SNS platforms is being used, how often, and what outcomes are being achieved. The size, composition, and power of an entrepreneur's online social network should be measured and tracked over time and compared across gender. Qualitative studies could be employed to better understand what roles context collapse and gendertrolling play in keeping female and male entrepreneurs from participating on SNS, or limiting their participation to innocuous topics, and whether that leads to heterogeneous outcomes based on gender.

It would also be helpful to develop a gender-aware framework to explore the relationship between social media affordances and entrepreneur's network outcomes. This requires a better understanding of the structure and density of entrepreneurial social networks and an examination of whether there are fundamental SNS differences based on gender. We believe the integration of theories such as role congruity theory (Eagly, 1987) and social identity theory (Tajfel & Turner, 1986) holds particular promise for developing a gender-aware framework of entrepreneur behavior on SNS platforms. Although, in the present work, we have presented a few exploratory proposals that can inform a gender-aware framework that utilizes role congruity theory, some more specific research questions future scholars might explore include: (1) whether women and men's entrepreneurial SNS networks are made up primarily of same-gender connections or more equally distributed across both genders and (2) whether men and women entrepreneurs are equally likely to be network brokers online (i.e., individuals whose network position provides them with the opportunity to mediate/broker between other people).

Another area of interest to scholars may be an examination of potential connections between self-leadership and SNS behavior. As SNS social networks are generally larger than an individual's friend group, entrepreneurs may prefer to use SNS to other mechanisms as they actively (or passively) solicit support and encouragement for their self-leadership behaviors. A recent study by Bendell, Sullivan, and Marvel (2019) suggests that there are gender differences in the use of, and outcomes derived from, the employment of key self-leadership behaviors among high-growth entrepreneurs. For example, the authors' study showed that men and women entrepreneurs employ significantly different levels of self-goal setting and self-cueing behaviors. Additionally, Bendell et al. (2019) found that male entrepreneurs extract greater benefit from high self-goal setting behaviors than female entrepreneurs and that, at low levels of self-cueing, male entrepreneurs generate greater intellectual property compared to females while, at high levels of self-cueing, female high-growth entrepreneurs generate greater intellectual property compared to males. Given these findings, future research could explore whether there are gender differences in the degree to which entrepreneurs use SNS in self-goal setting and self-cueing, which platforms they prefer when employing these behaviors (e.g., LinkedIn, Twitter, Facebook), and whether using SNS to support these behaviors leads to positive or negative outcomes. Additional research questions of particular interest might include whether women entrepreneurs, relative to male entrepreneurs and female non-entrepreneurs, prefer to use one or multiple SNS platforms for self-goal setting and whether the same SNS platform is used at all stages of the self-goal setting process (e.g., formulating, executing, evaluation, and revising) versus using a different platform depending on the stage in the process.

Scholars may also find value in examining the role SNS platforms play in the decision-making process for entrepreneurs. For example, recent studies suggest that gender may play a role in founder resource acquisition and market positioning (Elliott & Orser, 2018) or in innovation purchase decisions among small and medium enterprise owners (Bendell et al., 2019). Therefore a better understanding is needed of the degree to which SNS currently plays a role in entrepreneurial decision-making processes (e.g., informational, exerting peer pressure), or how it might in the future, and whether gender is a moderator.

Finally, the present research emphasized the individual difference of gender relative to social media usage and network outcomes realized. However, future research would be well advised to examine other individual differences related to entrepreneurship and social media. For example, scholarship in entrepreneurship has meaningfully explored how entrepreneurial phenomena might be influenced by culture. Research in this vein has discovered that facets of culture, such as distinctions between eastern and western societies, religious differences, and varying organizational cultures, need to be intentionally explored in order to more fully understand entrepreneurial phenomena (cf., Balkin & Schjoedt, 2012; Lin, Carsrud, Jagoda, & Shen, 2013; Sebah, Carsrud, & Kocak, 2014). In line with this research, we believe future scholarship studying social media and networking could benefit from exploring how these technologies might be differentially used toward the achievement of varying outcomes based on culture.

5.11 Concluding Remarks

In the present chapter, we explain how men and women entrepreneurs might differentially utilize features of social media to impact SNS networking outcomes. In addition, we also explore how the social media phenomena of context collapse and trolling may be subject to gender effects that relate to entrepreneur's networking. Drawing from role congruity theory, we developed initial proposals that explain how gender role norms might relate to an entrepreneurs' SNS network. Specifically, we suggest: (1) due to conformity to gender roles, the profile content of men and women entrepreneurs will vary, which will impact SNS network composition and content access; (2) SNS network size growth and network resource access will vary by men and women entrepreneurs as a consequence of how congruent their broadcasting communication behaviors are with gender role expectations; (3) social grooming will be less effective for women entrepreneurs compared to men in terms of realizing larger networks and networks with more weak ties; (4) women entrepreneurs are more prone to experiencing the ill effects of SNS context collapse, thus limiting the networking benefits they might otherwise realize; and (5) gendertrolling will have significant effects on women's online presence and self-presentation, which will relate to how women entrepreneurs might cultivate and/or engage current or potential network partners. Despite being a nascent effort exploring gender, networking, and social media, we hope this research can contribute to the burgeoning scholarship on social media and that future researchers might be inspired to explore these and other important relationships associated with new technology and entrepreneurship.

References

Ahl, H. (2006). Why research on women entrepreneurs needs new directions. *Entrepreneurship Theory & Practice, 30*(5), 595–622.

Aidis, R. (2016). Three faces of innovation: Institutions, gender and entrepreneurship in Latin America. In G. Alsos, U. Hytti, & E. Ljunggren (Eds.), *Research handbook on gender and innovation* (pp. 72–90). Cheltenham, UK: Edward Elgar.

Akerlof, G. A., & Kranton, R. E. (2010). *Identity economics: How our identities shape our work, wages, and Well-being*. Princeton, NJ: Princeton University Press.

Alsos, G., Hytti, U., & Ljunggren, E. (2016). Gender and innovation – An introduction. In G. A. Alsos, U. Hytti, & E. Ljunggren (Eds.), *Research handbook on gender and innovation* (pp. 3–16). Cheltenham, UK: Edward Elgar.

Amanatullah, E. T., & Morris, M. W. (2010). Negotiating gender roles: Gender differences in assertive negotiating are mediated by women's fear of backlash and attenuated when negotiating on behalf of others. *Journal of Personality and Social Psychology, 98*(2), 256–267.

Amnesty International. (2019). Troll Patrol. Retrieved from https://decoders.amnesty.org/projects/troll-patrol

Balkin, D. B., & Schjoedt, L. (2012). The role of organizational cultural values in managing diversity. *Organizational Dynamics, 41*(1), 44–51.

Baron, R. A., Markman, G. D., & Hirsa, A. (2001). Perceptions of women and men as entrepreneurs: Evidence for differential effects of attributional augmenting. *Journal of Applied Psychology, 86*(5), 923–929.

Baym, N. K. (2010). *Personal connections in the digital age*. Cambridge, UK: Polity press.

Bendell, B., Sullivan, D. M. & Hanek, K. (2019). Are technology investment decisions gendered among SME owners. *White Paper*.

Bendell, B., Sullivan, D. M., & Marvel, M. (2019). A gender-aware study of self-leadership strategies among high-growth entrepreneurs. *Journal of Small Business Management, 57*(1), 110–130.

Bigelow, L., Lundmark, L., Parks, J. M., & Wuebker, R. (2014). Skirting the issues: Experimental evidence of gender bias in IPO prospectus evaluations. *Journal of Management, 40*(6), 1732–1759.

Bijekić, T., Brink, S., Ettl, K., Kriwolusky, S., & Welter, F. (2016). Women's innovation in Germany – Empirical facts and conceptual explanations. In G. Alsos, U. Hytti, & E. Ljunggren (Eds.), *Research handbook on gender and innovation* (pp. 51–71). Cheltenham, UK: Edward Elgar.

Bird, B., & Brush, C. (2002). A gendered perspective on organizational creation. *Entrepreneurship Theory and Practice, 26*(3), 41–65.

Brooks, A. W., Huang, L., Kearney, S. W., & Murray, F. E. (2014). Investors prefer entrepreneurial ventures pitched by attractive men. *Proceedings of the National Academy of Sciences*. https://doi.org/10.1073/pnas.1321202111

Carr, P. B., & Steele, C. M. (2010). Stereotype threat affects financial decision making. *Psychological Science, 21*(10), 1411–1416.

Carsrud, A., Gaglio, C. M., Olm, K. W., & Churchill, N. C. (1987). Entrepreneurs—Mentors, networks, and successful venture development: An exploratory study. *American Journal of Small Business, 12*(2), 13–18.

Carter, C., & Steiner, L. (2004). Introduction to critical readings: Media and gender. *Critical Readings: Media and Gender, 1*, 1–10.

Carter, N. M., Brush, C. G., Greene, P. G., Gatewood, E., & Hart, M. M. (2003). Women entrepreneurs who break through to equity financing: The influence of human, social and financial capital. *Venture Capital, 5*(1), 1–28.

Duffy, B. E., & Pruchniewska, U. (2017). Gender and self-enterprise in the social media age: A digital double bind. *Information, Communication & Society, 20*(6), 843–859.

Duggan, M. (2017). Online harassment report. Retrieved from https://www.pewinternet.org/2017/07/11/experiencing-online-harassment/

Dy, A. M., Marlow, S., & Martin, L. (2017). A web of opportunity or the same old story? Women digital entrepreneurs and the intersectionality theory. *Human Relations, 70*(3), 286–311.

Eagly, A. H. (1987). *Sex differences in social behavior: A social-role interpretation*. Hillsdale, NJ: Erlbaum.

Eagly, A. H., & Karau, S. J. (2002). Role congruity theory of prejudice toward female leaders. *Psychological Review, 109*(3), 573–598.

Eagly, A. H., & Wood, W. (2012). Social role theory. In P. van Lange, A. Kruglanski, & E. T. Higgins (Eds.), *Handbook of theories in social psychology* (pp. 458–476). Thousand Oaks, CA: Sage.

Elliott, C., & Orser, B. (2018). Feminist entrepreneurial identity: Reproducing gender through founder decision-making. In P. Greene & C. Brush (Eds.), *A research agenda for women and entrepreneurship: Identity through aspirations* (Behaviors and confidence) (pp. 114–136). Northampton, MA: Edward Elgar.

Ellison, N., & Vitak, J. (2015). Social media affordances and their relationship to social capital processes. In S. Sundar (Ed.), *The handbook of psychology of communication technology* (pp. 205–227). Boston: Wiley-Blackwell.

Ellison, N. B., & Boyd, D. (2013). Sociality through social network sites. In W. H. Dutton (Ed.), *The Oxford handbook of internet studies* (pp. 151–173). Oxford: Oxford University Press.

Ellison, N. B., Steinfield, C., & Lampe, C. (2010). Connection strategies: Social capital implications of Facebook-enabled communication processes. *New Media & Society, 13*(6), 873–892.

Ellison, N. B., Vitak, J., Gray, R., & Lampe, C. (2014). Cultivating social resources on social network sites: Facebook relationship maintenance behaviors and their role in social capital processes. *Journal of Computer Mediated Communication, 9*(4), 855–870.

Faraj, S., & Azad, B. (2012). The materiality of technology: An affordance perspective. In P. Leonardi, B. Nardi, & J. Kallinkikos (Eds.), *Materiality and organizing: Social interaction in a technological world* (pp. 237–258). Oxford: Oxford University Press.

Fine, C. (2010). *Delusions of gender: How our minds, society, and Neurosexism create difference*. New York: WW Norton & Company.

Fine, C. (2017). *Testosterone rex: Unmaking the myths of our gendered minds*. New York: WW Norton & Company.

Fischer, E., & Reuber, A. R. (2011). Social interaction via new social media: (How) can interactions on Twitter affect effectual thinking and behavior? *Journal of Business Venturing, 25*(1), 1–18.

Gardiner, B., Mansfield, M., Anderson, I., Holder, J., Louter, D., & Ulmanu, M. (2016). The dark side of Guardian comments. *The Guardian*. Retrieved from https://www.theguardian.com/technology/2016/apr/12/the-dark-side-of-guardian-comments

Gibson, E. J. (2000). Where is the information for affordances? *Ecological Psychology, 12*(1), 53–56.

Gibson, J. J. (2014). The theory of affordances. In *The ecological approach to visual perception* (Classic Edition). New York: Psychology Press, pp. 119–136.

Godwin, L. N., Stevens, C. E., & Brenner, N. L. (2006). Forced to play by the rules? Theorizing how mixed-sex founding teams benefit women entrepreneurs in male-dominated contexts. *Entrepreneurship, Theory and Practice, 30*(5), 623–642.

Granovetter, M. (1973). The strength of weak ties. *American Journal of Sociology, 78*(6), 1360–1380.

Greve, A., & Salaff, J. W. (2003). Social networks and entrepreneurship. *Entrepreneurship, Theory and Practice, 28*(1), 1–22.

Gupta, V. K., Goktan, A. B., & Gunay, G. (2014). Gender differences in evaluation of new business opportunity: A stereotype threat perspective. *Journal of Business Venturing, 29*(2), 273–388.

Hearn, A. (2008). Meat, mask, burden': Probing the contours of the branded 'self. *Journal of Consumer Culture, 8*(2), 197–217.

Heilman, M. E., Wallen, A. S., Fuchs, D., & Tamkins, M. M. (2004). Penalties for success: Reactions to women who succeed at male gender-typed tasks. *Journal of Applied Psychology, 89*(3), 416–427.

Jamieson, K. H. (1995). *Beyond the double bind: Women and leadership*. New York: Oxford University Press.

Kane, G. C., Alavi, M., Labianca, G., & Borgatti, S. P. (2014). What's different about social media networks? A framework and research agenda. *MIS Quarterly, 38*(1), 275–304.

Kanter, R. M. (2008). *Men and women of the corporation*. New York: Basic Books.

Kanze, D., Huang, L., Conley, M. A., & Higgins, E. T. (2018). We ask men to win and women not to lose: Closing the gender gap in startup funding. *Academy of Management Journal, 61*(2), 586–614.

Kastrenakes, J. (2019). Twitter's final monthly user count shows a company still struggling to grow. Retrieved from https://www.theverge.com/2019/4/23/18511383/twitter-q1-2019-earnings-report-mau

Kidder, D. L., & Parks, J. M. (2001). The good soldier: Who is s(he)? *Journal of Organizational Behavior, 22*(8), 939–959.

Krishnan, S. (2015). Why the online marketplace is perfect for women in business. *Entrepreneur.* Retrieved from https://www.entrepreneur.com/article/245495, January 3, 2019.

Leonardi, P. M. (2014). Social media, knowledge sharing, and innovation: Toward a theory of communication visibility. *Information Systems Research, 25*(4), 796–816.

Leonardi, P. M., & Vaast, E. (2017). Social media and their affordances for organizing: A review and agenda for research. *Academy of Management Annals, 11*(1), 150–188.

Lilleker, D., & Jackson, N. (2011). Microblogging, constituency service and impression management–UK MPs and the use of Twitter. *Journal of Legislative Studies, 17*(1), 86–105.

Lin, X., Carsrud, A., Jagoda, K., & Shen, W. (2013). Determinants of entrepreneurial intentions: Applying Western model to the Sri Lanka context. *Journal of Enterprising Culture, 21*(2), 153–174.

LinkedIn. (2019). LinkedIn Workforce Report, United States. https://economicgraph.linkedin.com/resources/linkedin-workforce-report-january-2019

Luckman, S. (2016). Micro-enterprise as work-life 'magical solution." In L. Adkins & M. Dever (Eds), The post-fordist sexual contract: Working and living in contingency, Basingstoke, UK: Palgrave Macmillan, pp. 91–108.

Manolova, T. S., Carter, N., Manev, I., & Gyoshev, B. (2007). The differential effect of men and women entrepreneurs' human capital and networking on growth expectancies in Bulgaria. *Entrepreneurship, Theory and Practice, 31*(3), 407–426.

Mantilla, K. (2013). Gendertrolling: Misogyny adapts to new media. *Feminist Studies, 39*(2), 563–570.

Marwick, A. E., & Boyd, D. (2011). I tweet honestly, I tweet passionately: Twitter users, context collapse, and the imagined audience. *New Media & Society, 13*(1), 114–133.

Marwick, A. E., & Caplan, R. (2018). Drinking male tears: Language, the manosphere, and networked harassment. *Feminist Media Studies, 18*(4), 543–559.

McCarthy, E. D. (2016). Emotional performances as dramas of authenticity. In P. Vannini & J. P. Williams (Eds.), *Authenticity in culture, self, and society* (pp. 241–256). New York: Routledge.

Mickes, L., Walker, D. E., Parris, J. L., Mankoff, R., & Christenfeld, N. J. (2012). Who's funny: Gender stereotypes, humor production, and memory bias. *Psychonomic Bulletin & Review, 19*(1), 108–112.

Mitteness, C. R., Baucus, M. S., & Sudek, R. (2012). Horse vs. jockey? How stage of funding process and industry experience affect the evaluations of angel investors. *Venture Capital, 14*(4), 241–267.

Mumi, A., Obal, M., & Yang, Y. (2019). Investigating social media as a firm's signaling strategy through an IPO. *Small Business Economics, 53*(3), 631–645.

Nichols, N. A. (1993). Whatever happened to Rosie the riveter? *Harvard Business Review, 71*(4), 54.

Orhan, M. (2001). Women business owners in France: The issue of financing discrimination. *Journal of Small Business Management, 39*(1), 95–102.

Papacharissi, Z. (2010). *A private sphere: Democracy in a digital age*. Malden, MA/Cambridge, UK: Polity.

Pew Research Center. (2019). Social media fact sheet. https://www.pewinternet.org/fact-sheet/social-media/

Phillips, W. (2015). *This is why we can't have nice things: Mapping the relationship between online trolling and mainstream culture*. Cambridge, MA: MIT Press.

Rainie, L., Anderson, J., & Albright, J. (2017). The future of free speech, trolls, anonymity and fake news online. Retrieved from https://www.pewinternet.org/2017/03/29/the-future-of-free-speech-trolls-anonymity-and-fake-news-online/

Rudman, L. A., & Glick, P. (2001). Prescriptive gender stereotypes and backlash toward agentic women. *Journal of Social Issues, 57*(4), 743–762.

Sebah, S., Carsrud, A., & Kocak, A. (2014). The impact of cultural openness, religion, and nationalism on entrepreneurial intensity: Six prototypical cases of Turkish family firms. *Journal of Small Business Management, 52*(5), 306–324.

Smith, A., & Anderson, M. (2018). Social media use in 2018. *Pew Research Center*. https://www.pewinternet.org/2018/03/01/social-media-use-in-2018/

Smith, C., Smith, J. B., & Shaw, E. (2017). Embracing digital networks: Entrepreneurs' social capital online. *Journal of Business Venturing, 32*(1), 18–34.

Tajfel, H., & Turner, J. C. (1986). The social identity theory of inter-group behavior. In S. Worchel & W. G. Austin (Eds.), *Psychology of intergroup relations* (pp. 7–24). Chicago: Nelson-Hall.

Treem, J. W., & Leonardi, P. M. (2012). Social media use in organizations: Exploring the affordances of visibility, editability, persistence, and association. *Communication Yearbook, 36*(1), 143–189.

Uzzi, B. (1997). Social structure and competition in interfirm networks: The paradox of embeddedness. *Administrative Science Quarterly, 42*(1), 35–67.

Vannini, P., & Williams, J. P. (2016). Authenticity in culture, self, and society. In P. Vannini & J. P. Williams (Eds.), *Authenticity in culture, self, and society* (pp. 1–18). New York: Routledge.

Vitak, J., & Ellison, N. (2013). There's a network out there you might as well tap: Exploring the benefits of and barriers to exchanging informational and support-based resources on Facebook. *New Media & Society, 15*(2), 243–259.

Walker, N. A. (1988). *A Very Serious Thing: Women's Humor and American Culture* (Vol. Vol. 2). Minneapolis, MN: University of Minnesota Press.

Walter, N. (2011). *Living dolls: The return of sexism*. London: Little, Brown Book Group.

Chapter 6
How Is Social Media Adopted by Entrepreneurial Teams?

Sona Sareen, Etain Kidney, and Thomas M. Cooney

Abstract Research on social media and entrepreneurship highlights that entrepreneurs generally understand social media as a marketing and communication tool and have been using it to promote their businesses. The majority of studies that have analysed business use of social media have focused on entrepreneurs or new ventures, but there has been no research concerning how it is used by entrepreneurial teams (ETs). It has been agreed by many scholars that ETs are a relevant phenomenon and that a body of evidence exists to suggest that teams are more likely to enjoy high growth than firms founded by lone actors. Considering that an ET is a plural entity with two or more individuals involved in the entrepreneurial activity, it seems useful to explore a team's motive for using social media. This research gap was addressed by investigating the research question regarding "how ETs use social media" and an analysis of their strategy for social media preparedness. This study identified several new insights regarding how and why ETs use social media and established that social media use by ETs offers greater market accessibility and better customer relationship management opportunities to further build brand. The research revealed that women team members were spearheading the social media activity for their businesses which enabled the enterprise to grow. The selection of platforms and role of content also plays a critical role in social media usage. Though ETs do face challenges in terms of producing content and technical understanding of platforms, social media channels provide significant opportunities for enterprises to grow. Finally, the study provides a useful basis for future research in the area of social media use by ET.

Keywords Social media · Customer relationships · Platforms · Interactive media · Integrated omnichannel strategy · Influencer marketing · Branding · Customer engagement

---

S. Sareen · E. Kidney · T. M. Cooney (✉)
College of Business, Technological University Dublin (TU Dublin), Dublin, Ireland
e-mail: thomas.cooney@tudublin.ie

L. Schjoedt et al. (eds.), *Understanding Social Media and Entrepreneurship*, Exploring Diversity in Entrepreneurship,
https://doi.org/10.1007/978-3-030-43453-3_6

6.1 Introduction

Over the past decade, technological innovations have grown exponentially, thereby creating multiple opportunities in online commercial activities. Furthermore, the development of the Internet and social media networks has dramatically changed marketing dynamics. Social media has altered how businesses operate, introducing new ways of networking and doing business based on concepts such as sharing, collaboration and co-creation (Antes & Schuelke, 2011). According to PwC's Total Retail (2017) survey, 47% of consumers found social networks as their main source of inspiration to purchase. The survey also highlights that amongst the digital means shoppers use to make a purchase decision are social networks (e.g. Facebook, Twitter) and visual social networks (e.g. Instagram, Pinterest, Snapchat, YouTube), followed by the websites of brands and independent retailers. These online developments have significantly influenced how marketers today manage their strategies, as social media is now considered an essential part of their plan. Nascent and mature entrepreneurs are also increasingly using social media to interact with existing and potential customers, a circumstance that has enabled them to co-create product and service offerings (Fischer & Reuber, 2014). Although a significant proportion of business ventures are founded and managed by entrepreneurial teams (ETs), plus despite a lot of research being done on the relationship between entrepreneurs and social media, there is little knowledge in the existing body of literature regarding how entrepreneurial teams use social media.

This chapter aims to contribute to a deeper understanding of how entrepreneurial teams use social media by using semi-structured interviews, qualitative data analysis and responses from interviewed ETs in Dublin (Ireland). The selection of each team was determined by the research question and elements like characteristics of firm, profile of ET, social media engagements and teams who could provide new insights explaining how ETs use social media during different stages of the entrepreneurial process. Based on the selection criteria employed, three ETs were interviewed for the study. The findings suggest that participating ETs were highly aware of the changing marketing landscape and customer preferences, so they had developed social media marketing strategies for the changing times. This chapter also responds to the broader research question regarding how ETs adopt social media.

6.2 Understanding Entrepreneurial Teams

The term "entrepreneurial team" has received a number of definitions and it is essential to consider them to understand the various perspectives taken by different authors. Though the studies have presented several distinctive views, some common beliefs are held regarding ET members owning equity, being part of founding company and working within the firm. Gartner, Shaver, Gatewood, and Katz (1994) argued that the focus of entrepreneurial activity often resides not with one person, but in many. According to Watson, Ponthieu, and Critelli (1995), an ET occurs when two or more individuals establish a firm in which they have equity and continue running the business together. Further definitions are represented in Table 6.1.

The need to form a team arises when an entrepreneur recognises the opportunity to start a new venture and looks for resources in driving the growth (Schjoedt, Monsen, Pearson, Barnett, & Chrisman, 2013). The process of forming an entrepreneurial team as explained by Kamm and Nurick (1993) includes identification, selection and compensation. Entrepreneurs are advised to identify team members from their informal social networks (Leung, Zhang, Wong, & Der Foo, 2006) which includes friends and acquaintances or organised networks (Aldrich & Zimmer, 1986). Aldrich and Kim (2007), Beckman (2006) and Birley (1985) highlighted that entrepreneurs will look for the financial and human capital they need from amongst their existing networks (consisting of family, friends, relatives, business connections and institutional contacts) and will rarely think of including a stranger in the team (Blatt, 2009). When selecting desired team members, some aspects that entrepreneurs consider include matters such as a member's skills (instrumental perspective) and their cultural fit within the team (Aldrich & Kim, 2007; Forbes, Borchert, Zellmer-Bruhn, & Sapienza, 2006). Further, a founder's selection may also depend on the venture's life cycle stage as pointed by Leung et al. (2006). Once the members are identified and selected, Tetrick,

Table 6.1 Overview of different definitions of entrepreneurial team

Kamm and Nurick (1993), Kamm, Shuman, Seeger, and Nurick (1989, 1990)	Two or more people who are involved in pre-start-up activities and who formally establish and share ownership of their new organization
Ensley, Pearson, and Amason (2002)	Founders hold more than 10% equity, be involved in strategic decision-making. The CEO, president and vice president of critical functions are also included
Ruef, Aldrich, and Carter (2003)	Co-founder sharing ownership and affirmed that entrepreneurship is an exceedingly social phenomenon involving more than one person
Cooney (2005)	Two or more individuals who have a significant financial interest and participate actively in the development of the enterprise
Harper (2008)	A group of entrepreneurs with a common goal that can only be achieved by appropriate combinations of individual entrepreneurial actions
Schjoedt and Kraus (2009)	Two or more persons who have an interest, both financial and otherwise, and commitment to a venture's future and success; whose work is interdependent in the pursuit of common goals and venture success; who are considered to be at the executive level with executive responsibility in the early phases of the venture, including founding and pre-start-up; and who are seen as a social entity by themselves and by others
Klotz, Hmieleski, Bradley, and Busenitz (2014)	The group of individuals that is chiefly responsible for the strategic decision-making and ongoing operations of a new venture

Weathington, Da Silva, and Hutcheson (2010) suggested that the compensation level is another challenge founders face and the outcome will depend on factors such as marital status, inducements received in previous employment and the level of one's prior achievements.

Team members are viewed as the most important resource of the team and the people within the group are likely to affect the development and effects of the team (Levine & Moreland, 1990). According to Leary and DeVaughn (2009), a well-established team is crucial for the success of an enterprise. Though scholars have studied several combinations of team members' characteristics, they have generally focused on heterogeneity/homogeneity amongst the team members (Schjoedt & Kraus, 2009). Under the lead entrepreneur approach, the group is selected based on the changing resource or competence needs of the team (Forbes et al., 2006; Kamm & Nurick, 1993; Ruef et al., 2003) and such teams are considered to be diverse when they possess a multiplicity of complementary skills and abilities (Gartner, 1985). Members are also chosen based on their human capital (individual and knowledge skills) and social capital (access to social services) (Aldrich & Kim, 2007; Forbes et al., 2006; Ucbasaran, Lockett, Wright, & Westhead, 2003). Therefore, the literature suggests that the primary approach to building an ET assumes that individuals form heterogenous teams (Ruef et al., 2003). Alternatively, when an ET is composed before any entrepreneurial activity is identified, it follows a more interpersonal approach and such teams are formed based on social-psychological needs.

When the dynamics of ETs are discussed, the focus frequently lies with the entries and exits of team members. Over a period of time, it is likely that the group composition changes in some way (Birley & Stockley, 2000; Cooper & Daily, 1997; Timmons, 1999). Empirical research suggests that when a team is highly diverse, changes in composition are more likely (O'Reilly, Caldwell, & Barnett, 1989). Much research on homophily has focused on group formation and group tie creation which is important for understanding team dynamics. Homophily constitutes the central principle behind times of crises (Hurlbert, Haines, & Beggs, 2000), since ties to dissimilar people are more likely to be dropped in such circumstances (McPherson, Smith-Lovin, & Cook, 2001). A highly homogenous team will likely have fewer turnovers (Chandler, Honig, & Wiklund, 2005; Ucbasaran et al., 2003). The more dissimilar an individual is within a group, the higher the possibility of that person leaving the group (Popielarz & McPherson, 1995). Further, leadership capability and style will play a major role when one considers performance and sustainability of the team, especially in small- and medium-sized businesses as they are more vulnerable to market fluctuations and competition. If the owner also happen to be the manager, the adaptation of the organization to market changes and its sustainable performance is even more dependent on the leadership style within the enterprise (Langowitz & Allen, 2010).

6.3 Social Media

Social media is a relatively new phenomenon regarding the marketing of business activity. Also known as Web 2.0, Solis (2007) *described* social media as the "democratization of information, transforming people from readers into content publishers. It is a shift from a broadcast medium, one to many models, rooted in conversation between authors, people and peers". Campbell, Pitt, Parent, and Berthon (2011) further highlighted that Web 2.0 had evolved into an interactivity, interoperability and collaboration platform. Zago (2018) referred to Web 2.0 as the "read-write-publisher" era where the spread of information is as simple as these three words. In the last decade, Web 2.0 has enabled the development of social media as a tool used by both individuals and organisations. Kaplan and Haenlein (2010) emphasised that social media is relevant even for small businesses and entrepreneurs, and it is not restricted just to large multinationals. The interaction between the consumers and the company forms one of the most prominent features of the web (Ghose & Dou, 1998). By using services of free platforms like Facebook, LinkedIn and Twitter, organisations can market their business and create awareness. In addition to relaying messages, the entry of Web 2.0 has significantly increased the level of interactivity between stakeholders.

Mangold and Faulds (2009) recognised that while social media allows an enterprise to connect with both existing and potential customers, it also engages with them and reinforces a sense of community around an enterprise's offering. Blackshaw (2011) observed that contrary to the traditional one-way system of communication of content being circulated by company/brand, because of social media use, consumer opinions and experiences of products and services can now be considered in real time. Globally, online social media is used as an effective marketing communication tool, leveraging its revolutionary characteristics of creating user-generated, interactive, fast and cheap content (Whelan, Moon, & Grant, 2013). Consumers now react and share their viewpoint about brands, advertisements, products, consumption experience and so forth. According to Duggan and Brenner (2013), in the survey conducted for Pew Research Center's Internet & American Life Project (2012), they found that 62% of American men and 71% of women are actively creating new content on Facebook. O'Hern and Kahle (2013) identified four forms of user-generated content (UGC) as informing, innovating, co-communicating and co-creating. By this definition, consumers have now become "co-producers" or "prosumers" (Tapscott & Williams, 2006) along with the company.

The benefits of using social media by entrepreneurs as categorised by Olanrewaju, Hossain, Whiteside, and Mercieca (2019) comprise of uses such as value creation, enhancing entrepreneurial business process, improved performance and driving business innovation. Social media can help create value for the business by factors such as reduction in transaction costs, enhancement of information access and transmission through better communication channels (Lehmkuhl & Jung, 2013) and improved marketing strategies (Hitchen, Nylund, Ferràs, & Mussons, 2017; Scuotto,

Del Giudice, Peruta, & Tarba, 2017). Researchers have additionally observed that social media has been found to affect entrepreneurial business processes such as effectuation and opportunity recognition (Fischer & Reuber, 2011; Gustafsson & Khan, 2017; Mack, Marie-Pierre, & Redican, 2017). Women entrepreneurs in developing countries have immensely benefitted from social media use as it has helped them in creating and developing businesses, thereby achieving social and economic advancement (Beninger, Ajjan, Mostafa, & Crittenden, 2016; Nord, Riggio, & Paliszkiewicz, 2017; Steel, 2017). Finally, Bocconcelli, Cioppi, and Pagano (2017) and Mack et al. (2017) emphasised that social media plays a crucial role in running the venture, if the venture is in the growth phase.

With the development of unified metrics to measure the impact of social media on business, research studies have found a positive association between social media usage and business performance. According to Alarcón-del-Amo, Rialp-Criado, and Rialp-Criado (2018), higher levels of social media use will result in improved business performance. Grimmer, Grimmer, and Mortimer (2018) stressed that businesses which are in the nascent stage or businesses that have not invested heavily in social media (Gavino, Williams, Jacobson, & Smith, 2018) may not observe improved performance. Overall, social media usage has a positive impact on the business performance in terms of market expansion (Sasatanun & Charoensukmongkol, 2016) or building better customer relations (Ainin, Parveen, Moghavvemi, Jaafar, & Shuib, 2015). Although few entrepreneurs are strategically using social media to drive innovation, researchers have stated that co-creation with customers can also achieve innovation (Barnes & Mattsson, 2016; Hitchen et al., 2017). Innovation can also be supported on social media by ideas, interactions, knowledge search and transfer as highlighted by Scuotto et al. (2017). The business-client interaction on social media can help businesses to redesign their products which can lead to further innovation (Wang, Pauleen, & Zhang, 2016). Innovation can also be achieved through knowledge sharing, especially for manufacturing SMEs as submitted by Soto-Acosta, Popa, and Palacios-Marqués (2017).

The Internet-enabled communication media as mentioned by Chen, Chen, and Yang (2008) has helped organisations to conduct business anytime and from anywhere. Ainin et al. (2015) emphasised that factors such as compatibility, cost-effectiveness and interactivity influence social media adoption. According to Cooper and Zmud (1990) and Wang, Wang, and Yang (2010), *compatibility* is considered as one of the key factors for innovation adoption. Firms will adopt new technology (social media) if it's compatible to their work application systems. Derham, Cragg, and Morrish (2011) further emphasised that using social media in business helps not only to target customers effectively but also to share content about products/services instantly. Cost-effectiveness has been considered as another important factor in the adoption of new technologies (Chong & Chan, 2012; Premkumar & Roberts, 1999). Kaplan and Haenlein (2010) argued that social media is a cost-effective technology as it provides opportunity to organisations to directly communicate with its customers at low costs, thus influencing organizations to use it. Derham et al. (2011) further added that for SMEs (small- and medium-sized enterprises), it is highly suitable to adopt social media as it is not expensive, there are low barriers in participation and low levels of IT skills are required. Social media is also considered interactive media, a medium that enables two-way communication rather than being one-directional (Mayfield, 2008). According to Agarwal and Venkatesh (2002), interactivity is an important factor in the adoption of this medium because it impacts user response.

Researchers have suggested many models to investigate the individual acceptance behaviour on information technology and information systems. The technology acceptance model (TAM) developed by Davis (1989) as shown in Fig. 6.1 is one of the most popular research models to predict the use and acceptance of information systems and technology by individual users. According to TAM, ease of use and perceived usefulness are the most important determinants of actual system use, but these are influenced by social and political factors. The social factors include language, skills and facilitating conditions, whereas political factors are mainly the impact of legislation on using technology. The issue of attitude to use is concerned with a user's evaluation of their desirability to employ a particular information system application. Behavioural intention is the measure of the likelihood of a person employing a specific application. Lee and Runge (2001) stressed that an owner-manager needs to understand the technology and how they are going to benefit from adopting the technology before making any investment decisions. Wamba and Carter (2014) observed that younger managers are more inclined than older managers to adopt social media to promote an innovative atmosphere. Damanpour and Schneider (2006) further emphasized that in addition to age, higher levels of education are believed to enhance the receptiveness of people to new ideas and acquiring information. Some managerial characteristics (such as gender and race) may play a very small role in social media adoption. While recent studies have found no differences in social media adoption amongst different genders (Anderson, 2015; Wamba & Carter, 2014), some differences exist in terms of social media platforms selected and used by men and women. Anderson (2015) explained that while men may prefer to use online fora such as Reddit, women on the other hand are more likely to use networks such as Facebook, Pinterest and Instagram. Social media studies have also found variations in platform choice by race and ethnicity (Krogstad, 2015). Such characteristics may influence the type of media adopted by an organisation based on the owner-manager or even the customer orientation of the firm, but nothing is

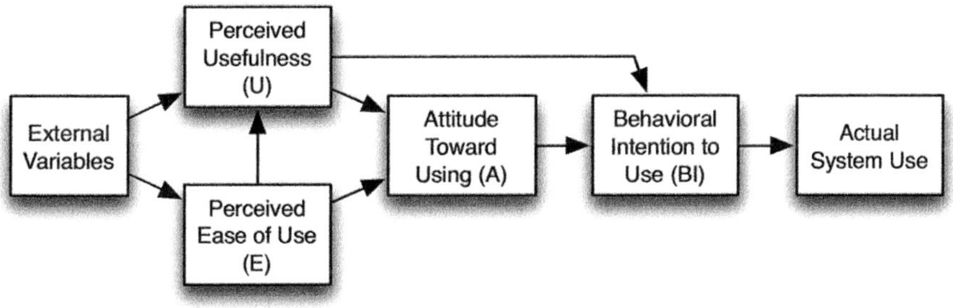

Fig. 6.1 Technology acceptance model (Source: Davis (1989))

known about the influence of ETs regarding the adoption of social media by an enterprise.

Social media is rapidly becoming critically important to businesses in countries across the world. Ireland is in sixth place on the 2018 Digital Economy and Society Index (DESI), up from eighth place in 2017, and behind Denmark, Sweden, Finland, the Netherlands and Luxembourg in the European Union (EU) (European Commission, 2018). When it comes to the integration of digital technologies by businesses, Ireland ranks very high because many SMEs have embraced e-commerce. Internet users increasingly take advantage of high-speed infrastructures and also make good use of online public services. Almost three-quarters (72%) of Irish SMEs now have a website and businesses have increased their usage of social media and other online tools. The following are some of the key statistics regarding the level of social media adoption in Ireland:

- According to Reuters (Newman, 2017), there is a 95% Internet penetration across Ireland.
- Seventy per cent of Irish Internet users surf the net every single day according to CS0 (2017).
- Data from Eurostat (European Commission, 2019) shows that 60% of Irish adults used social media in 2018.
- A study by Virgin media business survey (Virgin Media, 2018) found that 62% of SMEs use social media for business, but 4 in 10 feel it has delivered no growth.
- According to IPSOS/MRBI (2018), the most preferred social network in Ireland is Facebook with 62% of adults having a Facebook profile, followed by Instagram which is 41%.
- According to the IEDR Digital Health Index (IEDR, 2019), 77% of SMEs in Dublin have a website compared to a 72% national average.
- It was found that 34% of SMEs in Dublin allow consumers to purchase their products online against 32% national average.
- According to a PwC Irish Retail & Consumer (2019) report, 30% of consumers purchased online weekly in 2018.
- With the rise in mobile shopping, social media is considered a crucial touchpoint for retailers to create opportunity to engage as 28% of Irish consumers are influenced by social media.

While the above data is highly interesting, akin to the review of the literature, there are no statistics available regarding firms founded by ETs and their adoption and use of social media.

6.4 Methodology

According to the literature, entrepreneurs use social media for marketing, networking, crowdfunding and information search, but there exists a gap in relation to understanding how ETs use social media. The data for this study used an inductive approach using qualitative methods to explore the phenomenon and to identify patterns of ET use of social media (Saunders, Lewis, & Thornhill, 2016). As part of the research strategy, case studies using semi-structured interviews were applied to facilitate the emergence of new theories. The selection of ET was based on elements such as characteristics of the firm, profile of the team, together with each team member's age, demographic, education, professional background and their engagement on social media platforms (which was considered to ensure they were familiar with social media usage). The final sample included three SME firms representing three ETs engaged in different sectors and were at different stages of their business life cycle. During the fieldwork, semi-structured interviews were conducted with every member of each ET to capture their perceptions and experiences of the use of social media.

The interview guide was mainly divided into four blocks of questions. Firstly, a set of questions was formulated to briefly understand team characteristics and the profile of the respondents with an aim to capture the personal and professional background of the ET, their experience and the role of the members in the team. The second set of questions was designed to gather information about the respondent's industry, with questions such as the type of business, how long they had been running the business and insights regarding the respondent's social media participation and engagement. The main aim was to know whether respondents had changed their business strategy to be more aligned with digital opportunities. The third set of questions was dedicated to the new social media phenomenon and the respondent's views on why they use social media and what influenced their decision. The main aim was to capture the elements that drove them to engage in social media, the strategic choice in platform selection, how the digital aspects amongst the team was handled (meaning if the business roles had been divided and in what areas of business) and how they used social media. The main areas analysed were as cited by Olanrewaju et al. (2019): marketing, crowdfunding, networking and information search. Finally, the last set of questions was designed to ask the respondents the impact of their choices on business processes, how they had benefitted from using social media, the challenges they faced and what they expect to achieve from social media.

Three in-depth interviews were undertaken before the Braun and Clarke's (2006) six-step framework was adopted to identify the codes within the qualitative data. The first step was to familiarise oneself with the data (i.e. all the interviews conducted). The data was then organised into a more systematic fashion with a focus on coding. The process adopted was open coding analysis which meant there were no set pre-codes, but codes were developed and modified during the process. The codification process helped to bring in a set of theoretical concepts that allowed one to analyse why and how ETs use social media. Following the coding process, the next step was to identify emerging themes. All the relevant data relating to specific themes was gathered together and studied to see if the data supported the theme. In the final refinement stage, the aim was to identify the essence of what each theme/pattern was about and to address the research question.

6.5 Data Analysis

The environment today is dominated by several social media platforms, which both big and small firms are increasingly using to promote their products or services and also to engage with their existing and potential customers. Based on the analysis of data generated, interesting insights emerged regarding how and why ETs adopt and use social media. Figure 6.2 highlights the main findings from the analysis of the data. The ET identified the need to connect with their customers and to build customer relationships, plus the results highlight that they were able to promote themselves in a more cost-effective way to larger audiences, thus garnering visibility quickly which was possible only by using these platforms.

Based on the analysis of how ETs use social media, the key insights that emerged during the interviews are explained below.

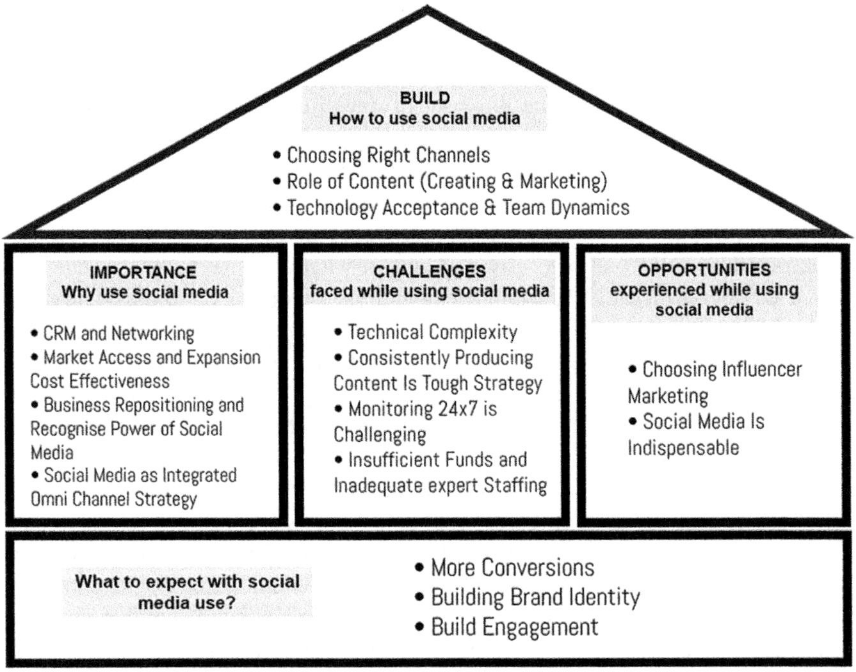

Fig. 6.2 Social media adoption by entrepreneurial teams

6.5.1 Choosing the Right Channels

In today's market scenario, having an online presence is considered a necessity. All the ETs interviewed agreed that in today's world, social media usage is important. All the ETs had adopted an organic approach in their platform selection, especially with reference to Facebook where they started promoting with their personal account and then switched to opening a business account for the enterprise. Initially, the ET tried to be on all platforms as they are free to join, but teams later reduced or even stopped using some platforms as they realised that they were not suited to their business. They were more active on Facebook and Instagram because of the visual nature of the platforms that helped them showcase their products and services. Team NB commented that:

> Yes, initially we used my personal Instagram, Facebook and Twitter account to promote the product. I never posted personally, but used the business account for our products as a cross between personal and business. We never got much engagement through Twitter as our product is more visual and Twitter is more announcing. One good thing with Facebook and Instagram…we have more core engaged followers.

Team FF shared similar views and stated that:

> The only platforms we use are FB and Instagram. We did have a Twitter account, but I found it totally frustrating. I don't think its suitable for fashion, so I don't use it anymore. We started with FB and grew from there and our website did help. Instagram is a new phenomenon and we went on board because literally everybody was doing it. We were told that it was the platform to go to.

In contrast to the literature review, this factor provides fresh insight from ETs regarding how businesses need to be strategic when choosing platforms to build their social media presence as some platforms may align/not align with an enterprise's brand and its customers.

6.5.2 Role of Content (Creating and Marketing)

Along with selecting the right channel, another crucial issue regarding using social media is creating content that suits the unique consumers of each social network. Moreover, it is not just creating content, but understanding how customers will benefit from this type of content. All the participating ET interviewed understood the role that content plays in promoting the brand and strategically focused on creating and marketing valuable content that appealed to their audience to drive results. Team FF mentioned that:

> Yes, we have a strategy, but the nature of fashion is such that you can only put so much into a content plan. The weather and deliveries schedules change everything. What's trending, what bloggers and celebrities are wearing is a constant game changer. One cannot plan too far with Instagram or Facebook scheduling….. Instagram posts have to be picture perfect which make it difficult and this has forced me to take photography and videography courses.

Similar views were presented by Team NB, where they pointed out that:

> Social media is more competitive. The content standard is much higher…. We have tried to plan a calendar, but it never really works. It is more spontaneous. We do a mix on our content based on product or people or stockist and keep it more focused; our customers like certain things like recipes, food, news about new products. Also, we have to ensure our images are constant as we have kept to our initial style.

While this finding briefly supports the need for a strategy prior to work on social media by entrepreneurs (Olanrewaju et al., 2019; Shih, Lin, & Luarn, 2014), it does not really emphasise the role of strategy within content overall. Thus, this particular insight from ETs on importance of content creation and marketing is essential in using social media.

6.5.3 Technology Acceptance and Team Dynamics

For the purposes of this research, it was important to understand who amongst the team used social media accounts, if the work roles had been divided, if all the members were comfortable in using technology, and how the team benefits from the diverse skills in the group. Leary and DeVaughn (2009) argued that a well-established team is crucial for the success of a business. The ET interviewed stated that roles and activities were divided. The teams showed excellent team dynamics and where one member lacked a particular skill, the other supported with their skill set, ensuring that team cohesion was balanced. This highlighted that there was efficient communication between team members which is critical for a team's performance on social media. Another factor that supports strong team cohesion was the clarity of roles when members took ownership of their duties. While all the ETs interviewed were homogenous in structure as team members were in some form related to each other, it was still interesting to observe how "women" team members were spearheading the social media activity for the firms. Team CB stated that:

> CB1 is front of the house and deals with everything in the bar really. Buying & purchasing is all he does. I help more if there is food requirement, interiors, décor and layout improvement based on customer requirement. And yes, a little bit of marketing. We take help from our daughter with regards to social media like Facebook.

Team FF shared similar views and stated that:

> We both are involved in buying and merchandising of range. FF2 is not much involved in selling. When it comes to IT or digital marketing related activities, FF1 is queen of DM. While FF2 is active on social media platforms, she would not be very good with digital marketing strategy or its functioning.

This factor provides fresh insight about team composition in terms of social media and entrepreneurship. Though Anderson (2015) did highlight that characteristics such as gender may impact selection of the type of SM channel, overall there is limited research on the use of SM by women entrepreneurs in a team setting.

6.5.4 Customer Relationship Management (CRM) and Networking

Today, customers are playing a critical role regarding online platforms and expect to move between different communication channels of a firm while expecting businesses to respond promptly. They have become part of the sale process and the CRM is being adapted to Social CRM to support this development. Team NB acknowledged that:

> For us, social media has been amazing as I am not sure how else we would have got our message out to customers…. making business visible among consumers, talking about our business journey, about the product.

Team FF stated that:

> Customers expect you to be on all these channels and platforms because the decision making is not like what it used to be. Customers don't want to go into the shops, but they want to do their research online.

The data from all ETs identified the need to connect and engage with consumers on social media to build customer relationship (CRM) and the ETs had proactively changed their strategies in accordance to prior research (Evans & Mckee, 2010; Guha, Harrigan, & Soutar, 2018; Harrigan & Miles, 2014; Olanrewaju et al., 2019).

6.5.5 Market Access and Expansion

Marketing through social media platforms helps to enhance one's digital knowledge and assists in an organisation's growth by providing opportunities for businesses to access new customers and markets. The ETs interviewed expressed similar views as Team NB who highlighted that:

> This lady Instagram user in Canada, in her post she tagged 5 shops/retailers asking them to order our product as she loved it. The shops contacted us and enquired about our products and now it's available in those shops.

Another team member further highlighted that:

> Social media is global and you can promote the business in several markets. I am not sure without social media how we would have become connected, exported or be engaged with our customers across world.

This insight is aligned to prior work on improved business performance (Olanrewaju et al., 2019; Sasatanun & Charoensukmongkol, 2016) where the ETs have also used social media, not only to build relations but to expand their business in new markets as they have the capacity in terms of personnel in the ET to undertake such activity.

6.5.6 Cost-Effectiveness

With a high number of users associated with several social media platforms, social media undoubtedly has massive reach and is considered one of the most cost-effective ways to promote business. This strategy has revolutionized how enterprises can expand their businesses activities. The ET interviewed advised how this strategy had worked to their advantage. Teams emphasised that initially they used their personal social media accounts to promote the business and later moved to business accounts which is also provided free by the majority of the networks. Team NB highlighted that:

> From the beginning we used Instagram, Facebook and also Twitter. I think we were lucky as we would not exist without social media as that was our way of promoting ourselves. We were lucky when we started as Facebook were less interested in making money – it was more about getting people to connect. They were not charging small businesses like us and we were able to create good visibility.

Team FF reiterated this by stating that:

> And, rather than investing in a bricks & mortar store, we decided to try the website to broaden our customer base. The initial investment was quite small and was less risky than taking on another store. We were promoting on Facebook – even though we could not Tag products on Facebook … we used our website address and people could browse the site for more information or buy if they wanted to.

This insight aligns to prior work on cost-effectiveness and good reach (Brink, 2017; Chong & Chan, 2012; Derham et al., 2011; Kaplan & Haenlein, 2010; Olanrewaju et al., 2019; Premkumar & Roberts, 1999) where firms felt that low cost was indeed a key factor that influenced social media use.

6.5.7 Recognising the Power of Social Media and Business Repositioning

In the last decade, many digital platforms have been launched which have dramatically changed the business and retail landscape. Today, marketers and entrepreneurs acknowledge that social media is essential to their business, as initially it can create a buzz about their products or services, while later it can generate word of mouth advocacy. Team NB who had established their business just 5 years previously stated that:

> We had a social media platform account before we had the product. It was more like we brought customers along the process, before the launch of product and then as we launched the product.

Team CB highlighted that:

> We also have to align our business with social media as that's the trend right now.

Team FF commented that:

> I would say up to 2013 there was little need for IT in business. It was more a traditional retail business. When the recession hit … we saw a big change. The main supermarket in town closed and footfall fell drastically. The local enterprise board was encouraging people to set-up a website. The timing of social media seems to happen together – Facebook started to grow in Ireland. Everyone had a mobile phone and people started using FB as a connection point. We saw lot of people liking our FB page and browsing our website and though we didn't convert these people into our customers, it definitely was a way forward for marketing purpose for our business.

This finding supports the strategy to prior work on enhanced entrepreneurial business processes (Olanrewaju et al., 2019) where interviewed ETs were not only aware of the benefits of using social media, but they also adapted and adopted the changes promptly, thus taking advantage of new capabilities in a positive way.

6.5.8 Social Media as an Integrated Omnichannel Strategy

Customers now use multiple shopping channels such as bricks and mortar stores, social media platforms, e-commerce sites or just a telephone call to either enquire about a product/service or to make a purchase. Consumers expect consistency across all channels and want businesses to engage with them. This has led to traditional retail processes being integrated with the digital processes. The ETs interviewed highlighted similar views. Team FF emphasised that:

> Social media is used for sales, contacts, messaging, for marketing promotion and to drive people to our website (awareness). It's the whole omni-channel journey of the customer. Customers expect you to be on all these channels and platforms because the decision-making is not like what it used to be.

This finding supports the strategy to prior work on enhanced entrepreneurial business processes used by lone entrepreneurs (Olanrewaju et al., 2019) as ETs also realise the potential of promoting business on social media and engaging with their customers.

6.5.9 Technical Complexity

Social media is ever evolving. The ETs interviewed spoke about having limited professional knowledge to use social media and continuous algorithm changes. Their lack of technical understanding was the main challenge to their use of the platforms. Team FF mentioned that:

> Like Facebook, before they brought in all the algorithm changes – it was fantastic to use. Now only 10% of our customers, our 20,000 followers, get to see our post because of what we post. It's very hard to keep on top of all the changes that are brought in by all the different platforms, like Google algorithms, Facebook algorithms and Instagram. It's very hard to

> keep on top of all this social media and run a physical business, especially for a small independent business, even though we are a team.

Team CB mentioned that:

> We are not educated on SM aspects really and we depend on our daughters to do it.

In contrast to the prior findings, this insight provided fresh insight from ET wherein one team spoke about not having knowledge to professionally use SM and depended on others, while other teams pointed to the challenges faced with having continuous algorithm changes.

6.5.10 Insufficient Funds and Inadequate Expert Staffing

Due to insufficient funds, teams are not able to recruit expert staff who could guide them regarding continuous social media updates or even regularly pay for advertisements to boost posts. The ET pointed out that platforms now charge extra to "boost" posts compared to a few years back. Team NB stated that:

> Even for posts, even if you put up a general post today … only 100 followers can see it. Compared to few years back when we started, each of our 27,000 followers were able to see our posts. But today if you want your followers to see your content, you have to nearly pay to boost the post. We tried doing advertising, but one needs to spend a lot of money…. it forces businesses to think of other ways to try and create content and engage with customers.

While time is precious for entrepreneurs, having inadequate expert staff supports the need for strategy on prior work as found with lone actor entrepreneurs (Kuhn, Galloway, & Collins-Williams, 2016; Olanrewaju et al., 2019; Quinton & Wilson, 2016). This is further related to the factor about insufficient funds as ETs with small/medium enterprises are not able to recruit expert staff who could guide them about continuous social media updates or even pay for advertisements to boost posts regularly.

6.5.11 Consistently Producing Content Is a Tough Strategy

To produce high-quality content, one needs to be able to identify and organise a list of ideas which requires creativity and strategic planning. The ETs emphasized that they found it challenging to decide what content to post regularly. While some members found it too corporate to post on a regular basis, others pointed out that planning content does not work always. Team CB talks about:

> Every day there is nothing much happening to post. I think some activity should be going on to post and we will be hard pressed to figure out what to post every day.

Team FF acknowledged that:

> We have a strategy, but the nature of fashion is such you can only put so much into a plan.

In contrast to the prior findings, this insight provided fresh insight about the challenges ETs face when using social media. It also demonstrates that even though there is an ET running the business, they still have difficulty in producing content regularly.

6.5.12 *Monitoring 24/7 Is Challenging*

While social media monitoring is beneficial to help boost a brand's communication and although several tools are available today to help businesses, still the ETs interviewed found it challenging to monitor the platforms continuously. Team FF acknowledged that:

> One has to be switched on 24/7, all the time. If you do not respond to a customer at night time … you will lose the sale. Initially, the likes and comments from customers were a great boost and also for one's confidence, especially in a small business you don't get feedback on a day-to-day basis that you get through social platforms – the instant feedback. If you don't get the feedback you expect, or that your competitor gets, then you do worry about social media matters. You have to train all the time, you cannot sit on your laurels. Someone else will wipe you off the social media platform. It's a treadmill, you cannot get off it.

The notion of the demands of social media being a treadmill that one cannot get off is very powerful as it highlights one of the critical challenges of social media use for businesses – if one is to engage in it effectively, then one has to be totally committed to keeping it proactive. This requirement is the same for firms founded by an individual or by an ET.

6.5.13 *Choosing Influencer Marketing*

Influencer marketing is a strategy being adopted by businesses to reach out to their specific audiences. The ETs interviewed were forthcoming in mentioning plans to include this strategy in their future digital plans. Team NB shared that:

> Initially we spent a lot on ads, but did not see any returns, so we are using that same budget now on sending sample packs to Influencers who have 10,000 to 20,000 followers. We do not actually pay them, but we share our product samples with people who may have similar interests. We contact them to see if they would be interested in sampling. And if they do genuinely like them, they talk about it. And nowadays, consumers can tell if its organic or if is paid for and looks more fake. Something that comes genuine, it makes a difference and we focus on that strategy.

Team FF stated:

> This year I have cut back a lot on the paid advertising. I did lot of ads in 2018 but felt we did not get much ROI. I probably should use more influencers, bloggers or stylists and that I have planned for next season.

The use of key influencers is a growing trend across all types and sizes of businesses. The use of this strategy by ETs only reflects the wider developments in social media activity.

6.5.14 Social Media Is Indispensable

Businesses now exist in a digital age which provides myriad opportunities for enterprises to market their product and services in faster and more cost-effective ways to millions of customers than was previously available. The ETs interviewed acknowledged that social media is a fantastic marketing tool that is here to stay. Team NB stated:

> I think we were lucky as we would not exist without social media. In many ways our first focus was Facebook and then things moved to Instagram. Probably it's a cycle and maybe some new platform will come up. There was period when Snapchat was huge for certain businesses. I think they are ever-evolving platforms.

Team FF explained that:

> Social media is not going anywhere, its gonna stay. People are using their mobile phones more and more. And if you cannot be found online, you are not going to exist. While your local customers will shop with you, if you want to grow, you have to be on such platforms. People do everything on their phone. The next generation cannot live without their phone and everything is fed through the phone…so if you are not there, you will definitely lose out. I don't think retailers will be 100% online, but I do think that they have to have a presence online, more for brand awareness.

The findings here are similar to those voiced more generally in businesses and do not suggest any new thoughts on the role of social media in modern business activity.

6.5.15 More Conversions/Sales

Currently there are several platforms through which a business can interact with their current and potential customers, to share content and engage with them. All ETs interviewed were of the view that they expected to achieve extra sales from social media use. Team NB said that:

> The top thing right now is sales, bringing customers to our online shop or to our stockists. We also talk about our stockist on social media channels and that drives people to stores to buy. We even get orders as social media is coming into the operational side of business as well.

NB2 further added that:

> We see massive potential to sell direct to consumers as we see constant orders coming in, even though we do not do much to promote.

Team FF mentioned:

> More sales, that's what it is all about. That's what keeps the door open.

Team CB also agreed that:

> extra business, extra sales.

This factor supports insight to prior findings that social media marketing enhances product awareness and drives sales (Dutot & Bergeron, 2016; Olanrewaju et al., 2019; Taneja & Toombs, 2014). The ETs also emphasized that by sharing details about their products or services and by engaging with their respective audiences on social media, their essential motive in using social media was to increase sales.

6.5.16 Building Brand Identity

Many businesses are active on several social media platforms because billions of users across the world use social media and the ET interviewed emphasized that building brand identity is one of the key reasons for using social media. Team FF spoke about:

> Sales, loyalty, you want to paint the right picture of your business, of who you are and what you represent. How you are viewed, how you are reviewed – all of that is important because now people judge you by the reviews and the likes.

Team NB said that:

> The awareness about our brand, plus the individual products, is critical. The stockists also promote the brand on the platforms they are active on. The platforms help us share more about the brand and the stories, and social media is helping us build that.

This insight is aligned to prior work on brand management (Ahmad, Ahmad, & Bakar, 2018; Ananda, Hernández-García, & Lamberti, 2017; Olanrewaju et al., 2019) where ETs highlighted that they were conscious about the standard of content. They ensured that the posts represented the voice of the brand and they effectively wanted their brand to stand out and keep customers engaged and interested.

6.5.17 Build Engagement

One of the key priorities of any business, irrespective of any industry, should be social media marketing. The focus should be to engage with followers and convert them into customers. The ETs interviewed agreed with this view and highlighted that by using social media platforms, they want to better engage with their customers and understand their needs so that they can better serve them. Above all, they were keen to nurture their relationships with customers further. Team CB stated that:

> We expect to get in more customers. We are not very sure as we have not really engaged fully with social media. I am sure if we engage more, we would get in more business. It will be good to get feedback from customers on what they like or not like as that is good to grow business further. I guess we have to be open to suggestions, new ideas.

Team FF pointed out:

> The likes and comments from customers was a great boost for the business and also for one's confidence, especially in a small business where you don't get feedback on a day-to-day basis that you get through social platforms – the instant feedback.

The ETs highlighted that by using social media platforms, they want to better engage with their customers and understand their needs so they can better serve them.

On the whole, ET recognised the importance of social media and repositioned their marketing strategy to use social media to their advantage. Moreover, they adopted an omnichannel strategy integrating traditional processes with digital processes. ETs also spoke about the challenges they faced while managing social media, like the technical complexity of using the platforms due to continuous upgrades as they could not invest time to understand these platforms' technicalities. They further added that inadequate expert staff was another issue and being a small business with limited funds, they could not hire social media experts. ETs expressed their concern regarding consistently producing content and also stressed that monitoring the platforms 24/7 was difficult considering they had to manage their businesses as well. However, the overall view of ETs highlighted the positive opportunities they experienced using social media. To summarise, the findings in the chapter reveal that compared to firms founded by lone actors, ETs have also incorporated social media as part of their sales and marketing strategy to engage and enhance their relationship with existing and potential customers, but few differences existed in terms of how they utilised social media. Perhaps the only difference that existed between firms founded by a lone individual versus those founded by a team was that in ETs, it was more likely that would possess the knowledge, skills and interest to manage the social media activity for an enterprise.

6.6 Conclusion

In recent years, the advent of Web 2.0 and the development of social media as a communication tool has revolutionised the way in which individuals and businesses interact with each other, making everyone more connected. Similar to lone actors, ETs also have access to these new tools and the ETs interviewed were highly aware of the changing marketing landscape and changing customer preferences. They had repositioned their marketing approach and incorporated social media into their business. While there are challenges faced when using social media, the ETs were excited by the opportunity that social media provides to engage with existing and potential customers. Interesting insights emerged where the ETs agreed that in today's market scenario having a digital presence for the business is a necessity. Rather than being on all platforms, ETs had adopted a systematic approach and had evaluated the platforms and their customers and then selected the platforms that align best with their business and customers. The results of the study also highlight that ETs did not consider producing content as a simple tactic, but rather all ETs understood the importance and role of content in a marketing strategy and how it should be optimised for each platform being used. It was interesting to observe that female team members across all three teams were leading the social media activity for their firm. This chapter has emphasized that social media is a crucial tool in today's commercial world to engage with wider audiences. It has substantial potential to develop business opportunities and ETs have strategically adopted social media and managed business social media strategy. ETs expect to build a positive image about their business in the minds of the customers, build better engagement with their followers and achieve extra sales by using social media platforms.

References

Agarwal, R., & Venkatesh, V. (2002). Assessing a firm's web presence: A heuristic evaluation procedure for the measurement of usability. *Information Systems Research, 13*(2), 168–186.

Ahmad, S. Z., Ahmad, N., & Bakar, A. R. A. (2018). Reflections of entrepreneurs of small and medium-sized enterprises concerning the adoption of social media and its impact on performance outcomes: Evidence from the UAE. *Telematics and Informatics, 35*, 6–17.

Ainin, S., Parveen, F., Moghavvemi, S., Jaafar, N. I., & Shuib, N. L. M. (2015). Factors influencing the use of social media by SMEs and its performance outcomes. *Industrial Management & Data Systems, 115*(3), 570–588.

Alarcón-del-Amo, M.-d.-C., Rialp-Criado, A., & Rialp-Criado, J. (2018). Examining the impact of managerial involvement with social media on exporting firm performance. *International Business Review, 27*(2), 355–366.

Aldrich, H. E., & Kim, P. H. (2007). Small worlds, infinite possibilities? How social networks affect entrepreneurial team formation and search. *Strategic Entrepreneurship Journal, 1*, 147–165.

Aldrich, H. E., & Zimmer, C. (1986). Entrepreneurship through social networks. In D. Sexton & R. Smiler (Eds.), *The art and science Of entrepreneurship* (pp. 3–23). Cambridge, MA: Ballinger.

Ananda, A. S., Hernández-García, Á., & Lamberti, L. (2017). SME fashion brands and social media marketing: From strategies to actions. *International Journal of Web Based Communities, 13*(4), 468–498.

Anderson, M. (2015). *Men catch up with women on overall social media use*. Retrieved August 28, 2015 from https://www.pewresearch.org/fact-tank/2015/08/28/men-catch-up-with-women-on-overall-social-media-use/

Antes, A. L., & Schuelke, M. J. (2011). Leveraging technology to develop creative leadership capacity. *Advances in Developing Human Resources, 13*(3), 318–365.

Barnes, S. J., & Mattsson, J. (2016). Building tribal communities in the collaborative economy: An innovation framework. *Prometheus, 34*(2), 95–113.

Beckman, C. M. (2006). The influence of founding team company affiliations on firm behavior. *Academy of Management Journal, 49*(4), 741–758.

Beninger, S., Ajjan, H., Mostafa, R. B., & Crittenden, V. L. (2016). A road to empowerment: Social media use by women entrepreneurs in Egypt. *International Journal of Entrepreneurship and Small Business, 27*(2–3), 308–332.

Birley, S. (1985). The role of networks in the entrepreneurial process. *Journal of Business Venturing, 1*, 107–117.

Birley, S., & Stockley, S. (2000). Entrepreneurial teams and venture growth. In D. L. Sexton & H. Landström (Eds.), *The Blackwell handbook of entrepreneurship*. Oxford, UK: Blackwell Publishing.

Blackshaw, P. (2011). User-generated content in context. *Journal of Advertising Research, 51*, 108–111.

Blatt, R. (2009). Tough love: How communal schemas and contracting practices build relational capital in entrepreneurial teams. *Academy of Management Review, 34*, 533–551.

Bocconcelli, R., Cioppi, M., & Pagano, A. (2017). Social media as a source in SMEs' sales process. *Journal of Business and Industrial Marketing, 32*(5), 693–709.

Braun, V., & Clarke, V. (2006). Using thematic analysis in psychology. *Qualitative Research in Psychology, 3*, 77–101.

Brink, T. (2017). B2B SME management of antecedents to the application of social media. *Industrial Marketing Management, 64*, 57–65.

Campbell, C., Pitt, L. F., Parent, M., & Berthon, P. R. (2011). Understanding consumer conversations around Ads in a Web 2.0 world. *Journal of Advertising, 40*, 87–102.

Chandler, G. N., Honig, B., & Wiklund, J. (2005). Antecedents, moderators, and performance consequences of membership change in new venture teams. *Journal of Business Venturing, 2*(5), 705–725.

Chen, J. V., Chen, C. C., & Yang, H. (2008). An empirical evaluation of key factors contributing to internet abuse in the workplace. *Industrial Management and Data Systems, 108*(1), 87–106.

Chong, A. Y.-L., & Chan, F. T. (2012). Structural equation modelling for multi-stage analysis on radio frequency identification (RFID) diffusion in the health care industry. *Expert Systems with Applications, 39*(10), 8645–8654.

Cooney, T. M. (2005). Editorial: What is an entrepreneurial team? *International Small Business Journal, 23*(3), 226–235.

Cooper, A. C., & Daily, C. M. (1997). Entrepreneurial teams. In D. L. Sexton & R. W. Smilor (Eds.), *Entrepreneurship 2000* (pp. 127–150). Chicago: Upstart Publishing Company.

Cooper, R. B., & Zmud, R. W. (1990). Information technology implementation research: A technological diffusion approach. *Management Science, 36*(2), 123–139.

Damanpour, F., & Schneider, M. (2006). Phases of the adoption of innovation in organizations: Effects of environment, organization and top managers. *British Journal of Management, 17*(3), 215–236.

Davis, F. D. (1989). Perceived usefulness, perceived ease of use, and user acceptance of information technology. *MIS Quarterly, 13*, 319–340.

Derham, R., Cragg, P., & Morrish, S. (2011). *Creating value: an SME and social media. PACIS 2011 proceedings, paper 53*. Paper presented at Pacific Asia Conference on Information Systems, PACIS 2011: Quality Research in Pacific Asia, Brisbane, QLD, Australia.

Duggan, M., & Brenner, J. (2013). *The demographics of social media users – 2012*. Pew Research Center's Internet & American Life Project. Retrieved from https://www.pewinternet.org/2013/02/14/the-demographics-of-social-media-users-2012/

Dutot, V., & Bergeron, F. (2016). From strategic orientation to social media orientation: Improving SMEs' performance on social media. *Journal of Small Business and Enterprise Development, 23*(4), 1165–1190.

Ensley, M. D., Pearson, A. W., & Amason, A. C. (2002). Understanding the dynamics of new venture top management teams: Cohesion, conflict, and new venture performance. *Journal of Business Venturing, 17*, 365–386.

European Commission. (2018). *Ireland in 6th place on this year's Eu Digital Economy and Society Index*. Retrieved from https://ec.europa.eu/ireland/news/ireland-in-6th-place-on-this-year-s-eu-digital-economy-and-society-index_en

European Commission. (2019). *Are you using social networks?* Retrieved June 29, 2019 from https://ec.europa.eu/eurostat/web/products-eurostat-news/-/EDN-20190629-1

Evans, D., & McKee, J. (2010). *Social media marketing: The next generation of business engagement*. Indianapolis, IN: Wiley Publishing.

Fischer, E., & Reuber, A. R. (2011). Social interaction via new social media: (How) can interactions on Twitter affect effectual thinking and behavior? *Journal of Business Venturing, 26*(1), 1–18.

Fischer, E., & Reuber, A. R. (2014). Online entrepreneurial communication: Mitigating uncertainty and increasing differentiation via Twitter. *Journal of Business Venturing, 29*(4), 565–583.

Forbes, D. P., Borchert, P. S., Zellmer-Bruhn, M. E., & Sapienza, J. J. (2006). Entrepreneurial team formation: An exploration of new member addition. *Entrepreneurship Theory and Practice, 30*, 225–248.

Gartner, W. B. (1985). A conceptual framework for describing the phenomenon of new venture creation. *Academy of Management Review, 10*(4), 696–706.

Gartner, W. B., Shaver, K. G., Gatewood, E., & Katz, J. A. (1994). Finding the entrepreneur in entrepreneurship. *Entrepreneurship Theory & Practice, 18*(3), 5–10.

Gavino, M. C., Williams, D. E., Jacobson, D., & Smith, I. (2018). Latino entrepreneurs and social media adoption: Personal and business social network platforms. *Management Research Review, 42*(4), 469–494.

Ghose, S., & Dou, W. (1998). Interactive functions and their impacts on the appeal of internet presence sites. *Journal of Advertising Research, 38*(2), 29–43.

Grimmer, L., Grimmer, M., & Mortimer, G. (2018). The more things change the more they stay the same: A replicated study of small retail firm resources. *Journal of Retailing and Consumer Services, 44*, 54–63.

Guha, S., Harrigan, P., & Soutar, G. (2018). Linking social media to customer relationship management (CRM): A qualitative study on SMEs. *Journal of Small Business & Entrepreneurship, 30*(3), 193–214.

Gustafsson, V., & Khan, M. S. (2017). Monetising blogs: Enterprising behaviour, co-creation of opportunities and social media entrepreneurship. *Journal of Business Venturing Insights, 7*, 26–31.

Harper, D. A. (2008). Towards a theory of entrepreneurial teams. *Journal of Business Venturing, 23*, 613–626.

Harrigan, P., & Miles, M. (2014). From e-CRM to s-CRM. Critical factors underpinning the social CRM activities of SMEs. *Small Enterprise Research, 21*(1), 99–116.

Hitchen, E. L., Nylund, P. A., Ferràs, X., & Mussons, S. (2017). Social media: Open innovation in SMEs finds new support. *Journal of Business Strategy, 38*(3), 21–29.

Hurlbert, J. S., Haines, V. A., & Beggs, J. J. (2000). Core networks and tie activation: What kinds of routine networks allocate resources in nonroutine situations? *American Sociological Review, 65*(4), 598–618.

IEDR. (2019). *SME Digital Health Index 2019*. Retrieved from https://www.iedr.ie/wp-content/uploads/2019/11/04624-IE-Domain-Registry-DHI-2019.pdf

IPSOS/MRBI. (2018, June). *Social networking tracker*. Retrieved from https://www.ipsos.com/sites/default/files/ct/news/documents/2018-11/soc_net_june_18.pdf

Kamm, J. B., & Nurick, A. J. (1993). The stages of team venture formation: A decision-making model. *Entrepreneurship Theory and Practice, 17*, 17–27.

Kamm, J. B., Shuman, J. C., Seeger, J. A., & Nurick, A. J. (1989). *Are well balanced teams more successful?* Paper presented at the Babson College Entrepreneurship Research Conference 9, St. Louis.

Kamm, J. B., Shuman, J. C., Seeger, J. A., & Nurick, A. J. (1990). Entrepreneurial teams in new venture creation: A research agenda. *Entrepreneurship Theory and Practice, 14*(4), 7–17.

Kaplan, A. M., & Haenlein, M. (2010). Users of the world, unite: The challenges and opportunities of social media. *Business Horizons, 53*, 59–68.

Klotz, A. C., Hmieleski, K. M., Bradley, B. H., & Busenitz, L. W. (2014). New venture teams: A review of the literature and roadmap for future research. *Journal of Management, 40*, 226–255.

Krogstad, J. M. (2015). *Social media preferences vary by race and ethnicity*. Retrieved February 3, 2015 from http://www.pewresearch.org/fact-tank/2015/02/03/social-mediapreferences-vary-by-race-and-ethnicity
Kuhn, K., Galloway, T., & Collins-Williams, M. (2016). Near, far, and online: Small business owners' advice-seeking from peers. *Journal of Small Business and Enterprise Development, 23*(1), 189–206.
Langowitz, N. S., & Allen, I. E. (2010). Small business leadership: Does being the founder matter? *Journal of Small Business Entrepreneurship, 23*(1), 53–63.
Leary, M. M., & DeVaughn, M. L. (2009). Entrepreneurial team characteristics that influence the successful launch of a new venture. *Management Research News, 32*(6), 567–579.
Lee, J., & Runge, J. (2001). Adoption of information technology in small business: Testing drivers of adoption for entrepreneurs. *Journal of Computer Information Systems, 42*, 44–57.
Lehmkuhl, T., & Jung, R. (2013). Value creation potential of web 2.0 for SME: Insights and lessons learnt from a European producer of consumer electronics. *International Journal of Cooperative Information Systems, 22*(03), 1340003.
Leung, A., Zhang, J., Wong, P. K., & Der Foo, M. (2006). The use of networks in human resource acquisition for entrepreneurial firms: Multiple "fit" considerations. *Journal of Business Venturing, 21*, 664–686.
Levine, J. M., & Moreland, R. L. (1990). Progress in small group research. *Annual Review of Psychology, 41*, 585–634.
Mack, E. A., Marie-Pierre, L., & Redican, K. (2017). Entrepreneurs' use of internet and social media applications. *Telecommunications Policy, 41*(2), 120–139.
Mangold, W. G., & Faulds, D. J. (2009). Social media: The new hybrid element of the promotion mix. *Business Horizons, 52*, 357–365.
Mayfield, A. (2008). *What is social media?* iCrossing eBook. Retrieved from https://www.icrossing.com/uk/sites/default/files_uk/insight_pdf_files/What%20is%20Social%20Media_iCrossing_ebook.pdf
McPherson, M., Smith-Lovin, L., & Cook, J. M. (2001). Birds of a feather: Homophily in social networks. *Annual Review of Sociology, 27*, 415–444.
Newman, N. (2017). *Overview and key findings of the 2017 report*. Reuters Institute for the Study of Journalism. Retrieved from http://www.digitalnewsreport.org/survey/2017/overview-key-findings-2017/
Nord, J. H., Riggio, M. T., & Paliszkiewicz, J. (2017). Social and economic development through information and communications technologies: Italy. *Journal of Computer Information Systems, 57*(3), 278–285.
O'Hern, M. S., & Kahle, L. (2013). The empowered customer: User-generated content and the future of marketing. *Global Economics and Management Review, 18*, 22–30.
O'Reilly, C. A., Caldwell, D. F., & Barnett, W. P. (1989). Work group demography, social integration, and turnover. *Administrative Science Quarterly, 34*(1), 21–37.
Olanrewaju, A.-S. T., Hossain, M. A., Whiteside, N., & Mercieca, P. (2019). Social media and entrepreneurship research: A literature review. *International Journal of Information Management, 50*, 90–110.
Popielarz, P. A., & McPherson, M. (1995). On the edge or in between: Niche position, niche overlap, and the duration of voluntary association memberships. *The American Journal of Sociology, 101*(3), 698–720.
Premkumar, G., & Roberts, M. (1999). Adoption of new information technologies in rural small businesses. *Omega, 27*(4), 467–484.
PwC. (2017). *2017 Total Retail survey*. Retrieved from https://www.pwc.com/gx/en/industries/assets/total-retail-2017.pdf
PwC. (2019). *Irish Retail and Consumer report 2019*. Retrieved from https://www.pwc.ie/publications/2019/irish-retail-consumer-report-investing-in-experience.pdf
Quinton, S., & Wilson, D. (2016). Tensions and ties in social media networks: Towards a model of understanding business relationship development and business performance enhancement through the use of LinkedIn. *Industrial Marketing Management, 54*, 15–24.

Ruef, M., Aldrich, H. E., & Carter, N. M. (2003). The structure of founding teams: Homophily, strong ties, and isolation among U.S. entrepreneurs. *American Sociological Review, 68*, 195–222.
Sasatanun, P., & Charoensukmongkol, P. (2016). Antecedents and outcomes associated with social media use in customer relationship management of Thai micro enterprises. *International Journal of Technoentrepreneurship, 3*(2), 127–149.
Saunders, M., Lewis, P., & Thornhill, A. (2016). *Research methods for business students* (7th ed.). Harlow, UK: Pearson Education Limited.
Schjoedt, L., & Kraus, S. (2009). Entrepreneurial teams: Definition and performance factors. *Management Research News, 32*, 513–524.
Schjoedt, L., Monsen, E., Pearson, A., Barnett, T., & Chrisman, J. J. (2013). New venture and family business teams: Understanding team formation, composition, behaviours, and performance. *Entrepreneurship: Theory & Practice, 37*, 1–15.
Scuotto, V., Del Giudice, M., Peruta, M. R., & Tarba, S. (2017). The performance implications of leveraging internal innovation through social media networks: An empirical verification of the smart fashion industry. *Technological Forecasting and Social Change, 120*, 184–194.
Shih, C.-C., Lin, T. M. Y., & Luarn, P. (2014). Fan-centric social media: The Xiaomi phenomenon in China. *Business Horizons, 57*(3), 349–358.
Solis, B. (2007). *Defining social media*. Retrieved June 28, 2007 from https://www.briansolis.com/2007/06/defining-social-media
Soto-Acosta, P., Popa, S., & Palacios-Marqués, D. (2017). Social web knowledge sharing and innovation performance in knowledge-intensive manufacturing SMEs. *The Journal of Technology Transfer, 42*(2), 425–440.
Steel, G. (2017). Navigating (im) mobility: Female entrepreneurship and social media in Khartoum. *Africa: Journal of International African Institute, 87*(2), 233–252.
Taneja, S., & Toombs, L. (2014). Putting a face on small businesses: Visibility, viability, and sustainability the impact of social media on small business marketing. *Academy of Marketing Studies Journal, 18*(1), 249.
Tapscott, D., & Williams, A. D. (2006). *Wikinomics: How mass collaboration changes everything*. New York: Portfolio Trade.
Tetrick, L. E., Weathington, B. L., Da Silva, N., & Hutcheson, J. M. (2010). Individual differences in attractiveness of jobs based on compensation package components. *Employee Responsibilities and Rights Journal, 22*, 195–211.
Timmons, J. A. (1999). *New venture creation: Entrepreneurship for the 21st century* (5th ed.). Boston: Irwin/McGraw-Hill.
Ucbasaran, D., Lockett, A., Wright, M., & Westhead, P. (2003). Entrepreneurial founder teams: Factors associated with member entry and exit. *Entrepreneurship Theory and Practice, 28*(2), 107–125.
Virgin Media. (2018). *Virgin media business survey*. Retrieved December 2, 2018 from https://www.virginmedia.ie/img/Business/achieving-business-growth-with-facebook-ads-irish-SME-case-studies.pdf
Wamba, S. F., & Carter, L. (2014). Social media tools adoption and use by SMES: An empirical study. *Journal of Organizational and End User Computing, 26*(2), 1–17.
Wang, W., Pauleen, D. J., & Zhang, T. (2016). How social media applications affect B2B communication and improve business performance in SMEs. *Industrial Marketing Management, 54*, 4.
Wang, Y.-M., Wang, Y. S., & Yang, Y.-F. (2010). Understanding the determinants of RFID adoption in the manufacturing industry. *Technological Forecasting and Social Change, 77*(5), 803–815.
Watson, W. E., Ponthieu, L. D., & Critelli, J. W. (1995). Team interpersonal process effectiveness in venture partnerships and its connection to perceived success. *Journal of Business Venturing, 10*, 393–411.
Whelan, G., Moon, J., & Grant, B. (2013). Corporations and citizenship arenas in the age of social media. *Journal of Business Ethics, 118*(4), 777–790.
Zago, M. G. (2018). *Why the web 3.0 matters and you should know about it?* Retrieved January 30, 2018 from https://medium.com/@matteozago/why-the-web-3-0-matters-and-you-should-know-about-it-a5851d63c949

Part III
Social Media in Entrepreneurship Research: Where Do We Go Internationally?

Chapter 7
Entrepreneurship and Social Media Influencers in an Islamic Context

Khyati Shetty Datta, Olivia Adkins, and Jason R. Fitzsimmons

Abstract Social media has provided significant opportunities for individuals to pursue entrepreneurial endeavors. One phenomenon, in particular, has been the rise of social media influencers as a driving force in the entrepreneurial landscape. In this chapter we investigate the social media influencers in an Islamic context, exploring how institutional factors influence their behavior in such contexts.

Keywords Influencers · Islamic · Institutions · Middle East · Women entrepreneurs

7.1 Introduction

Entrepreneurship is widely regarded as an important driver of economic growth with governments around the world encouraging entrepreneurial activities through various programs and incentives. Moreover, the rise of social media has allowed many individuals to pursue self-employment through the many opportunities and low-cost entry into entrepreneurship. Social media platforms such as Facebook, Twitter, YouTube, and Instagram have enabled many users to create considerable value through enabling enterprising individuals to contribute their ideas, share information, and influence the opinions of their followers. As a consequence, social media influencers have become a considerable force driving public opinion through

K. S. Datta
Curtin University, Dubai, United Arab Emirates

O. Adkins
University of Birmingham, Dubai, United Arab Emirates

J. R. Fitzsimmons (✉)
School of Business, Manipal University, Dubai, United Arab Emirates
e-mail: jason.fitzsimmons@manipaldubai.com

L. Schjoedt et al. (eds.), *Understanding Social Media and Entrepreneurship*, Exploring Diversity in Entrepreneurship,
https://doi.org/10.1007/978-3-030-43453-3_7

their vast networks of followers. This has created significant opportunities for public relations and advertising firms. Marketers, in particular, have recognized this and have been actively integrating social media influencers into their mainstream marketing activities to reach potential customers.

The phenomena of social media influencers have also enabled many individuals, particularly women, to engage in entrepreneurial activities. Women, in particular, dominate the social media influencer community with women accounting for around 77% of the total number of influencers across the domains of food, travel, fashion, leisure, and entertainment (Gesenhues, 2019). For the most part, though, social media influencers have not traditionally been regarded as entrepreneurs, since their activities have largely been informally organized and seen as more of hobby activity. However, this view has been changing as many governments have recognized the considerable influence that social media influencers have, with many seeing the need to regulate influencers and encourage them to register their activities. The government of the United Arab Emirates, for example, has recently passed laws requiring social media influencers to obtain a social media license as well as obtain a trade license (Euronews, 2019). This has effectively legitimized social media influencers as business owners and entrepreneurs.

Also, the increasing number of women becoming social media influencers has created several issues, particularly in Islamic societies where women have traditionally been discouraged from entering the workforce or to actively voice their opinions. This has created a dilemma for many social media influencers in these regions. In this chapter, we explore these issues by drawing on institutional theory (North, 1990) and investigate the extent to which a sample of United Arab Emirates social media influencers see themselves as entrepreneurs and how regulatory, social, and cultural forces impact their social media activities.

7.2 Entrepreneurship in the United Arab Emirates

Encouraging entrepreneurial activity is important for sustaining economic growth. Dana and Dana (2005), for instance, point out that various governments around the world have been encouraging entrepreneurship since recognizing the social and economic value of entrepreneurship. Entrepreneurs are crucial to the future development of economies particularly those in emerging economies like the United Arab Emirates (UAE) where they play a key role in increasing market orientation and economic foundation.

Religion is perhaps one of the most important aspects of life in the UAE. It is, therefore, crucial to consider it when thinking about entrepreneurship. A strong correlation has been found between religion and entrepreneurship (Adas, 2006; Dana, 2009). In an Islamic context, entrepreneurship has an important place as Prophet Muhammad (peace be upon him) was a business leader himself. Consequently, Islamic culture encourages and promotes entrepreneurial values provided it is done following the teachings of the Prophet Muhammad (peace be upon him) who was known as "Al-Amin" (the honest, in Arabic) (Gümüsay, 2015). Entrepreneurship is seen as an integral part of the Islamic culture, with Islamic teachings promoting trade and commercial activities, illustrated, for example, by verse 4:33 of the Holy Quran Surah An-Nisa (The Women) "O believers, consume not your goods between you in vanity, except there be trading, by your agreeing together" (Ghoul, 2015).

Entrepreneurship from an Islamic perspective is based on three pillars. The first of these is based on the classic definition of entrepreneurship and is the pursuit of opportunities to make a profit. The second pillar is ethical and socioeconomic. Islam, being itself guided by a set of norms, values, and recommendations, entrepreneurship from an Islamic perspective is as well. The last but not least pillar is religio-spiritual and links people to God intending to please Allah (Gümüsay, 2015).

Since the Muslim population covers a large percentage of the world's total population, this growth has strengthened Islam as a religion and put Islamic teachings in various sectors, including entrepreneurship. Muslim entrepreneurs may choose to incorporate Islamic principles in their business, and this can be reflected in the corporate culture and procedure while running their businesses (Anggadwita, Ramadani, Alamanda, Ratten, & Hashani, 2017).

Based on the Quran, Islam supports free trade, with profit seen as legitimate provided it is consistent with Islamic ethics and does not seek to exploit others (Ludwig, 2001; Yousef, 2000). The singular pursuit of profit is discouraged as the main motivation of entrepreneurship in Islamic contexts. The Sharia promotes products and services that are beneficial to society and cautions against engaging in enterprises involved with alcohol, pornography, gambling and speculation, violence, riba, and other prohibited activities, unless necessary (Ghoul, 2015). Even if a government is compliant with the Sharia law, entrepreneurs are accountable to God and are expected to remain truthful through their business dealings, which is viewed as executing Islamic law.

In the UAE, perceptions of entrepreneurship have developed over the past few decades. A survey conducted in 2011 found that only around 6.3% of the adult population had aspirations to start a business (Van Horne, Huang, & Al Awad, 2011). The perception that students have about entrepreneurship and innovation is also highly influenced by their university education. It is also argued that one will tend to have more positive perceptions and values related to entrepreneurship if their families or friends have been involved in business activities (Saji & Nair, 2018). This situation has changed over time in line with the introduction of the National Agenda 2021, which aims to see the United Arab Emirates among the world's best in entrepreneurship. According to the director general of the Department of Economic Development in Dubai, more than 34,000 entrepreneurs have benefited from the new venture start-up advisory and development services of Dubai SME, and over 6000 Emirati enterprises were formed from their assistance (Sadaqat, 2019). The Hamdan Innovation Incubator of Dubai SME was launched by the Mohammed bin Rashid establishment to work with Emirati entrepreneurs and has helped 571 projects take off.

Entrepreneurship involves utilizing skills to bring innovation to established firms or toward the development of new firms. Whether one puts into practice new ideas or simply modify the existing one to better suit the circumstances, innovation is in the heart of entrepreneurship (Jamali, 2014). Entrepreneurship in the world and especially in the Middle East has also been highly influenced by the trend toward digitalization. In 2016, for example, it was reported that 2500 new jobs were created and \$1.5 billion generated for every 10 successful new enterprises (Alkasmi, El Hamamsy, Khoury, & Syed, 2016). However, despite the immense economic potential (projected to reach a GDP of \$3.4 trillion in 2020), the Middle East and North Africa (MENA) region has only realized 8.4% of its digital potential (Benni, Elmasry, Parel, & Moore, 2016). Aware of the potential of entrepreneurship, the Dubai Chamber of Commerce and Industry mentors, trains, and advises UAE nationals to develop their natural entrepreneurship ability. The program is called Tejar Dubai. As per the general coordinator of Tejar Dubai, it is a full program that was founded around three pillars: assess, assist, and attain. The program, therefore, has a mission to create young Emirati entrepreneurs and ensure the sustainability of the UAE economy. Women are largely included in the program, which counts 70% of female participants. For instance, a woman launched a venture called Potential Nursery as a result of participation in the program. The program also helped launch projects like Gravity Gym and Garden Depot, both financed by banks thanks to the influence of Tejar Dubai (ArabianBusiness.com, 2015).

The MENA region is also experiencing a youth bulge offering considerable entrepreneurial potential with the largest proportion of youths to adults in the region's history, with 60% of the population under the age 30 and 30% between the age 15 and 29 (Alkasmi et al., 2016). Therefore, it is not a surprise that the region is one of the most digitally connected in the world with an average of 94% of the population owning a smartphone and 88% of the population being connected daily (Alkasmi et al., 2016). Given these, entrepreneurship in the MENA region is highly influenced by social media, and digital entrepreneurship offers considerable opportunities for entrepreneurship in the region. A few examples illustrate the growth of local digital entrepreneurship. In the sector of e-commerce, the United Arab Emirates leads with entrepreneurial solutions such as dubizzle in Dubai which is the perfect example of pure-play marketplace (a platform to sell and buy goods); Namshi, a full-fledged e-retailer (which provides digital storefronts, payment facilities, and delivery solutions); and Amazon's Souq.com, which is a hybrid model (offering both e-retail offerings and marketplace). Another Dubai-based company, Fetchr, uses smartphone GPS technology to accurately locate users for package delivery. As e-commerce is an important industry in the region, this type of innovative solutions will prosper from complementary effects.

Aside from digital entrepreneurship, social media is perceived as a factor that can help to promote entrepreneurship in the United Arab Emirates. Social media can help businesses build trusted and valued relationships by sharing assessments, surveys, news, etc. (Metcalfe, Minouni, & Murfin, 2011). However, Samuel and Sarprasatha (2015) argue that many entrepreneurs have not fully appreciated the immense benefits that social media can have in their business; hence, they do not optimally use it.

7.3 Social Media in the United Arab Emirates

7.3.1 Social Media Usage

The technology landscape of the world has drastically changed over the last few decades. The rise of social media has resulted in important changes in how individuals and businesses communicate with each other and share information. Social media as defined by Kaplan and Haenlein (2010) is "a group of Internet-based applications that build on the ideological and technological foundations of Web 2.0, and allow the creation and exchange of user-generated content." Social media helps foster old relations and create new ones, at an individual level and global one, and therefore has become a vital part of our daily life (Hatab, 2016). Indeed, social media usage is one of the most popular online activities.

Statista (2019) records an estimate of 2.65 billion people using social media worldwide in 2018, with a projected increase to almost 3.1 billion in 2021. The most widely used social media platforms are social networking sites such as Twitter, Facebook, YouTube, and Instagram which are popular communication tools among adolescents and young adults with usage growing at tremendous rates (Subrahmanyam, Reich, Waechter, & Espinoza, 2008).

In the UAE, the digital landscape has been reshaped with the use of social media among youths and businesses with the UAE growing into one of the most digital-friendly countries in the Middle East. According to the latest statistics on social media usage, 99.06% of the UAE population remain active on social media with social media usage recording a 1.5% increase from the previous year (Global Media Insights, 2019). The most popular social media platforms in the UAE continue to be Facebook, YouTube, and Instagram with Instagram being the most popular platform among younger users.

Social media has significant potential for business owners and entrepreneurs across the UAE as a marketing tool and a method of increasing sales. Social media makes it possible for individuals to create, share, and exchange information and consequently has become an important advertising channel and communication tool for brands to shape their presence online. According to a January 2019 survey of marketers worldwide, increased exposure and traffic were two of the leading benefits of using social media for marketing purposes, followed by lead generation (Statista, 2019). Additionally, social media is a source of news for youth, as findings by ASDA'A Burson-Marsteller revealed that young Arabs look first to social media for news updates (Radcliffe & Bruni, 2018). Given the connectedness of individuals in the UAE, local businesses have begun to leverage sites such as Facebook and Instagram as a web portal for retail activities (Samuel & Sarprasatha, 2015). Social media has impacted multiple organizational phenomena and processes through various implications from organizing to the dissemination of information (Leonardi & Vaast, 2016).

7.3.2 Social Media and Entrepreneurship

As discussed in the previous section, social media has been transforming the digital landscape, allowing entrepreneurs to utilize social media platforms to manage their business activities including marketing and customer relationship management (Alalwan, Rana, Dwivedi, & Algharabat, 2017; Misirlis & Vlachopoulou, 2018). The rise of social media has impacted on how entrepreneurs carry out day-to-day activities. Social media has provided entrepreneurs with better opportunities to connect with individuals, overcoming common challenges such as reaching out for expert advice. Social media also drives innovation and co-creation through networks where entrepreneurs can establish relationships with other entrepreneurs.

Social media has allowed entrepreneurs to enhance marketing efforts with the ability to promote and advertise their products and services on various platforms, using to their advantage the cost-effectiveness of this proposition compared to traditional marketing and other marketing processes (Olanrewaju, Hossain, Whiteside, & Mercieca, 2020). Marketing on social media is more visible with business to customer organizations where activities such as customer relationship management, brand management, and advertising are a key focus. These activities not only drive their sales by improving visibility but also play a role in improving customer relationships through endorsements, promotions, and business activities with responses of customer likes, shares, and comments. The rise of social media influencers discussed in the next section also provides an insight into the powerful means used by brands to reach out to customers through social media campaigns.

The ease and reachability of social media also play a huge role in the way entrepreneurs search for and access information. Social media has changed how they seek, search, and gather information (Olanrewaju, Hossain, Whiteside, & Mercieca, 2020). Various social media affordances enable this process (Smith, Smith, & Shaw, 2017). Entrepreneurs often lack funds for activities such as hiring experts in their areas to assist with their business needs. It is seen that social media provides entrepreneurs with the confidence to search for and gather information as it is easily available on the platforms. Information regarding competitors, how to run business, and more is easily accessible through social media. There is an exchange of tacit and non-tacit knowledge (Wang, Mack, & Maciewjewski, 2017) whereby entrepreneurs can follow users on platforms, therefore fulfilling the information needs of entrepreneurs. Entrepreneurs often seek advice on social media platforms from altruistic information providers (Kuhn, Galloway, & Collins-Williams, 2016; Quinton & Wilson, 2016). Entrepreneurs make use of the different platforms to not only market their product or search for information but also create, enlarge, and strengthen networks (Ahmad, Ahmad, & Abu Bakar, 2018; Fischer & Reuber, 2011; Quinton & Wilson, 2016).

Entrepreneurship is no longer restricted by geographical location, thanks to social media, which has opened the doors to networking and interacting with people from all over the globe with similar or diverse socioeconomic and demographic statuses (Fischer & Reuber, 2011; Wang et al., 2017). Through social media, entrepreneurs can develop strong and weak ties, by creating strategic or emergent networks that can add value depending on the transactional offer from the entrepreneurs (Olanrewaju, Hossain, Whiteside, & Mercieca, 2020).

Moreover, entrepreneurs can use the data gathered from social media to drive innovation for their business. On Instagram, for example, users can use insights to find how their customers react to products and service offerings. Another emerging area has been the role of social media in raising capital which is often described as one of the hindering factors for entrepreneurs. Social media can play crucial roles in entrepreneur crowdfunding. With the use of audio-visuals and crowdfunding videos, entrepreneurs can raise funds through the various platforms available on the Internet (Song & van Boeschoten, 2015). Metrics such as the number of friends or followers and social capital accrued are also factors that drive crowdfunding. Social media, therefore, provides a platform that eases communication, social capital, marketing, and other activities entrepreneurs need to be successful.

7.3.3 The Rise of Instagram Influencers

The rise of social networks has brought a new generation of influencers. Even though social networks are rather new, influencers are not. For years, brands have been using celebrities and leaders to promote their products. Recently, brands have started to accept the rise of social media, and influencers now serve as the connection between a brand and its consumers. As opposed to celebrities, influencers use their personal lives to connect with their audience and can provide a sense of relatability (Nouri, 2018). Where traditional marketing focuses on targeting mass audiences, influencers have a niche that until now has been unreachable, making this phenomenon successful. Social media influencers in this sense are more than opinion leaders.

This growth of social media influencers has led to the establishment of a new type of agency who provide services to identify the right influencers and offer various tools to create interesting content and reach their target groups. Social media influencers are usually divided into bloggers, vloggers, celebrities, and influencers. Bloggers are usually website owners who create content for their blogs and often share their thoughts and passions via social media. Vloggers are mostly present on social media sites such as YouTube and use audio-visual content to connect with their audiences. Celebrities are often actors, singers, and others who are followed for being widely known. Finally, Instagrammers are influencers who have been able to attract audiences through photo sharing and stories on the Instagram social media platform (Kadekova & Holienčinová, 2018).

7.4 Methodology

The sample for the study consisted of semi-structured interviews and focus group discussions with six female social media influencers in the United Arab Emirates. Interviews with the influencers were carried out in 2019. A range of open-ended questions was asked about their social media activities as well as their views on how institutional factors related to regulatory, values and norms, and cultural issues impact on their social media activities.

7.5 Institutional Contexts in the UAE

7.5.1 Regulatory Framework

The regulatory framework represents the models of individual and organization behavior denoted by policies, rules, sanctions laws, and regulations that affect individual behavior in society (Stenholm, Acs, & Wuebker, 2013). North (1990) likens the regulatory framework to the written rules of a sport. Some rules including the ones formulated by external agents (league officials, referees) and the ones accepted and enforced by the players themselves. Several lines of evidence support the influence of these rules on the legitimacy and acceptance of entrepreneurship (Webb, Kistruck, Ireland, & Ketchen Jr, 2010). These laws and framework can have an impact on entrepreneurial ventures as it can create opportunities, support or constrain formation of new business, influence the extent to which women entrepreneurs can grow and develop, diminish or trigger risks for entrepreneurs, affect the types of ventures women can engage in, or constraint the access of financial resources (Amine & Staub, 2009; Ellis, Blackden, Cutura, MacCulloch, & Seebens, 2007; Naser, Rashid Mohammed, & Nuseibeh, 2009). While some of these policies and regulations may have the same effect on male and female entrepreneurs, others have gendered effects like labor market laws, family policies that specify childcare provisions, work permits, and residency regulations (Bianco, Lombe, & Bolis, 2017; Langevang, Gough, Yankson, Owusu, & Osei, 2015; Welter & Smallbone, 2010).

The open constitutional framework for work opportunities in the UAE believes that women are entitled to fulfill active roles in society, and the vision was promulgated from UAE's founding father Sheikh Zayed bin Sultan Al Nahyan who believed that "Women have the right to work everywhere." Under the constitution, women are assured the same legal status, claims to titles, access to education, and similar rights to practice professions as men. As a result, the UAE Business Women Council was formed in 2002 and is regarded as a very important business organization in the UAE (ElGurg, 2005). The Abu Dhabi Business Women Group (ADBW) and Dubai Business Women Council (DBWC) strive to provide assistance to women in the entrepreneurial space, and The National Investor TNI, a UAE Blue Chip Fund, announced the launch of its new TNI Dana Women Fund and the FORSA fund that have been created to cater toward women wishing to invest amounts over USD273,000, and ENMAA, a boutique bank catering to both small and large investors in the MENA region (Gallant, Weeks, & Niethammer, 2007).

In spite of the abundant support provided by the UAE government authorities, the legal framework of the country makes it challenging for budding female influencers to establish a foothold in the country. In 2019, the National Media Council announced new regulations for social media influencers to require a trade license and an e-media license for carrying out all online activities (print, video, audio, and electronically published activities) for commercial purposes (Al-Balushi, 2018). The regulation also requires influencers to mark sponsored content with clear borders between paid-for-promotion and other content. The new guidelines also mandated the post to include hashtags (e.g., #advertisement, #paid:ad, #sponsored) and not to include too many other hashtags which made it confusing to the reader. While these regulations were put in place to systematize the social media industry in the UAE, these rules may act to deter people from entering into the influencer marketing business as monetizing from these ventures can get challenging. As expressed by one of the established Emirati influencers:

> Being a social media influencer is a long term game as far as online monetization goes. To most people, it takes a year or two to start making money. When I started I didn't see a penny in my bank account for more than a year. With the current licensing requirements, the industry may no longer look lucrative to budding influencers.

Additionally, there are very stringent cybercrime laws that govern photography, privacy and confidentiality, and cultural sensitivities. For instance, it is an offense to take and post someone else's picture without their consent. This could potentially curb the creative freedom of style bloggers who feature other people on their platforms. The penal code in the UAE makes it an offense to make defamatory statements against another person or their company. This makes it binding for influencers to exercise caution while writing a negative review against a company or service provider. It is also illegal to post content that is considered inconsistent with public morals which could include un-Islamic and lewd content or anything that mocks leaders of the nation or hurts national unity (Grant, 2017). These regulations asphyxiate the space to voice out and the creative freedom of influencers which is one of the main intrinsic motivations to venture into this career. Commenting on the cybercrime laws, an influencer commented:

> As influencers, our freedom of speech and activity should be bounded by personal responsibility. I completely join the call of these rules but there is a lack of awareness of these laws. Because I very often catch myself questioning if my content would be appropriate as per the regulations.

7.5.2 Normative Framework

Normative systems typically include the values and norms that further establish the underlying assumptions and ground rules that people conform to (Scott, 2008). However, these are informal and intangible and establish the "rules of the game" and further determine the acceptance and social desirability of entrepreneurship as a legitimate career option (Busenitz, Gomez, & Spencer, 2000). While some cultures are socially acceptable of entrepreneurial careers of women, others make it daunting by looking down upon women pursuing it (Baumol, Litan, & Schramm, 2009; De Soto, 2000; Luthans, Stajkovic, & Ibrayeva, 2000; Mueller & Thomas, 2001). This, in turn, affects entrepreneurial intentions and affects the planned behavior of starting an entrepreneurial activity (Krueger, Reilly, & Carsrud, 2000).

Past studies have confirmed that respect, legitimacy, and admiration are important factors for entrepreneurial participation by women (Baughn, Chua, & Neupert, 2006). The traditional Arab environment attaches less reverence for professions that require women to mix with men. Any jobs that require women being exposed to large audiences are not acceptable by families and, as a result, are typically discouraged. Being an influencer requires one to build and engage with a large audience over time to stand out eventually to start making money. The challenge of keeping up with expected norms of society will require Emirati influencers to exclude male followers from their targeted audience, thereby narrowing their audience base.

Furthermore, the UAE society is strongly influenced by religion and tradition, and the level of women's involvement in the workforce has been determined by the strong patriarchal culture (Naser, Nuseibeh, & Al-Hussaini, 2012) and traditional Islamic standards (Javadian & Singh, 2012). Some conservative sections of society still look down upon women entrepreneurs on social media and often describe them as aggressive and bold (Marlow, 2002). These stereotypes are not considered desirable to describe women in traditional Arab societies which in turn discourages women (Bird & Brush, 2002; Langowitz & Minniti, 2007; Marlow & Patton, 2005) from entering into social media platforms. Some women also face active dissuasion from the male family members (Baud & Mahgoub, 1999), as social media is seen as a platform that objectifies women and is associated with latent sexism. Thus, the lack of normative support, which refers to the extent to which there is acceptance of women venturing into self-employment in social media given their traditional roles (Holmén, Min, & Saarelainen, 2011; Preiss & McCrohan, 2006) and the general tendency of female entrepreneurs being more conscious to their threats to legitimacy and validation, diminishes their keenness to enter into this line of self-employment (Kourilsky & Walstad, 1998). One influencer reinforced this point by saying:

> As influencers, we are often scrutinized by the public eye. And some of our followers feel entitled to comment just not on the area of work but also our personal lives, especially about how we express our religion. We are often accused by haters for drifting away from religion. This can get exhausting at times.

Aspiring female entrepreneurs are also frozen by the fear of negative social attitude (Woldie & Adersua, 2004) as the traditional Arab society still emphasizes the primary role of women in household and family responsibilities. As Goffee and Scase (1985) suggest, female entrepreneurs in the Arab world differ from male entrepreneurs in the sense that they tend to view their business as one aspect of a wider system that includes family, friends, and community. In this respect, there is a tendency for Emirati female entrepreneurs to manage their business activities in ways that do not interfere or cause an unnecessary conflict with the interests of their family (Carter & Cannon, 1992). However, as an influencer, being an expert in a domain requires one to build a following or a cult around them and cater to the needs of the base who follow them. This makes it vital for them to spend extraordinary time and effort with their platforms functioning on a 24/7 basis, engaging with audiences at all hours and delivering a constant stream of notifications. As aptly put by one of the influencers:

> I know of people who think of influencers as people who only post pictures and look pretty. Very few know that there is a lot of time and effort that goes into building your audience, constantly engaging with them and building a standalone brand for yourself. You may work from home, but when you have family responsibilities to tend to, your work takes a back-seat. There have been days when I don't compose a single post as I let other parts of my personal life takeover.

Yet another Emirati influencer raised her concern stating:

> As an influencer, I work from home and don't have set job timings. Thus I constantly stressing if I am dedicating enough time to my daughters or if I am overdoing it. Even though I am at home, I am not sure if they feel like I am there for them as I am constantly connected to my laptop. There are so many times I have considered going back to my 9 to 3 pm job with the government.

However, this deep-rooted culture makes it extremely challenging for UAE women entrepreneurs to devote time to these entrepreneurial ventures, especially due to the familial and societal demands placed on them (Preiss & McCrohan, 2006). Adding to this, given the volatile nature of this social media industry and the presence of very stiff competition, there is a very high perceived risk associated with the profession. And given the relatively small and well-knit characteristic of the Emirati community (Haan, 2003), there is increased fear among Emirati women for the loss of credibility as the news of failure quickly permeates in society.

Thus most Emirati women shun the options of starting an entrepreneurial venture on social media and instead opt for public sector jobs which are known for their more comfortable working hours, stability in pay, and generally less demanding work regimes (Erogul & McCrohan, 2008).

7.5.3 *Cognitive Framework*

The cognitive pillar summarized by Scott (1995) is "the shared conceptions that constitute the nature of social reality and the frames through which meaning is made." This pillar is important to entrepreneurship as it curates how societies accept and ascribe value to certain careers and also creates a cultural milieu (Bosma, Acs, Autio, Coduras, & Levie, 2009). This plays a crucial role in curating the social meaning that individuals attach to careers like social media influencing and determines the extent of risks, fears, and rewards associated with it (Amine & Staub, 2009; Baughn et al., 2006), which also establishes the desirability and perceived feasibility of starting a business (Welter & Smallbone, 2010). Several lines of evidence from past studies support the high correlation between perceptions of feasibility on intentions of entrepreneurship (Rasheed, 2004). Thus, if an individual perceives an action as infeasible, there is a less likelihood of the individual to pursue such an action. In the words of an Emirati influencer:

> Getting into social media full time is a risky option. It is extremely competitive and there are shoots, deadlines, and brand guidelines. Very few of us stand out and if you fail to do so, brands will decide to go to other people in the industry who are more than willing to do it for free.

Drawing from prior research, several studies have sought to examine the importance of entrepreneurial networks, the presence of strong female role models, and the availability of entrepreneurial education in determining the propensity to act in relation to entrepreneurial acceptance (Davis & Shaver, 2012). Like most ventures, social media is an industry where networking is considered an essential skill for success (McGregor & Tweed, 2000; St-Cyr & Gagnon, 2004). It is not only about what you know but who you know. You need an audience to grow your audience, but developing one is a process. The GEM 2004 report on female entrepreneurs additionally supported those female entrepreneurs who connected with other entrepreneurs, and role models in the same line of business are more likely to venture into the same line of business themselves (Minniti, Arenius, & Langowitz, 2005). While there are some networking platforms for influencers within the UAE, like the Arab Social Media Influencers Summit, most of these platforms are tapped by expatriates rather than their Emirati counterparts (Haan, 2004). The reason for this slow engagement might be attributed to the preconceived norms of gender separation. This leads to women drawing on their networks limited to immediate family and friends. This dependence on a narrow network, absence of access to male industry contacts, and lack of opportunities to practice networking skills may rouse low self-confidence and act as an impediment to female Emirati influencers.

Cognitive institutions are largely built from the culture of the society. Countries may differ in terms of the value placed on various streams of entrepreneurship that people pursue (Bruton, Fried, & Manigart, 2005). The UAE society has a modern outlook but is still strongly influenced by local traditions, norms, and religion. Perceptions of entrepreneurial roles as a social media influencer may be devalued in a country, not because of gender discrimination but the stream of work itself may not be respected and held in high regard. Consistent with this, various studies have examined the national difference in the social acceptability of various entrepreneurial careers (Luthans et al., 2000; Mueller & Thomas, 2001). The deep-seated cultural norms curated by role models, family, friends, and society as a whole act as a moderating variable between the individual and his/her self-efficacy to get involved in entrepreneurial activity (Krueger et al., 2000). Consequently, these norms which prevail at a macrolevel are internalized by women which in turn trickle to the cultural cognitive pillar and in turn influence their conceptions of appropriate actions at a microlevel. The following two quotes offer a good illustration of this internalization process:

> As a fashion blogger and influencer, I have to post pictures. It gets challenging sometimes to take pictures that do not expose my face and not accentuate my body too much. I am constantly striving to make the photos look stylish, cheek and at the same time maintain my modesty as it is of utmost importance in my society. Personally, for me, everything must follow Islamic guidelines.

Another influencer reinforced this point when she said:

> Like other countries, we are not legally required to take permission from the men in the family to pursue a career. But our career choices need validation and acceptance from the male member of the family. It is less legal and more cultural.

Furthermore, an access and control over finances (Jamali, 2009; Minniti, 2009) play an important role in shaping the perception of women entrepreneurs about the suitability of the environment they are going to venture into (Zhao, Seibert, & Hills, 2005). However, not getting paid or not getting paid on time is the most frustrating part for social media influencers in the UAE, where the average lead time for payments by most agencies is a minimum of 60 days. Adding to this is the gender pay gap in the industry where female influencers are earning 23% less than their male counterparts (Klear Influencer Marketing Report, 2019). As a result, Langowitz and Minniti (2007: 356) found that "women tend to perceive themselves and such business environment in a less favorable light." As expressed by one Emirati micro-influencer:

> As a micro-influencer, you do not have a steady flow of income. My earnings are very unstable, for instance during Ramadan time the market slows. Thus you cannot think of being an influencer as a full- time job. For most of us, it's a side gig. It cannot be more than making some extra bucks on the side.

7.6 Discussion

Building on institutional theory, this paper endeavors to document how female social media influencers in the Emirates navigate the complex institutional environment in the UAE and how the interplay of these factors shape and mold the expressions of these women in the UAE. Examining the influencing factors through the institutional theory lens, by conceptualizing the institutional pillars impacting female entrepreneurship, has been highlighted in previous studies (Welter, 2005; Yeung, 2002).

The findings regarding female Emirati influencers highlight the high degree of institutional uncertainty, incongruity, and inconsistency between the different pillars. In the regulatory domain, the dominance of the news laws and regulations on obtaining new licenses makes the process of entering into this business complex, expensive, and cumbersome. While the objective of the new framework is to protect the privacy of individuals and to produce balanced and responsible media content, it is leaving a chilling effect on a burgeoning industry. The increased difficulty and the very high barrier to entry may hollow out the roster of emerging female influencers in the region. While the larger, more established influencers are happy with this law as it wipes out the competition, the regulatory framework in the UAE will discount the vast swathes of micro-influencers. Adding to this, the very high scrutiny of the kinds of content posted limits the entrepreneurial intentions to enter the industry. Regarding the normative pillar, in spite of the encouragement given to female entrepreneurs by the UAE government for women entrepreneurs, the social media industry as an entrepreneurial career for women is slow to gain acceptance, acknowledgment, and inclusivity. Plus, the role of the importance of gender segregation and the lack of networking opportunities with the male stakeholders in the industry limit their potential to expand. In the cognitive domain, the role of the cognitive patriarchal norms is salient and is often internalized by women to the point of reducing motivation and their potential for self-fulfillment and actualization through entrepreneurship (Rehan, Block, & Fisch, 2019).

While the government of UAE is completely in support of women entrepreneurship and has set up many institutions such as Mohammed bin Rashid Establishment for Young Business Leader and Khalifa Fund to finance upcoming entrepreneurs, the social media entrepreneurs are still not a formalized industry and lack a level of support. And as evidenced by previous studies, female entrepreneurs in unregulated industries face several challenges that have no one single remedy (Pardo-del-Val & Ribeiro-Soriano, 2007). Several recommendations can be suggested to tackle these challenges. The female influencers interviewed in the study provided several useful insights that should be corroborated by future research. Though the UAE is making strides in empowering women through government initiatives, there is still a deep underlying concern of acceptance of social media as a respected profession for women, coupled with a lack of support from their environment and fear of failure. There is a change needed at the society level.

One of the limiting factors stated by the influencers was local and cultural norms prevalent in society. Most women did not desire a far-reaching change in the social and religious customs as they held very high reverence for the existing traditions; however, they hoped that a modern interpretation of careers in the field of social media will gain them respect and mark their presence in the field. There is a need to establish a formal institutional framework for social media entrepreneurs in collaboration with other women entrepreneur associations in the UAE. There should also be training and workshops set for influencers to sharpen their skills in digital marketing, content creation, and SEO. Rolling out such programs will help sharpen their knowledge and gain confidence in venturing into this line of business. Success stories of popular Emirati female influencers should be publicized. This will gain better acceptance and help break stereotypes and help women battle their cognitive inner hurdles.

7.7 Conclusions

Social media has witnessed a significant rise in usage in the Middle East, and social media influencers are at the center of the spotlight. The Emirati women influencers are taking over the mainstream with fearless ideas, overcoming hurdles, and growing into a power to be reckoned with. However, there is a dire need to provide constant support and guidance and empower these women in their efforts to overcome regulatory, normative, and cognitive hurdles.

References

Adas, E. (2006). The making of entrepreneurial Islam and the Islamic spirit of capitalism. *Journal for Cultural Research, 10*(2), 113–137. https://doi.org/10.1080/14797580600624745

Ahmad, S., Ahmad, N., & Abu Bakar, A. (2018). Reflections of entrepreneurs of small and medium-sized enterprises concerning the adoption of social media and its impact on performance outcomes: Evidence from the UAE. *Telematics and Informatics, 35*(1), 6–17.

Alalwan, A., Rana, N., Dwivedi, Y., & Algharabat, R. (2017). Social media in marketing: A review and analysis of the existing literature. *Telematics and Informatics, 34*(7), 1177–1190.

Al-Balushi, R. (2018). Social media influencers require permits to operate in the UAE. *Journal of Intellectual Property Law & Practice, 13*, 858–859.

Alkasmi, A. J., El Hamamsy, O., Khoury, L., & Syed, A. (2016). *Entrepreneurship in the Middle East and North Africa: How investors can support and enable growth*. McKinsey & Company, N.Y.

Amine, L. S., & Staub, K. M. (2009). Women entrepreneurs in sub-Saharan Africa: An institutional theory analysis from a social marketing point of view. *Entrepreneurship & Regional Development, 21*(2), 183–211.

Anggadwita, G., Ramadani, V., Alamanda, D. T., Ratten, V., & Hashani, M. (2017). Entrepreneurial intentions from an Islamic perspective: A study of Muslim entrepreneurs in Indonesia. *International Journal of Entrepreneurship and Small Business, 31*(2), 165–179. https://doi.org/10.1504/ijesb.2017.10004845

ArabianBusiness.com (2015). *Charting the rise of the Emirati Entrepreneur*. Retrieved 2 December 2019, from https://www.arabianbusiness.com/charting-rise-of-emirati-entrepreneur-615114.html

Baud, I., & Mahgoub, H. K. (1999, June). *Towards increasing national female participation in the labour force*. Research Report 2, Center for Labour Market Research and Information, Tanmia, Dubai.

Baughn, C., Chua, B., & Neupert, K. (2006). The normative context for women's participation in entreprenerusnip: A multicountry study. *Entrepreneurship Theory and Practice, 30*(5), 687–708.

Baumol, W. J., Litan, R. E., & Schramm, C. J. (2009). *Good capitalism, bad capitalism, and the economics of growth and prosperity*. New Haven, CT: Yale University Press.

Benni, E., Elmasry, T., Parel, J., & Moore, J. P. (2016, October). *Digital Middle East: Transforming the region into a leading global economy*. McKinsey & Company, N.Y.

Bianco, M., Lombe, M., & Bolis, M. (2017). Challenging gender norms and practices through women's entrepreneurship. *International Journal of Gender and Entrepreneurship, 9*(4), 338–358. https://doi.org/10.1108/ijge-10-2017-0060

Bird, B., & Brush, C. (2002). A gendered perspective on organizational creation. *Entrepreneurship Theory and Practice, 26*(3), 41–65.

Bosma, N., Acs, Z., Autio, E., Coduras, A., & Levie, J. (2009). *Global entrepreneurship monitor, 2008 executive report*. Wellesley, MA: Babson College.
Bruton, G., Fried, V., & Manigart, S. (2005). Institutional influences on the worldwide expansion of venture capital. *Entrepreneurship Theory and Practice, 29*(6), 737–760.
Busenitz, L., Gomez, C., & Spencer, J. (2000). Country institutional profiles: Unlocking entrepreneurial phenomena. *Academy of Management Journal, 43*(5), 994–1003.
Carter, S., & Cannon, T. (1992). *Women as entrepreneurs*. London: Academic Press. Challenges facing entrepreneurial develop-context. In C. G. Brush & E. J. De Bruin (Eds.), *Women entrepreneurs and the global environment*.
Dana, L. (2009). Religion as an explanatory variable for entrepreneurship. *The International Journal of Entrepreneurship and Innovation, 10*(2), 87–99.
Dana, L., & Dana, T. (2005). Expanding the scope of methodologies used in entrepreneurship research. *International Journal of Entrepreneurship and Small Business, 2*(1), 79.
Davis, A. E., & Shaver, K. G. (2012). Understanding gendered variations in business growth intentions across the life course. *Entrepreneurship Theory and Practice, 36*(3), 495–512.
De Soto, H. (2000). *The mystery of capital: Why capitalism triumphs in the west and fails everywhere else*. New York: Basic Books.
ElGurg, R. E. (2005, March). *The development March of Emirates' woman: Experiment of the UAE Businesswomen Council, a model that can be followed*. Proceedings of the First Forum for Businesswomen in OIC Countries, Sharjah, UAE, pp. 71–80.
Ellis, A., Blackden, M., Cutura, J., MacCulloch, F., & Seebens, H. (2007). *Gender and economic growth in Tanzania: Creating opportunities for women*. Washington, DC: World Bank.
Erogul, M. S., & McCrohan, D. (2008). Preliminary investigation of Emirati women entrepreneurs in the UAE. *African Journal of Business Management, 2*(10), 177.
Euronews. (2019). *License to influence: UAE law regulates social media players*. Retrieved 2 December 2019, from https://www.euronews.com/2019/07/19/license-to-influence-uae-law-regulates-social-media-players
Fischer, E., & Reuber, A. R. (2011). Social interaction via new social media: (How) can interactions on Twitter affect effectual thinking and behavior?. *Journal of Business Venturing, 26*(1), 1–18.
Gallant, M., Weeks, J., & Niethammer, C. (2007). Women business owners in the United Arab Emirates. The Center of Arab Women for Training and Research and the International Finance Corporation, Dubai/UAE December. Gender entrepreneurship markets (2007). International Finance Corporation (IFC). *GEM Country Brief – Lebanon Geography, 91*(4), 449–473.
Gesenhues, A. (2019). Women make up majority of influencer community, still earn less than male influencers. *Marketing Land*. Retrieved 2 December 2019, from https://marketingland.com/women-make-up-majority-of-influencer-community-earn-less-than-male-influencers-262193
Ghoul, W. (2015). Entrepreneurship within the framework of Shari'ah. *International Journal of Business and Globalisation, 15*(3), 262.
Global Media Insights. (2019). UAE social media usage statistics (2019). [online] *Official GMI Blog*. Available at: https://www.globalmediainsight.com/blog/uae-social-media-statistics/
Goffee, R., & Scase, R. (1985). *Women in charge: The experience of women entrepreneurs*. London: Allen & Unwin.
Grant Thorton. (2017). *Cyber-crime: Avoid paying the price*. Retrieved from https://www.grantthornton.ae/globalassets/1.-member-firms/uae/may-2017-onwards/cybercrime_avoid-paying-the-price_2017.pdf
Gümüsay, A. A. (2015). Entrepreneurship from an Islamic perspective. *Journal of Business Ethics, 130*(1), 199–208.
Haan, H. C. (2004). *Small enterprises: Women entrepreneurs in the UAE*. Labour market study no. 19, Center for Labour Market Research and Information, Tanmia/CLMRI, Dubai.
Haan, H. C. (2003). *Fingers of one hand: Experiences of small businesses in Northern Emirates*. Dubai: Tanmia/CLMRI.
Hatab, A. W. (2016). Islam and social media: Attitudes and views. *Asian Social Science, 12*(5), 221.

Holmén, M., Min, T. T., & Saarelainen, E. (2011). Female entrepreneurship in Afghanistan. *Journal of Developmental Entrepreneurship, 16*(03), 307–331.

Jamali, D. (2009). Constraints and opportunities facing women entrepreneurs in developing countries. *Gender in Management: An International Journal, 24*(4), 232–251.

Jamali, D. (2014). Overview of corporate social responsibility in the Middle East. *The World Financial Review*, pp. 71–72.

Javadian, G., & Singh, R. (2012). Examining successful Iranian women entrepreneurs: An exploratory study. *Gender in Management: An International Journal, 27*(3), 148–164.

Kadekova, Z., & Holienčinová, M. (2018). Influencer marketing as a modern phenomenon creating a new frontier of virtual opportunities. *Communication Today, 9*, 90–104.

Kaplan, A. M., & Haenlein, M. (2010). Users of the world, unite! The challenges and opportunities of Social Media. *Business Horizons, 53*(1), 59–68.

Klear. (2019). *Klear Influencer Marketing report 2019*. Retrieved from https://klear.com/KlearRateCard.pdf

Kourilsky, M. L., & Walstad, W. B. (1998). Entrepreneurship and female youth: Knowledge, attitudes, gender differences, and educational practices. *Journal of Business Venturing, 13*, 77–88.

Krueger, N. F., Reilly, M. D., & Carsrud, A. L. (2000). Competing models of entrepreneurial intentions. *Journal of Business Venturing, 15*(5–6), 411–432.

Kuhn, K., Galloway, T., & Collins-Williams, M. (2016). Near, far, and online: Small business owners' advice-seeking from peers. *Journal of Small Business and Enterprise Development, 23*(1), 189–206.

Langevang, T., Gough, K. V., Yankson, P. W., Owusu, G., & Osei, R. (2015). Bounded entrepreneurial vitality: The mixed embeddedness of female entrepreneurship. *Economic Geography, 91*(4), 449–473.

Langowitz, N., & Minniti, M. (2007). The entrepreneurial propensity of women. *Entrepreneurship Theory and Practice, 31*(3), 341–364.

Leonardi, P., & Vaast, E. (2016). Social media and their affordances for organizing: A review and agenda for research. *Academy of Management Annals, 11*(1), 150–188.

Ludwig, T. M. (2001). *The sacred paths*. Upper Saddle River, NJ: Prentice Hall.

Luthans, F., Stajkovic, A. D., & Ibrayeva, E. (2000). Environmental and psychological challenges facing entrepreneurial development in transitional economies. *Journal of World Business, 35*(1), 95–110.

Marlow, S. (2002). Women and self-employment: A part of or apart from theoretical construct? *The International Journal of Entrepreneurship and Innovation, 3*(2), 83–91.

Marlow, S., & Patton, D. (2005). All credit to men? Entrepreneurship, finance, and gender. *Entrepreneurship Theory and Practice, 29*(6), 717–735.

McGregor, J., & Tweed, D. (2000). Women managers and business owners in New Zealand. *Women in Management: Current Research Issues, 2*, 40–52.

Metcalfe, B., Minouni, F., & Murfin, T. (2011). Turning neither to East nor West: Social reform and a liberating ethics for leadership development. In *Leadership development in the Middle East* (pp. 371–400). Cheltenham, UK: Edward Elgar.

Minniti, M. (2009). Gender issues in entrepreneurship. *Foundations and Trends® in Entrepreneurship, 5*(7–8), 497–621.

Minniti, M., Arenius, P., & Langowitz, N. (2005). *Global entrepreneurship monitor – 2005 report on women and entrepreneurship*. Center for Women's Leadership at Babson College, Babson Park, 40 pages.

Misirlis, N., & Vlachopoulou, M. (2018). Social media metrics and analytics in marketing–S3M: A mapping literature review. *International Journal of Information Management, 38*(1), 270–276.

Mueller, S. L., & Thomas, A. S. (2001). Culture and entrepreneurial potential: A nine country study of locus of control and innovativeness. *Journal of Business Venturing, 16*(1), 51–75.

Naser, K., Nuseibeh, R., & Al-Hussaini, A. (2012). Personal and external factors effect on women entrepreneurs: Evidence from Kuwait. *Journal of Developmental Entrepreneurship, 17*(02), 1250008.

Naser, K., Rashid Mohammed, W., & Nuseibeh, R. (2009). Factors that affect women entrepreneurs: Evidence from an emerging economy. *International Journal of Organizational Analysis, 17*(3), 225–247.

North, D. (1990). *Institutions, institutional change and economic performance*. Cambridge, UK/ New York: Cambridge University Press.

Nouri, M. (2018). The power of influence: Traditional celebrity vs social media influencer. *Advanced Writing: Pop Culture Intersections, 32*, 1–20.

Olanrewaju, A. S. T., Hossain, M. A., Whiteside, N., & Mercieca, P. (2020). Social media and entrepreneurship research: A literature review. *International Journal of Information Management, 50*, 90–110.

Pardo-del-Val, M., & Ribeiro-Soriano, D. (2007). Political support for women entrepreneurs. *Equality, Diversity and Inclusion: An International Journal, 26*(8), 761.

Preiss, K., & McCrohan, D. (2006). *GEM global summary 2006: United Arab Emirates*. London: London School of Economics/Babson.

Quinton, S., & Wilson, D. (2016). Tensions and ties in social media networks: Towards a model of understanding business relationship development and business performance enhancement through the use of LinkedIn. *Industrial Marketing Management, 54*, 15–24.

Radcliffe, D., & Bruni, P. (2018). State of social media, Middle East: 2018. *Middle East*.

Rasheed, H. S. (2004). Capital access barriers to public procurement performance: The moderating effects of ethnicity, gender and education. *Journal of Developmental Entrepreneurship, 9*(2), 22–43.

Rehan, F., Block, J. H., & Fisch, C. (2019). Entrepreneurship in Islamic communities: How do Islamic values and Islamic practices influence entrepreneurship intentions? *Journal of Enterprising Communities: People and Places in the Global Economy, 13*, 557–583.

Sadaqat, R. (2019). Entrepreneurial growth set to accelerate in 2019. [online] *Khaleej Times*. Available at: https://www.khaleejtimes.com/entrepreneurial-growth-set-to-accelerate-in-2019.

Saji, B. S., & Nair, A. R. (2018). Effectiveness of innovation and entrepreneurship education in UAE higher education. *Academy of Strategic Management Journal, 17*(4), 1–12.

Samuel, B. S., & Sarprasatha, J. (2015). Social media as a factor for promoting entrepreneurship – the Middle East & Oman Scenario. *International Journal of Economics, Finance and Management Sciences, 3*(5), 483–493.

Scott, W. R. (1995). *Institutions and organizations: Ideas, interests, and identities*. London: SAGE Publications.

Scott, W. R. (2008). *Institutions and organizations: Ideas and interests*. London: Sage.

Smith, C., Smith, J. B., & Shaw, E. (2017). Embracing digital networks: Entrepreneurs' social capital online. *Journal of Business Venturing, 32*(1), 18–34.

Song, Y., & van Boeschoten, R. (2015). Success factors for Crowdfunding founders and funders. *arXiv preprint arXiv:1503.00288*.

Statista. (2019). Number of social media users worldwide 2010–2021. *Statista*. [online] Available at: https://www.statista.com/statistics/278414/number-of-worldwide-social-network-users/

St-Cyr, L., & Gagnon, S. (2004). *Les entrepreneures Québécoises: taille des entreprises et performance*. Congrès International Francophone en Entreprenneurship et PME, Montpellier, France.

Stenholm, P., Acs, Z. J., & Wuebker, R. (2013). Exploring country-level institutional arrangements on the rate and type of entrepreneurial activity. *Journal of Business Venturing, 28*(1), 176–193.

Subrahmanyam, K., Reich, S. M., Waechter, N., & Espinoza, G. (2008). Online and offline social networks: Use of social networking sites by emerging adults. *Journal of Applied Developmental Psychology, 29*(6), 420–433.

Van Horne, C., Huang, V. Z., & Al Awad, M. (2011). *Global entrepreneurship monitor (GEM) report on entrepreneurship in the United Arab Emirates*. Zayed University.

Wang, F., Mack, E. A., & Maciewjewski, R. (2017). Analyzing entrepreneurial social networks with big data. *Annals of the American Association of Geographers, 107*(1), 130–150.

Webb, J. W., Kistruck, G. M., Ireland, R. D., & Ketchen Jr., D. J. (2010). The entrepreneurship process in base of the pyramid markets: The case of multinational enterprise/nongovernment organization alliances. *Entrepreneurship Theory and Practice, 34*(3), 555–581.

Welter, F. (2005). Entrepreneurial behavior in differing environments. In *Local heroes in the global village* (pp. 93–112). Boston: Springer.

Welter, F., & Smallbone, D. (2010). The embeddedness of women's entrepreneurship in a transition context. In *Women entrepreneurs and the global environment for growth: A research perspective* (pp. 96–117). Cheltenham, UK/Northampton, MA: Edward Elgar.

Woldie, A., & Adersua, A. (2004). Female entrepreneurs in a transitional economy: Businesswomen in Nigeria. *International Journal of Social Economics, 31*(1/2), 78–93.

Yeung, H. W. C. (2002). Entrepreneurship in international business: An institutional perspective. *Asia Pacific Journal of Management, 19*(1), 29–61.

Yousef, D. A. (2000). Organizational commitment as a mediator of the relationship between Islamic work ethic and attitudes toward organizational change. *Human Relations, 53*(4), 513–537.

Zhao, H., Seibert, S. E., & Hills, G. E. (2005). The mediating role of self-efficacy in the development of entrepreneurial intentions. *Journal of Applied Psychology, 90*(6), 1265. Retrieved from https://www.government.ae/en/information-and-services/justice-safety-and-the-law/cyber-safety-and-digital-security

Chapter 8
Social Media and Small Entrepreneurial Firms' Internationalization

Pia Hurmelinna-Laukkanen, Lauri Haapanen, and Saara Holma

Abstract Small entrepreneurial firms often need to be quite creative when allocating and deploying their limited resources. Especially in grasping international opportunities, social media provides a seemingly affordable and far-reaching medium. However, challenges—such as the controllability of the content and the outcomes of using social media—become apparent as the reach of social media marketing expands beyond certain threshold limits. In this study, we rely on data from multiple case studies to evaluate to what extent and under which conditions social media can support small entrepreneurial firms' international expansion. Thereby, we contribute to research on SME internationalization and business implications of digitalization. Our findings indicate that small entrepreneurial firms face somewhat different social media–related challenges in the international business environment compared to domestic settings. The controllability of the contents comes with new tones. Furthermore, small firms' resources, both in terms of social media use and in different functions, play an important role in determining the extent to which the use of social media supports these firms' internationalization.

Keywords Social media · Entrepreneurial firms · Internationalization

8.1 Introduction

Entering new, foreign markets comes with uncertainty and risks. International expansion requires developing and harnessing a portfolio of key resources and capabilities (Haapanen, Juntunen, & Juntunen, 2016; Knight & Cavusgil, 2004). Among these, relevant marketing resources provide a means to learn about the

P. Hurmelinna-Laukkanen (✉) · L. Haapanen
University of Oulu, Oulu Business School, Oulu, Finland
e-mail: pia.hurmelinna@oulu.fi; lauri.haapanen@oulu.fi

S. Holma
University of Oulu, Oulu Business School/Duunitori Oy, Helsinki, Finland

L. Schjoedt et al. (eds.), *Understanding Social Media and Entrepreneurship*,
Exploring Diversity in Entrepreneurship,
https://doi.org/10.1007/978-3-030-43453-3_8

markets, make the firm known, and interact with foreign customers (Knight, Koed Madsen, & Servais, 2004). Hence, investments in marketing typically have a positive influence on internationalization (Aspelund, Koed Madsen, & Moen, 2007).

Yet, in many cases, small entrepreneurial firms need to cope with scarce resources and capabilities (Dahnil, Marzuki, Langgat, & Fabeil, 2014; Kahiya & Dean, 2016). Limited resource endowments narrow down available options (Jane Hewerdine, Rumyantseva, & Welch, 2014; Kumar, 2009; Lecerf, 2012), and therefore, especially internationalizing, small entrepreneurial firms need to be innovative to overcome such resource limitations. In this regard, the internet, and digitalization in general, has had a revolutionary impact on multiple fronts. First, digitalization—the use of digital technologies such as the internet, mobile technologies, digital media, and communications—has provided small entrepreneurial firms with totally new instruments to deliver their products and services online with minor overhead costs (Davidson & Vaast, 2010). Consequently, digital technologies have started breeding a new form of digital entrepreneurship (Giones & Brem, 2017; Nambisan, 2017; Sussan & Acs, 2017), such as mobile application developers (Shaheer & Li, 2020), which lean heavily on the various possibilities provided by digital platforms (Kraus, Palmer, Kailer, Kallinger, & Spitzer, 2019; Ojala, Evers, & Rialp, 2018).

Second, digitalization and social media, in particular, have enabled firms to share and exchange information at very low costs (Kraus, Harms, & Fink, 2010; Miller, Fabian, & Lin, 2009; Nakara, Benmoussa, & Jaouen, 2012). Social media provides firms with tools for online advertising, sales, after sales support, and collecting market information (Bianchi & Mathews, 2016). Low thresholds of using social media have even brought forth a new generation of social media entrepreneurs who are highly skilled in efficiently capitalizing on the social network ecosystems and respective co-creation opportunities (Gustafsson & Khan, 2017).

Social media has already received a fair share of scholarly interest—specifically in marketing research. Social media refers to web-based and mobile tools that enable users and group members to share, co-create, discuss, and modify user-generated content (Kietzmann, Hermkens, Mccarthy, & Silvestre, 2011). Current research indicates that as social media provides a platform for public communication, firms use it to establish relationships, build trust, identify business partners, increase sales, and support their brands (Kaplan, 2012; Leonardi & Vaast, 2017; Shih, 2009; Wang, Pauleen, & Zhang, 2016). In a similar manner, Rapp, Beitelspacher, Grewal, and Hughes (2013) point out that prudent use of social media enhances brand performance, retail performance, and consumer-retailer loyalty.

At best, social media is an interdisciplinary and cross-functional marketing tool, which is often combined with other traditional communication channels (Felix, Rauschnabel, & Hinsch, 2017). Scholars agree that since consumers do not have single purchasing paths, firms reach their customers better when they select, combine, and integrate their traditional marketing with digital communication channels (Batra & Keller, 2016; Dinner, van Heerde, & Neslin, 2014; Kumar, Choi, & Greene, 2017). Regarding this terminology, Lamberton and Stephen (2016) note that as digitalization has become a new norm, the precipitous distinction between traditional and digital marketing is becoming less important—it is all about marketing.

Literature shows that for small entrepreneurial firms, digital marketing—social media in particular—is quite a natural means to build networks, and thus, social media constitutes a key business resource in order to maintain the relationships between firms and their customers (Durkin, McGowan, & McKeown, 2013). When this notion is coupled with the features of social media as a relatively affordable, user-oriented, and far-reaching channel (Miller et al., 2009; Zahoor & Qureshi, 2017; Zolkepli & Kamarulzaman, 2015) for building and maintaining relationships (De Vries, Gensler, & Leeflang, 2012), not to mention brand building (Coulter, Bruhn, Schoenmueller, & Schäfer, 2012), it is not surprising that SMEs have discovered social media as a very useful marketing platform. However, existing research has also acknowledged that the coin has two sides. Implementing social media requires both organizational competencies (Durkin et al., 2013), resources, and commitment (Felix et al., 2017). In this respect, the measurement of effectiveness and usefulness is difficult (Michaelidou, Siamagka, & Christodoulides, 2011; Siamagka, Christodoulides, Michaelidou, & Valvi, 2015). Another challenge is that social media marketing not only enables customers to get information provided by the organization online but also allows them to post and share their opinions, experiences, and reviews across an extensive social network in a manner that the firm cannot control (Gopinath, Thomas, & Krishnamurthi, 2014; Kannan, 2017). Therefore, firms need to comprehend how to approach and utilize these tools.

The international expansion of those entrepreneurial firms that lean strongly on digitalization differs from traditional firms' internationalization processes; still only few studies on this stream exist (Brouthers, Geisser, & Rothlauf, 2016). Some of these earlier studies focus on specific ibusiness firms or born-digitals (Monaghan, Tippmann, & Coviello, 2019; Shaheer & Li, 2020; Vadana, Torkkeli, Kuivalainen, & Saarenketo, 2019), which are firms providing internet-based platforms or digital artifacts (Brouthers et al., 2016; Stallkamp & Schotter, 2018). Within this stream of studies, Ojala et al. (2018) argue that technology-related bottlenecks may limit entrepreneurial firms' early-phase internationalization, whereas Fraccastoro and Gabrielsson (2018) show that the use of social media increases the speed of a software firm's (digital artifact) early-phase internationalization, yet acknowledging that more studies are needed.

The relationship between digitalization and small entrepreneurial firms' internationalization (manufacturing products other than digital artifacts and mainly utilizing digitalization in their marketing) is somewhat unclear. For these small firms, digitalization in general decreases the liability of foreignness (Arenius, Sasi, & Gabrielsson, 2006), lowers search costs (Petersen, Welch, & Liesch, 2002), reduces risks (Barrutia & Echebarria, 2007), provides firms with direct interface with customers and suppliers, and at the same time, strengthens promotion and market knowledge (Mathews, Bianchi, Perks, Healy, & Wickramasekera, 2016). Arenius et al. (2006) argue that digitalization may increase the speed of small entrepreneurial firms' internationalization. Mathews et al. (2016) suggest that digitalization improves international marketing activities but enhances firms' exports only in the presence of other supporting organizational capabilities. In a similar vein, Sinkovics, Sinkovics, and Jean (2013) call this overwhelming trust in online tools as a "virtuality trap," and Gabrielsson and Gabrielsson (2011) note that those entrepreneurial firms that have reached a sufficient degree of internationalization are able to rely more on digitalization compared to their counterparts in the beginning of their internationalization journey.

Gaps remain. First, as we show above, prior research on how social media in particular impacts small entrepreneurial firms' internationalization is still in its infancy. The extension of social media coverage into foreign countries, cultures, and different legislation might come with unexpected consequences; thus, there is a need for understanding. Second, and more importantly, social media has drastically changed the role of firms' marketing from being informing and influencing to co-creation; consumers are no longer bystanders but are dictating the nature, extent, and context of marketing content (Hanna, Rohm, & Crittenden, 2011). We argue that causal studies that explain whether social media influences small entrepreneurial firms' internationalization positively or negatively are too simplistic, and this relationship requires considering how this two-way communication (the most elementary feature in social media) between a firm and its customers evolves and, in particular, how this trajectory influences international expansion over time.

In this study, we acknowledge that more research is needed that combines insights gained in different scholarly areas and that introduces related empirical evidence. For example, while the benefits and challenges of social media use are already quite well known considering marketing and brand-building purposes, there might be adverse effects for internationalization that are yet to be uncovered. We turn attention to these issues, pulling together information on how small entrepreneurial firms utilize social media and in what circumstances and to what extent social media can support small entrepreneurial firms' pursuit for international expansion. Likewise, we are interested in specific problems associated with small entrepreneurial firms using social media in the international context. The research question that guides our work is *to what extent and under which conditions social media can support small entrepreneurial firms to grasp international opportunities.* In the search for the answers, we rely on empirical evidence from a qualitative study conducted among five case firms. The empirical evidence allows us to gain insight on the factors determining the means and extent to which social media can be incorporated feasibly as a part of the marketing and internationalization strategies of growing small entrepreneurial firms.

In the following, we first briefly introduce the theoretical background on small entrepreneurial firms' use of social media and social media's role in international business activities. Empirical examination follows this discussion, and toward the end of the paper, we present the analysis combining the theoretical and empirical views, conclusions drawn from them, and implications and limitations.

8.2 Social Media in the Business Promotion of Small Entrepreneurial Firms

Social media generally refers to internet-based applications that carry user-generated content. The original uses of social media do not necessarily relate to business promotion as such, but this too has become a phenomenon to be reckoned. Business promotion in social media can take different forms from competitions to brand fan pages (e.g., see De Vries et al., 2012).

Existing literature has mainly focused on marketing as a primary reason for SMEs to utilize social media (Durkin et al., 2013). Social media marketing has been defined in earlier literature "as the process that empowers individuals to promote their websites, products, or services through online social channels and tap into a much larger community that may not have been available via traditional channels" (Erdoğmuş & Cicek, 2012, 1354). As a marketing tool, social media may reinforce sales as firms can use it to provide information on offerings, gain new customers, improve their brand image, and increase brand awareness—at least to an extent (Coulter et al., 2012; Karjaluoto, Mustonen, & Ulkuniemi, 2015). In addition, social media enables a firm to facilitate online platforms, reduce marketing costs, and promote user interactivity (Barashi, 2012; Felix et al., 2017; Michaelidou et al., 2011). Different social media channels, for example, Facebook, Twitter, blogs, Instagram, and YouTube, are pieces of an integrated social media ecosystem and they should not be treated as stand-alone elements (Hanna et al., 2011). The efficient use of social media is about creating and influencing the consumer experience (Hanna et al., 2011), and contemporary social media tools even enable firms to adopt location-based and context-based marketing (Buhalis & Foerste, 2015). However, Coulter et al. (2012) point out that traditional media may still have an important role, in particular, with regard to the familiarity of a brand—even if the brand image is simultaneously prone to be affected by the use of social media.

Considering these potential benefits, the marketing budgets for social media use—as the use of social media among end users and other customers—are constantly increasing (De Vries et al., 2012). In general, social media is a relatively affordable, scalable, and far-reaching channel (e.g., Miller et al., 2009; Zahoor & Qureshi, 2017; Zolkepli & Kamarulzaman, 2015). Such media is lucrative, especially for those smaller firms that have limited financial resources to develop and execute their marketing and keep it continuously in the core of the firm's functions. Reaching potential customers and communication with stakeholders do not necessarily require similar investments in social media as traditional high-quality and high-resolution advertisements in the printed media channels do. Surely, the use of social media also requires careful planning, but already relatively small efforts may draw attention for the company using social media. Furthermore, social media gives degrees of freedom to use marketing in a more responsive, spontaneous, and interactive manner (e.g., see Agnihotri, Dingus, Hu, & Krush, 2016) than traditional channels that always require upfront planning and reservations for publication.

Such flexibility can be quite relevant for small entrepreneurial firms trying to capture emerging international opportunities.

Nevertheless, using social media as a part of a firm's marketing mix is not completely unproblematic, especially for small entrepreneurial firms. Increasing sales profitably based on social media may end up being a time-consuming and complex process despite the apparent initial inexpensiveness (Keller, 2003). Also, the efficient use of social media requires organizational competence and commitment (Guesalaga, 2016). Often in small entrepreneurial firms, the top management and owners are the ones taking care of all firm activities, including social media use, and the requirements of social media to be active may be too much to handle (Krake, 2005). Even with dedicated marketing personnel, the top managers need to be closely involved.

In addition, since social media comprises, first and foremost, user-generated content and because it allows customers and end users to take part in generating the contents and sharing insights (Tsimonis & Dimitriadis, 2014), the contents are never solely controlled by the firms. As a result of the interactivity of social media, customers exchange information on the firm and its offerings with each other, and they may even find this information more reliable than the information provided by the firm (Muntinga, Moorman, & Smit, 2011; Thackeray, Neiger, Hanson, & McKenzie, 2008; Tsimonis & Dimitriadis, 2014). Prior studies note that consumers' opinions, in particular, their mutual opinions, do matter; "what people think" is highly important (Gopinath et al., 2014). In effect, this means that the influence power shifts—at least partly—from the firm to its customers (Okazaki & Taylor, 2013).

Furthermore, the increasing of visibility takes time also when using social media. Hence, the use of such media brings results typically only after a while, so especially small growing firms may not benefit from the use of social media immediately, even if it otherwise would be more usable than many other traditional marketing and promotion tools (Ghodeswar, 2008). Yet another issue is that social media can substitute traditional business approaches on selling and marketing only to a point. Rather, it needs to be used jointly with other marketing means (Neti, 2011). For example, product packaging and user guides are an elementary part of product marketing that needs to meet local requirements and expectations. Furthermore, the complexity of social media use increases when a firm expands its coverage into foreign markets, that is, into different cultures and languages.

8.3 Operating in the International Business Environment

As noted above, internationalization and social media are still rarely explicitly combined in existing scholarly discussion, and when they are, the results can be somewhat contradictory. Some initial insights provide valuable points of departure for growing understanding on these issues. Arenius et al. (2006) argue that digitalization may increase the speed of small entrepreneurial firms' internationalization, and

Gabrielsson and Gabrielsson (2011) add more detail by noting that the adoption of social media increases the speed of international expansion during an early internationalization phase. Mathews et al. (2016) suggest that in order to support exporting, social media requires the presence of other supporting organizational capabilities. This indicates that growing, internationalizing small entrepreneurial firms are, in fact, likely to be very much influenced by social media and that the use of social media can bear notable importance for them.

Generally speaking, scholars in international entrepreneurship indicate that the use of social media can ease entry to online networks and allow managing of multiple international relationships (Sigfusson & Chetty, 2013). Social media decreases the liability of outsidership that foreign firms face (Fraccastoro & Gabrielsson, 2018). This is relevant, as limited resources set constraints and, consequently, push expanding SMEs to cooperate with other actors (Oviatt & McDougall, 1994). Previous research has comprehensively described that personal networks, partnerships, and strategic alliances are important enablers of early and rapid internationalization of firms (Bell, 1995; Coviello & Munro, 1997; McDougall, Shane, & Oviatt, 1994). However, also in the international entrepreneurship field, the studies on how social media marketing in particular impacts small entrepreneurial firms' internationalization are still in their early stage.

Based on the above considerations, while there are challenges also, the benefits of social media for internationalizing small entrepreneurial firms seem to be at least twofold. It may open the access to the international markets relatively directly by increasing brand awareness/image and by reducing uncertainty regarding a firm among potential customers (Andzulis, Panagopoulos, & Rapp, 2012; Fraccastoro & Gabrielsson, 2018). Additionally, support for internationalization may be reached also more indirectly, through the improved chances to entering different networks that enable foreign entry (Durkin et al., 2013; Laurell, Achtenhagen, & Andersson, 2017). However, as literature is still relatively silent on the connections between social media and internationalization efforts of small entrepreneurial firms—with regard to the positive and negative elements and the cause-effect relationships, for example—we turn next to empirical evidence for further insight.

8.4 Empirical Evidence: Case Study of Five Internationalizing Small Entrepreneurial Firms

Considering that the topic of our study calls for both theoretical and empirical research work, we found the qualitative case study approach appropriate to enable the exploration of a poorly understood phenomenon (see Eisenhardt, 1989) without prior theories and, hence, with no testable hypothesis (Ketokivi & Choi, 2014). In our exploratory study (Patton, 2002), we examined five young small entrepreneurial firms that have made efforts to build strong, internationalizing brands by using the means of social media. The companies in our study focus on customers that value individualism and uniqueness. These five small entrepreneurial firms represent different fields of industry, but they are similar in many respects, especially in their international expansion aims and emphasis on transparency, responsibility, and their roots and origins.

The data comprises interviews (semi-structured expert interviews) and documentary data. We focused on key themes, and the interviews were conducted with the firm representatives responsible for the use and development of the digital marketing tools—especially social media—in their firms. As the companies are young and relatively small (see Table 8.1 for firm and interviewee information), these interviewees are well informed about the developments and strategies of the organizations that they represent. This data was completed with information gained by studying the firms' web pages and social media channels. The contents of these materials were examined already before the interviews, but they were also scrutinized again after the interviews in order to capture the themes emerging from the discussions with the firm representatives. The interviews were recorded and transcribed for content analysis (Table 8.1).

For analyzing the data, we took several interrelated steps. We first wrote case descriptions, showing the approaches adopted by the firms to their businesses and to the use of social media. We also documented information on their experiences in regard to social media use and internationalization at this phase. The individual case analyses were followed by case comparison, in which the extent and conditions of social media use were taken under closer scrutiny. In parallel, we organized the information from the cases following the steps introduced in the study by Gioia,

Table 8.1 Case companies and summary of interview data

Firm	Year of establishment/ international market entry; international coverage	Turnover (1000 €)/ personnel (2017)	Social media channels in use	Interviewee (position)	Time and place of interview/ duration
Kyrö distillery	2012; 28 countries	4500/25	Facebook, Instagram, Twitter	Marketing director	17 Jan 2018/ 43:50
Goodio	2015; 13 countries (especially Nordic countries, the USA)	640/3	Facebook, Instagram, Twitter, blog	Marketing director	13 Feb 2018/27:59
Supermood	2014/2016; the USA and other English-speaking markets, EU	176/0	Facebook, Instagram	Entrepreneur, CEO	26 Jan 2018/1:09:28
Népra	2015/2018 Germany	55/2	Facebook, Instagram, blog	Owner-entrepreneur (founder)	24 Jan 2018/ 28:58
Vimma company	2013; EU	2400/8	Facebook, Instagram, YouTube	Development director	23 Jan 2018/ 35:05

Corley, and Hamilton (2013) to identify central constructs and their relationships as they emerged in the data. In the following, we discuss each of the case organizations, introduce the combined insights from them, and propose a framework that captures relevant aspects in social media use for internationalizing small entrepreneurial firms.

8.5 Case Firms

8.5.1 Kyrö Distillery

Five friends founded Kyrö Distillery in 2012. The firm builds on rye, and the brand reflects this strongly. Kyrö Distillery's marketing director highlights the brand values, "Rye. In the very heart. In everything. Our slogan is 'In rye we trust' and it shows in everything we do." The firm was originally established for distilling whisky, but as it takes 3 years to mature, the owners decided to make some gin on the side. The outcome, Napue Gin, has become an international success, winning the "World's Best Gin for Gin and Tonic" prize in 2015 and, in 2016, a gold medal in the San Francisco World Spirits Competition premium gin series. The brand reflects the wish of the owners to break distillery stereotypes. Kyrö Distillery is positioning itself as an easy-to-approach premium-house and, consequently, is emphasizing transparency and openness, an adventurous spirit, and the founding members' Finnish origins.

Kyrö Distillery delivers most of its products in Finland but is aiming at being a globally significant gin and whiskey manufacturer, the world's best-known rye distillery by 2022. Hence, internationalization is an inseparable part of the firm's strategy. Today, Kyrö Distillery operates in 28 markets and is actively building its brand in 8 of these countries. When expanding into international markets, Kyrö Distillery first approaches its distributors. Kyrö Distillery supports its dealers in marketing by doing consumer marketing and by building their brand awareness globally. "Brand is everything ... especially in the gin industry, in which we have thousands of competitors, it is very difficult to stand out only by relying on products" as Kyrö Distillery marketing director notes.

With regard social media marketing, Kyrö Distillery uses various channels. The contents of social media are tightly connected to the distillery and its everyday activity. It is not fancy or sugarcoated, but—following firm values—openness is important, and the firm shows on social media that things do not always go as they are planned. Regarding the design, Kyrö Distillery has a black and white look. They consider this as a distinctive feature that connects to the local origin of the firm.

The international reach gained with social media use is secured by the strong reliance on the distinctive brand, which is accompanied with segmentation based on interests rather than demographical factors. The firm seeks to address customers that are genuinely curious and appreciate new experiences. Design, unique story, and Nordic minimalism are in a central role for Kyrö to be distinguished from the competitors. Kyrö Distillery does not localize its brand visually, but regarding communication, they always carefully plan what elements they put in the frontline. For example, the picture of naked Finnish men (the five founders) running in a rye field may not be appropriate in some markets; hence, different marketing material is selected for illustrating the ideology of the firm.

The effective use of social media enables firms to expand on multiple foreign markets simultaneously. Kyrö Distillery admits that they are just in the beginning of their journey; nevertheless, as the firm's marketing director points out "Our brand is becoming international … and we do believe that today any brand can be global since end users are global, borders have faded away long time ago." For the firm, the highest priority is the building of an international brand. Firm sales have exceeded the set targets on many key markets, and to keep up this trend, Kyrö Distillery recognizes that it is highly important to ensure that distributors diffuse the brand awareness to their customers. The firm keeps a registry of users and stakeholders to keep them informed. Hence, the end users get the marketing messages from two separate channels, from the distributors and from the firm, "an extensive grapevine effect, which we need to control," notes the marketing director.

Facebook, Twitter, and Instagram are the three main social media marketing channels that Kyrö Distillery uses. Some media is targeted to specific market areas, for example, Twitter has a more important role in the UK compared to other markets. The channels are overlapping; the firm meets same individuals in more than one digital marketplace. "It does not matter in which channel you are present, as long as you are in conversation with people," explains the marketing director. The firm is using the social media marketing channels to bring people with similar interests together and, furthermore, to strengthen the feeling that the firm is all the time present. "We have continuous dialogue with our customers in various digital marketing channels, we aim at replying to all the messages, and for example, in Facebook our response rate is 100 percent. We use social media like any private person, we answer, we discuss, and we share what's up," explains the marketing director.

Social media enables the firm to collect such market information and industry trends that would not be otherwise available. "We are being rewarded for being present, information drifts to us from all over the world. As an example, a fan of ours told us about a spelling mistake in a Chinese airline catalogue … you would not believe how much these things happen. We always get back to the people who contacted us and in many cases, these individuals become our ambassadors," the marketing director explains. Kyrö Distillery also uses social media to get advice, for example, to get hints and information from the barrel owners on how to treat whisky while being matured.

The coin has another side as well. Active use of social media channels, particularly continuous presence in these media, is time-consuming and calls for resources. The marketing director admits that "… for us, to dedicate one person solely to digital marketing feels from time to time as a big investment, but it is very important." Furthermore, Kyrö Distillery acknowledges that their inventory needs to meet the demand they create by using social media marketing, "It does not make sense to start increasing demand until there are products to be delivered." The marketing director also points out that social media is not the only place where the users meet: "We cannot be sure that we follow all on-going discussions and moreover, there are discussions in many other forums in which we have no control over, nor have we any possibilities to impact on. In general, social media comes with vast benefits. Yet, on occasions opinions escalate; one must realize the nature of social media."

However, Kyrö Distillery does not only rely on social media marketing. Close personal contact with distributors and bar owners is an elementary part of the firm's marketing. "While speaking, one of the firm founders is skiing in Lapland with our German distributor … we have made it a personal mission … our brand ambassadors personally knock on bar doors … let the bar owners taste our products and tell our story … not a very internationally scalable business model, though" notes the marketing director. The firm believes in genuine bonds between individuals, "We travel a lot, and we spend hours and hours sitting at bar counters with bar owners and our distributors."

8.5.2 Goodio

Goodio started its current business in 2015. The founder, whose background is connected to Angry Birds, could not find chocolate that did not include any white sugar. He decided to start making healthier chocolate by himself, focusing on health and well-being. Today, the firm operates in a dozen countries, mainly in the Nordic countries, the USA, and the UK. In Goodio, one person is responsible for the firm's brand building. The newly appointed marketing director points out that "… our marketing is in its infancy, we have been focusing on selling and getting our chocolate in the stores, and until now, people have been doing social media marketing part time." Goodio is in the middle of the strategy process, and consequently, the firm is renewing its communication and brand-building strategy. Currently the marketing director has the overall responsibility for marketing and communications, including the firm's social media marketing. A trainee is helping him in this task, and he explains, "We go through what we post and the style we post, to keep social marketing aligned with our brand."

For social media marketing, Goodio is actively using web pages, its own blogs, Facebook, Instagram, and Twitter, all targeted to a global audience. In addition, in terms of marketing, they provide shops with sales promotion material and print media with press releases. However, Goodio has separate Facebook pages and Instagram account for their cafes. In these channels, Goodio shares their chocolate recipes and photographs of the chocolate packages. "We decided to have separate Facebook and Instagram for our cafes in order not disturb our foreign followers with these posts," explains the marketing director and continues, "Users like our recipes very much; obviously they use ours when they bake. We do not have too much time to spend on social media, hence, we also ask our employees to post what they have done."

Domestic markets are somewhat different from international markets. The marketing director gives an example, "Finns are happy to see a Finnish brand succeed, Swedish consumers are not that interested in Finnish brands, but the Japanese, then again, highly appreciate Finnish brands. This requires localization in marketing communications and in brand building, thus indicating that internationalization is not that easy." Goodio does not only sell chocolate but also focuses on well-being and environmental issues as they are "… issues that get people interested in the firm brand. The challenge is to get such issues highlighted and communicated," says the marketing director. In social media, Goodio is planning to shift from nice pictures toward videos to explain the firm's ideology, and the marketing director stresses that it is "Good that we have digital channels. I would like to tell more about our values and see how our followers accept them."

Goodio acknowledges that the active use of social media marketing requires more human and financial resources than the firm currently has. "On Facebook, one does not get visibility without investing huge amounts in advertising, and the fact is that a small firm has a small marketing budget. Hence, gaining visibility is more challenging for a small firm compared to a large one," concludes the marketing director. Due to limited resources, Goodio has not been able to follow and participate in the ongoing discussions in social media to the extent they would have liked to.

8.5.3 Supermood

Supermood is a Finnish firm established in 2014. The firm focuses on natural skincare with a fresh take on beauty and wellness. Supermood produces cosmetics and chocolate, the latter being 70% cold-pressed raw chocolate from organic cocoa beans. Supermood stresses entrepreneurial attitude, ethical business, and transparency. For the first 2 years, Supermood mainly focused on—and learned from—the domestic markets. From day 1, the firm's strategy has been to manufacture products for international markets. Since 2016, the firm has started to expand its sales in foreign markets. Early internationalization was rapid and chaotic as the CEO describes, "We had leads from Korea, Taiwan, Maldives, India, Russia, the UK, the US … four to five requests weekly from all over the world … and we realized that we were investing huge amounts of money to register our trademarks in markets in which we did not even sell yet. At the same time, we were paying lawyers to go through the contracts from these countries. We were spending all our money to find out if we are able to make sales … instead of investing in activities to make sales."

Supermood was also facing high risks in their early internationalization. The CEO gives an example of their Russian initiative, "We were discussing with a large local distributor for more than six months, and they send us an agreement … our lawyer needed just to have a quick glance, it was an absolute no go… with a big bill.

He said that if we would like to make this deal happen, it would require a number of iteration rounds, a new firm to be registered in Russia, and a remarkable invoice from him." According to the CEO, this was the turning point when Supermood started to reconsider its internationalization strategy. The firm decided to focus strictly on one market at time. Today, the firm has distributors in the EU, China, and the USA. The firm's expansion in foreign countries for the upcoming 2 years includes only English-speaking countries, the UK, Canada, and Australia.

As Supermood had a partner in the USA, the decision to focus on the USA was easy. In addition, existing sales promotion material and product packaging were suitable to the US markets. The local partner is screening potential distributors and ensures that they are capable and compatible with, for example, Amazon drop shipping policy. "Local distributors like the products. Sales in the US got a head start. Now our inventory is gone, and the production of a new batch takes time, which brings a new challenge in terms of cash flow. Also, the exchange fluctuations bring in an additional flavor," notes the CEO. Distributors in the USA also use their own marketing channels to promote Supermood products, which has led to further cooperation with other firms. The CEO continues, "It has been a bit confusing … stores that have taken our products to be sold … in such a short period of time. Lots of hard work and a hint of good luck." Empty inventories have made Supermood postpone its social media marketing and campaigns. "The risk is that I will sell and empty my stocks … and there is nothing to ship to our distributors … that is not good," the CEO points out.

One of the three firm founders has a background in cosmetics; the other two, including the CEO, have been in sales promotion and advertising agencies. The CEO is responsible for the product package design, web shop, and all brand-building-related activities and notes "Marketing, communications, and brand building are quite easy for us due to our sales promotion and advertising agency backgrounds. However, in previous firms there were plenty of people to delegate to and big customers with huge marketing budgets. Now I have had to learn how to cope with limited financial resources." The CEO continues, "How can you build a brand without resources. You may have campaigns with discounts … but having social media contents that improve your brand require time and resources; instead of discounts, you have to tempt users with emotionally attractive contents. This really requires delving, time and money."

Supermood recognizes the benefits of using social media marketing. Supermood is not only able to reach a vast number of potential customers but also can receive their opinions and feedback. Yet, the firm is using social media marketing channels cautiously; social media marketing also requires financial resources, capabilities, and time. The firm is short in all of these. The CEO explains, "We produce all the social media contents in-house. To use social media wisely, the contents must make sense and have to be interesting. For this reason, we do not post often, but share posts with substance … rather than crank out something meaningless." The majority of the contents is disposable, which means that the firm needs the capacity to produce new contents continuously. The CEO continues, "Digital marketing calls for both personal commitment and continuous involvement … as soon as we have enough money, I will trace a partner to help us with our social media. I am capable of doing it, you just need to select your battles and outsource the rest."

Supermood uses social media to communicate with its customers. The firm returns to posts and keeps up dialogue with its fans. Supermood does not utilize this ongoing communication in product development, though. The firm is not about to bring new products to the markets, as the main challenge for the time being is to build brand and awareness.

Supermood receives a large number of cooperation requests from bloggers and influencers. The firm has learned that many of them are only after free samples without any further reciprocity. The firm has now implemented criteria to verify engagement and possible reach. Moreover, as the CEO notes "We believe that true influencers find our products, buy our products, and like our products, without us paying them." As a departure from the core activity, the firm that provides Supermood with its product packages has a website, where end users can order varying products. This provider has a large online customer base and these customers are very active in social media. Supermood got on the provider's lists and consequently now receives high-quality end user reviews through this channel also.

8.5.4 Népra

In 2015, two young Finnish women established Népra, an ethical sportswear brand. Népra designs and manufactures sportswear especially to CrossFit trainers. The firm provides long-lasting activewear (e.g., tops, tights, socks, long-sleeved shirts, and shorts) and lazywear (e.g., T-shirts, sweaters, and hoodies). Népra is aiming at becoming a Europe-wide sportswear brand. Népra is currently selling its products mostly on the domestic market in Finland but also to some extent in the EU. The firm's current inventory limits the further expansion to foreign markets, and as the owner of Népra mentions, "Next year we will put more effort to foreign campaigns to enhance our foreign sales, in particular in Germany." The firm utilizes social media in their internationalization, especially in Germany. "When we take photos in Germany, we tag them to those locations in which they were taken," the owner notes.

Népra has been participating in carefully selected sales promotion events in order to build a team of athletes who wear Népra's sportswear. "Athletes are wearing our clothing, and in this way, they are also building our brand. We also use social media as a complementary marketing media, and also in order to interact with the customers," explains the owner. The firm owner believes that buyers trust the advocates wearing the firm's products, "Buyers follow highly ranked and appreciated sportsmen," points out the interviewee.

Through social media, the firm receives customer feedback, both positive and negative. Hence, Népra is continuously gathering information that the firm further transfers to product development. "For a small brand like us, it is extremely important to learn if there are any weak spots, specific problems, wishes where to place logos, etc. We have a hunch that people have accepted our products well, and as a token, they provide us with lengthy messages," points out the firm owner.

Népra is investing in the firm's web pages in order to provide relevant information for the buyers. In addition, Népra posts newsletters on a regular basis. For the firm, the most important social media channels are Instagram, Facebook, and a blog. In these media, the firm communicates daily and shares as much information as possible. "Social media is a good channel to share something daily, to share bits of our story, values, product news, and our athletes. Moreover, social media has become an intrinsic part of everyone's life. Since we are running a web shop, we need to be part of it," explains the owner. The firm pays close attention especially to the quality and colors of the pictures they use, even if there are limitations, "We usually have a color theme. At the time being, we are not able to have all the Instagram photographs taken by professionals, thus, the quality is not always the highest possible." The firm utilizes texts from its blogs in its other social marketing media, for example, on Instagram.

Népra uses the same social media marketing channels in all of its target markets. In order to differentiate the media in different geographical or language areas, they would need to hire additional resources. "Not at the time being, maybe within the next two years. We do see all the possibilities in communicating using customers' own language, but today, the workload is not in balance with the possible benefits," answers the firm owner when asked about this issue.

Népra considers that "Giving customers too green of an image, or giving them an impression that the firm does all things 100% right or provides the world's most ecological products," runs the risk of giving a misleading image in social media. "The world is not just black and white. We need to be cautious how much we want to build our brand based on the ecological premises. We need to be transparent. The problem is that if you make a claim in social media that is incorrect, you soon ruin your image," points out the owner of Népra. "Bad news travel fast," she concludes.

8.5.5 Vimma

Vimma is a Finnish company manufacturing design clothing. The firm was established in 2013 and originally focused on children's clothing. Over the past years, Vimma has been gradually including also clothing for adults into its pool of offerings. Vimma highlights transparency, honesty, ecological friendliness, and its roots in Scandinavia, particularly in Finland. Brand building leans on high-quality products that are made of ecological materials. Vimma sells its products mainly in Finland and, to some extent, also in Europe. The firm is seeking further foreign growth in Europe, regardless of the fact that the firm's products have gained interest also in Asia and North America. As the firm's development director notes, "Vimma is a respected brand. For the time being, we will focus on Europe, but in the future, we will not exclude other markets."

The CEO of the firm is responsible for the firm's product design and production planning but also for the firm's brand building. "She has been in this firm since day one, she knows the firm inside out, and she has been working hard to build our brand," explains the development director. As a strong personality, the CEO is the firm's figurehead, yet, she also gives guidelines for the firm's marketing and communication.

Vimma's main social media communication channels are Facebook, Instagram, and YouTube. In addition, the firm also uses print media, "We do not rely solely on digital marketing. One has to be versatile when it comes to the use of marketing media. We have also made some experiments of targeted printed advertisements in foreign markets, in Baltic countries, for example," notes the development director. Currently Vimma uses only English in its social media marketing, but the firm has plans to adopt more extensively local languages one geographic market area at the time. Vimma has local resellers to distribute its products, and they use influencers and bloggers to write stories of the firm. "Building a presence in social media calls for local actors. To get your products in local shops, a new brand requires familiar salespersons who believe in your products," points out the development director.

For Vimma, social media is a fast channel to share information. "For us, social media is an easy channel to handle, is responsive, real time, provides an opportunity to reach a large number of people in a short period of time, and when utilized in marketing, is inexpensive," lists the development director. On the other hand, Vimma recognizes that negative messages spread fast in social media, and hence, the use of social media calls for alertness and accurate information. "One has to take into account possible multiplicative effects," points out the Vimma development director. In foreign markets, Vimma uses social media in a similar manner as they do in Finland. The firm acknowledges that in the near future, it needs to adapt to the social media marketing channels that customers use in different countries. The development director says, "In some countries, Facebook and Instagram may be less used, say in Russia, for example."

Vimma notes that users use social media to give feedback. Social media is fast, and hence, it requires that the firm follows discussions continuously and reacts in real time. Vimma involves its customers also in product design, "We may ask about the patterns, if the users have any wishes. We do listen carefully what our customers say about our models. We are trying to genuinely meet our customers' needs," concludes the development director. At the same time, Vimma has experienced that social media is not without challenges. "… Problems in our on-line store, and then the problems in the functionality of the payment methods. Furthermore, operating in international markets comes with language challenges, and combining different languages, digital marketing, and logistics is far from straightforward. Moreover, the same clothing models that we sell in Finland do not necessarily suit every European country," says the development director.

8.6 Aggregate Findings

Our case study among the five internationalizing small entrepreneurial firms points toward some quite specific issues to which the management reacts in slightly different ways, not only compared to larger firms but also among our case firms.

For the firms in our study, the *benefits* accruing from utilizing social media involve the ones already identified in the prior research, such as the possibility to communicate the firm brand and share news about the products, wide (global) reach among customers, interactivity, and possibilities to tap into networks (see Andzulis et al., 2012). The conclusion that these benefits lead to a higher market awareness of the brand, and a subsequent increase in sales, seems quite straightforward.

However, our case firms also bring up some benefits that stem from using social media for quite specific purposes and in different manners. Internationalizing small entrepreneurial firms may approach the feedback and information from the international customer base—gained through social media—in different ways. Social media is a highly valuable source of foreign market information and, hence, provides a small firm with "an extended marketing resource," or, more specifically, a market intelligence resource. Social media provides an access to market information and feedback into the firms' R&D from such (potential) foreign customers and networks that small firms would otherwise not reach. Yet, our results indicate that not all firms capitalize on such an extended resource. This can be at least to an extent due to the nature of the firm offering. For example, fashion industry product development, which is more seasonal, benefits more naturally from wider international feedback than companies with longer product or service life cycles. The relevance level of the benefits varies, which can also be considered a relevant area of further research. For example, it could be studied if social medial usage facilitates dynamic consistency (cf. Demil & Lecocq, 2010), that is, the ability of companies to utilize their existing assets while at the same time exploring areas of renewal.

According to our findings, *some benefits are also controversial*, such as the speed of the media. While the firms appreciate the possibility to communicate fast and to promote visibility daily, they also acknowledge both the weight of the necessity to react rapidly and the burden of the information overload. This requires resources (see also Sigfusson & Chetty, 2013). The increased visibility, in particular, is a two-edged sword. Growing, especially international, audiences in social media acts like snowballs; demand may pass the level where the company cannot respond to customer needs. If the company does not have the inventory or good enough logistic services to match the demand, the benefits gained through social media use may be short-lived and, in the worst cases, even transform into bad reputation—a manifestation of the uncontrollability of social media. This has some implications on social media use also. For example, a need to limit promotional activity may emerge until there is certainty that the production can match the possibly emerging demand. Likewise, it may be necessary to design the content in a manner that makes the distribution challenges more understandable among the customer base (e.g., consider Kyrö Distillery posting also about problems and failures). In best cases, limited availability of products and services can be communicated in a positive light, making the offering a luxury item. Building on these notions, future research can uncover specific features of social media in this sense.

Figure 8.1 illustrates how social media can support internationalization to the extent that it increases, rather than effectively limits, marketing and production resources—the vertical arrow at the right-hand side of the figure indicates that input gained from markets can influence the level of resources at the firm's disposal and simultaneously illustrates the turning point where the risk of adverse effects emerges. Our data suggests that market awareness can promote sales but only to the level that marketing and production resources are adequate to handle the demand. If control is lost (and demand caused by awareness exceeds resources), a negative spiral may be initiated by the inability to respond to demand leading to negative reputation effects and lowering demand and lowering interest in social media. In the optimal case, market awareness leads to a situation where full capacity production and sales are balanced and where the effective marketing and production resources extended by the social media penetration are used to their fullest.

Indeed, as noted in the prior marketing literature (e.g., Huotari, Ulkuniemi, Saraniemi, & Mäläskä, 2015; Kannan, 2017), our results also indicate that the lack of controllability of social media content may become a notable *challenge* for internationalizing small entrepreneurial firms. In our data, social media audiences are considered an extension of the firms' resource base, although the firms have recognized the risk of abuse. While growing, especially by expanding into international markets, it is not always sure which contacts and ambassadors are appropriate. Social media and digital platforms (online stores, online sales, and order-delivery processes) are to an extent under a firm's influence. Small firms can control the contents they share themselves; however, the further spread of the information is beyond the firm's influence.

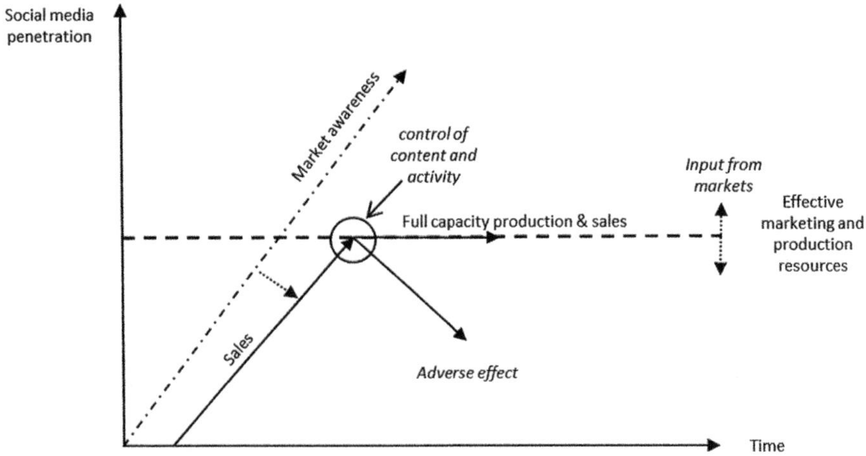

Fig. 8.1 Effective resources, control, and social media

To mitigate the controllability challenge, the small entrepreneurial firms in our case study have made some specific efforts. For example, they have utilized social media to lead their (potential) customers and collaborators to their web pages and blogs rather than left them in these platforms solely. The firms consider that in these forms of digital media, the content is more controllable and accurate. Small firms also utilize the replicability of the contents in different social media channels, thereby effectively localizing their social media use—not in terms of contents but in terms of making sure that the materials are available in the most used channels. Related to localization, the firms in our study also acknowledge that the norms and regulations of a specific international market area may be an important factor that influences social media use, especially in regard to content. Sometimes, this leads the firms to naturally adapt their social media contents. The contingencies and details of retaining and regaining control when it has been lost are interesting areas for future research.

We verified the initial findings illustrated in Fig. 8.1 also by organizing the data in a more structured manner, starting from the raw data, translating it into first-order concepts, which we further combined into second-order themes and, finally, aggregate dimensions (see Gioia et al., 2013). The Appendix shows the development of the main elements from the data. This step of data analysis provided us with a way to develop a framework that captures the logic illustrated in Fig. 8.2 in a concise manner. Initially, a firm can decide if it sets up social media and digital platforms to promote its internationalization and how these look like. However, beyond this point, the control starts to shift. At the core of the framework is the notion that "the grapevine effect" in social media is typically positive if a firm can deliver its promises, but if this fails, negative news, shortages in deliveries, disappointments, and doubts travel fast. Inherently, market awareness may enforce either a virtuous or vicious cycle, which is highly relevant for internationalizing SMEs. Market awareness influences buying behavior, but in social media, and especially international markets, this is largely beyond a firm's influence. On the other hand, with social

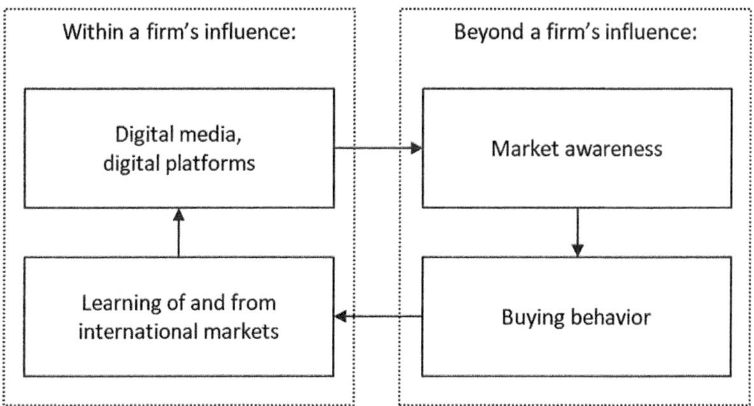

Fig. 8.2 Social media in supporting small entrepreneurial firm internationalization

media use, a firm can gather relevant and appropriate market information on the buying behavior of foreign customers, support favorable development trajectories, and try to avoid failures. This happens when the firm learns from markets (e.g., by experimenting) and—as a highly relevant issue—feeds this learning back to its use of social media. Firms need to react correctly and adjust their social media contents in order to improve customer experiences and expectations (see the Appendix for examples on these issues). The five internationalizing small entrepreneurial firms in our study seem to be in different stages of this learning. They use social media in different ways (as already depicted above). In managing the challenges and potential benefits, some of them use social media as the main marketing and communication channel, supported by other media. Others like to have it as a complement to the main channels that they find easier to control. How these decisions are made is one area where future research can add to existing knowledge building on the framing provided here.

8.7 Conclusions

Our study builds on, integrates, and extends various streams of existing scholarly knowledge. Marketing literature has already provided numerous insights on social media use, most notably as a marketing and brand-building tool (Andzulis et al., 2012; Kannan, 2017; Karjaluoto et al., 2015; Rapp et al., 2013). Many of these insights apply to international marketing, and international activity more in general, but there also are features related to international expansion that are less well covered and understood (e.g., Fraccastoro & Gabrielsson, 2018). Considering an even more specific context—that of internationalizing and growing small entrepreneurial firms—there is a need to understand the premises, benefits, and limits of social media use. In fact, existing research has almost completely neglected the relationship between social media and the internationalization endeavors of SMEs (Brouthers et al., 2016; Fraccastoro & Gabrielsson, 2018; Mathews et al., 2016). In a recent study, Cao, Ajjan, Hong, and Le (2018, 228) state that "[as] the research on social media evolves, more studies may examine what specific forms of social media are most influential in achieving the performance goals of organizations beyond national boundaries—in global market contexts." While beneficial in many ways in an international operations environment—even when considering the downsides related to the uncontrollability of the messages and contents that generally affect brand image, for example—social media also may bring some benefits and challenges that are not clearly visible.

Our study adds to existing knowledge on the internationalization of small entrepreneurial firms and digitalization by showing how social media may help overcome resource limitations in some respects, e.g., in regard to liabilities of foreignness, newness, and outsidership (e.g., see Arenius et al., 2006; Fraccastoro & Gabrielsson, 2018). However, somewhat paradoxically, the removal of these liabilities, and the increasing visibility and acceptance, may create such demand that the small entrepreneurial firm cannot respond to due to limited resources in its R&D and production. Control is therefore needed, which again demands resources. For example, the limited production resources generate the need to control promotional activities. Therefore, the extent to which social media is relied on, and used for different purposes, may change according to a firm's experiences and accumulated learning in regard to the influences of social media on the effective resources at the firms' disposal and on the need for control. The (expectations to gain) increasing sales are not, therefore, necessarily the most decisive issue, and dynamic consistency (Demil & Lecocq, 2010) throughout the organization is needed.

While our findings build on only five case firms, they reveal relevant features in the relationship between social media use and internationalization in small entrepreneurial firms. We acknowledge the need to study the connections between benefits and challenges and uses of social media in a more detailed manner still, as different interactive and mutual connections seem to emerge. Our within and between case analyses provide a good overview of and some in-depth insights on small firms' approaches to social media use and the related issues, but as the sample is limited and comprises companies in one country only, there is plenty of room for addressing other issues, such as those identified in the above sections. Likewise, for generalizability, a wider range of cases and practical examples should be examined through quantitative and qualitative means. This study provides a point of departure for those subsequent research endeavors.

Simultaneously, our study provides some guidance in terms of managerial practices. The experiences of the case firms can be a valuable learning point for other small entrepreneurial firms targeting international markets. Already acknowledging the different alternatives, such as whether to communicate about products or the corporate brand, whether to do everything in-house or to outsource some aspects of social media use, whether to limit or to increase communication, which channels to select, and so on, eases creating a strategy for social media use in internationalizing small entrepreneurial firms. The stories of the case firms, together with the theoretical considerations, form a basis for informed management. At the same time, each of these decision points for managers can be considered as relevant areas of deeper academic examination as well. We hope that both managerial and scientific work can be promoted based on our contribution.

Acknowledgments The authors thank Professor Tanja Leppäaho, Professor Olli Kuivalainen, and Professor Jorma Larimo for their valuable insights into an earlier version of the results, Editor Professor Leon Schjoedt for his helpful advice, and the Foundation for Economic Education for their financial support.

Appendix: Data Analysis (cf. Fig. 8.2)

Quotes from data	First-order concepts	Second-order themes	Aggregate dimensions
"…today any brand can be global since end users are global, borders have faded away long time ago"	International expansion	Nature of customer base	Buying behavior
"…we decided to have separate Facebook and Instagram for our cafes in order not disturb our foreign followers with these posts … [different markets] require localization … making internationalization not that easy" "… next year we will put more effort to foreign campaigns to enhance sales, in particular in Germany"	International activity		
"…we had … four to five requests weekly from all over the world …"	Customer contacts	Enlargement of customer base	
"…The risk is [social media] that I will sell and empty my stock and there is nothing to deliver our distributors" "It does not make sense to start increasing demand until there are products to be delivered" "…if only we have stock…we would have an event…"	Production challenges	Visibility/ awareness risks	Market awareness
"…an extensive grapevine effect, which we need to control … we cannot be sure that we follow all on-going discussions and moreover, there are discussions in many other places in which we have no control over." "…but we get an unbelievable amount of contact requests… there are so many networks…"	Uncontrollability		
"…we need to be cautious … if you make a claim in the social media that is incorrect, you soon ruin your image"	Wrong/false information		
"…for sure on daily basis we need to work on this." "… bad news travel fast"	Speed		
"possible to reach a lot of people within a short time" "…we had very fast a lot of followers in social media" "…world wide reach, definitely"	Wide reach	Marketing/ promotion-related gains	

Quotes from data	First-order concepts	Second-order themes	Aggregate dimensions
"Very important for brand visibility" "…every day we can tell our story" "It is very good that we have a channel where to communicate… We have seen that [posts] receive a lot of likes	Visibility		
"… we use social media as a complementary marketing media, and also in order to interact with the customers" "… I think it really is the interaction with the customer interface that is very valuable, from the ivory tower it is very difficult to do this, we need to know what people really think about our products" "…if someone posts us, we do open the dialogue…"	Interactivity		
"…the dealers without physical stores… you kind of create the customer streams to both sides" "…we spend hours and hours sitting at the bar counters with our distributors" "this is a network business, and we need to be there"	Networking/dealers and potential customers	Expansion of effective resources	Social media
"…small firm with a small budget" "In social media… there is reasonable cost in trying to reach even larger target groups" "lowering the costs"	Affordability		
"…information drifts to us from all over the world" "At any time, we can ask the barrel owners if we need further information, for example, on making whiskey" "… it is extremely important to learn if there are any weak spots, any specific problems, any wishes where to place logos, etc. … people has accepted our products well, and as a token, they provide us with lengthy messages" "… you get feedback all the time and you need to study it constantly and react to it"	Market knowledge		
"… we use social media as a complementary marketing media, and also in order to interact with the customers" "…we do not rely solely on digital marketing. One has to be versatile what comes to the use of marketing media…	Role in marketing	Social media use	

Quotes from data	First-order concepts	Second-order themes	Aggregate dimensions
"… Facebook is the main channel… Instagram and Twitter" "We need to use different channels, we can't rely on one channel reaching people in every country"	(Multi)channel approach		
"…to dedicate one person solely in digital marketing feels from time to time a big investment" "…we do not have too much time to spend on social media … a small firm has a small marketing budget, gaining a visibility is more challenging for a small firm compared to a large counterpart" "… having such social media … tempt users with emotionally attractive contents, this really requires delving, time and money"	Resource requirements	Resources allocated for social media	
"…We do see all the possibilities to communicate using customers' own language … the workload is not in balance with the possible benefits" "We wish to provide this to Europeans in their own languages" "Different channels for different countries – not yet anyway…we would need employees for that"	Activity type		
"… it has brought some sensitivity in marketing.. you need to be pretty careful"	Experiences	Learning as a means to develop social media use	Learning

References

Agnihotri, R., Dingus, R., Hu, M. Y., & Krush, M. T. (2016). Social media: Influencing customer satisfaction in B2B sales. *Industrial Marketing Management, 53*, 172–180.

Andzulis, J. M., Panagopoulos, N. G., & Rapp, A. (2012). A review of social media and implications for the sales process. *Journal of Personal Selling & Sales Management, 32*(3), 305–316.

Arenius, P., Sasi, V., & Gabrielsson, M. (2006). Rapid internationalization enabled by the Internet: The case of a knowledge-intensive company. *Journal of International Entrepreneurship, 3*, 279–290.

Aspelund, A., Koed Madsen, T., & Moen, Ø. (2007). A review of the foundation, international marketing strategies, and performance of international new ventures. *European Journal of Marketing, 41*(11/12), 1423–1448.

Barashi, R. (2012). The impact of using social networking site (SNS) on small and medium enterprises (SMEs) comparing to large enterprises. Flinders University—Adelaide, Australia.

Barrutia, J. M., & Echebarria, C. (2007). A new internet driven internationalisation framework. *The Service Industries Journal, 27*(7), 923–946.
Batra, R., & Keller, K. L. (2016). Integrating marketing communications: New findings, new lessons, and new ideas. *Journal of Marketing, 80*(6), 122–145.
Bell, J. (1995). The internationalization of small computer software firms: A further challenge to "stage" theories. *European Journal of Marketing, 29*(8), 60–75.
Bianchi, C., & Mathews, S. (2016). Internet marketing and export market growth in Chile. *Journal of Business Research, 69*(2), 426–434.
Brouthers, K. D., Geisser, K. D., & Rothlauf, F. (2016). Explaining the internationalization of ibusiness firms. *Journal of International Business Studies, 47*(5), 513–534.
Buhalis, D., & Foerste, M. (2015). SoCoMo marketing for travel and tourism: Empowering co-creation of value. *Journal of Destination Marketing & Management, 4*(3), 151–161.
Cao, Y., Ajjan, H., Hong, P., & Le, T. (2018). Using social media for competitive business outcomes: An empirical study of companies in China. *Journal of Advances in Management Research, 15*(2), 211–235.
Coulter, K. S., Bruhn, M., Schoenmueller, V., & Schäfer, D. B. (2012). Are social media replacing traditional media in terms of brand equity creation? *Management Research Review, 35*(9), 770–790.
Coviello, N., & Munro, H. (1997). Network relationships and the internationalisation process of small software firms. *International Business Review, 6*(4), 361–386.
Dahnil, M. I., Marzuki, K. M., Langgat, J., & Fabeil, N. F. (2014). Factors influencing SMEs adoption of social media marketing. *Procedia-Social and Behavioral Sciences, 148*, 119–126.
Davidson, E., & Vaast, E. (2010, January). Digital entrepreneurship and its sociomaterial enactment. In *2010 43rd Hawaii International Conference on System Sciences* (pp. 1–10). IEEE.
De Vries, L., Gensler, S., & Leeflang, P. S. (2012). Popularity of brand posts on brand fan pages: An investigation of the effects of social media marketing. *Journal of Interactive Marketing, 26*(2), 83–91.
Demil, B., & Lecocq, X. (2010). Business model evolution: In search of dynamic consistency. *Long Range Planning, 43*(2–3), 227–246.
Dinner, I. M., van Heerde, H. J., & Neslin, S. A. (2014). Driving online and offline sales: The cross-channel effects of traditional, online display, and paid search advertising. *Journal of Marketing Research, 51*(5), 527–545.
Durkin, M., McGowan, P., & McKeown, N. (2013). Exploring social media adoption in small to medium-sized enterprises in Ireland. *Journal of Small Business and Enterprise Development, 20*(4), 716–734.
Eisenhardt, K. M. (1989). Building theories from case study research. *Academy of Management Review, 14*(4), 532–550.
Erdoğmuş, İ. E., & Cicek, M. (2012). The impact of social media marketing on brand loyalty. *Procedia-Social and Behavioral Sciences, 58*, 1353–1360.
Felix, R., Rauschnabel, P. A., & Hinsch, C. (2017). Elements of strategic social media marketing: A holistic framework. *Journal of Business Research, 70*, 118–126.
Fraccastoro, S., & Gabrielsson, M. (2018, January). Effects of social media usage on the speed of international growth of an international new venture. In *Proceedings of the 51st Hawaii International Conference on System Sciences*.
Gabrielsson, M., & Gabrielsson, P. (2011). Internet-based sales channel strategies of born global firms. *International Business Review, 20*(1), 88–99.
Ghodeswar, B. M. (2008). Building brand identity in competitive markets: A conceptual model. *Journal of Product & Brand Management, 17*(1), 4–12.
Gioia, D. A., Corley, K. G., & Hamilton, A. L. (2013). Seeking qualitative rigor in inductive research: Notes on the Gioia methodology. *Organizational Research Methods, 16*(1), 15–31.
Giones, F., & Brem, A. (2017). Digital technology entrepreneurship: A definition and research agenda. *Technology Innovation Management Review, 7*(5), 44–51.

Gopinath, S., Thomas, J. S., & Krishnamurthi, L. (2014). Investigating the relationship between the content of online word of mouth, advertising, and brand performance. *Marketing Science, 33*(2), 241–258.

Guesalaga, R. (2016). The use of social media in sales: Individual and organizational antecedents, and the role of customer engagement in social media. *Industrial Marketing Management, 54*, 71–79.

Gustafsson, V., & Khan, M. S. (2017). Monetising blogs: Enterprising behaviour, co-creation of opportunities and social media entrepreneurship. *Journal of Business Venturing Insights, 7*, 26–31.

Haapanen, L., Juntunen, M., & Juntunen, J. (2016). Firms' capability portfolios throughout international expansion: A latent class approach. *Journal of Business Research, 69*(12), 5578–5586.

Hanna, R., Rohm, A., & Crittenden, V. L. (2011). We're all connected: The power of the social media ecosystem. *Business Horizons, 54*(3), 265–273.

Huotari, L., Ulkuniemi, P., Saraniemi, S., & Mäläskä, M. (2015). Analysis of content creation in social media by B2B companies. *Journal of Industrial & Business Marketing, 30*(6), 761–770.

Jane Hewerdine, L., Rumyantseva, M., & Welch, C. (2014). Resource scavenging: Another dimension of the internationalisation pattern of high-tech SMEs. *International Marketing Review, 31*(3), 237–258.

Kahiya, E. T., & Dean, D. L. (2016). Export stages and export barriers: Revisiting traditional export development. *Thunderbird International Business Review, 58*(1), 75–89.

Kannan, P. K. (2017). Digital marketing: A framework, review and research agenda. *International Journal of Research in Marketing, 34*(1), 22–45.

Kaplan, A. M. (2012). If you love something, let it go mobile: Mobile marketing and mobile social media 4 × 4. *Business Horizons, 55*(2), 129–139. https://doi.org/10.1016/j.bushor.2011.10.009

Karjaluoto, H., Mustonen, N., & Ulkuniemi, P. (2015). The role of digital channels in industrial marketing communications. *Journal of Business & Industrial Marketing, 30*(6), 703–710.

Keller, K. L. (2003). Brand synthesis: The multidimensionality of brand knowledge. *Journal of Consumer Research, 29*(4), 595–600.

Ketokivi, M., & Choi, T. (2014). Renaissance of case research as a scientific method. *Journal of Operations Management, 32*(5), 232–240.

Kietzmann, J. H., Hermkens, K., Mccarthy, I. P., & Silvestre, B. S. (2011). Social media? Get serious! Understanding the functional building blocks of social media. *Business Horizons, 54*(3), 241–251. https://doi.org/10.1016/j.bushor.2011.01.005

Knight, G., Koed Madsen, T., & Servais, P. (2004). An inquiry into born-global firms in Europe and the USA. *International Marketing Review, 21*(6), 645–665.

Knight, G. A., & Cavusgil, S. T. (2004). Innovation, organizational capabilities, and the born-global firm. *Journal of International Business Studies, 35*(2), 124–141.

Krake, F. B. (2005). Successful brand management in SMEs: A new theory and practical hints. *Journal of Product & Brand Management, 14*(4), 228–238.

Kraus, S., Harms, R., & Fink, M. (2010). Entrepreneurial marketing: Moving beyond marketing in new ventures. *International Journal of Entrepreneurship and Innovation Management, 11*(1), 19.

Kraus, S., Palmer, C., Kailer, N., Kallinger, F. L., & Spitzer, J. (2019). Digital entrepreneurship: A research agenda on new business models for the twenty-first century. *International Journal of Entrepreneurial Behavior & Research, 25*(2), 353–375.

Kumar, M. V. S. (2009). The relationship between product and international diversification: The effects of short-run constraints and endogeneity. *Strategic Management Journal, 30*(1), 99–116.

Kumar, V., Choi, J. B., & Greene, M. (2017). Synergistic effects of social media and traditional marketing on brand sales: Capturing the time-varying effects. *Journal of the Academy of Marketing Science, 45*(2), 268–288.

Lamberton, C., & Stephen, A. T. (2016). A thematic exploration of digital, social media, and mobile marketing: Research evolution from 2000 to 2015 and an agenda for future inquiry. *Journal of Marketing, 80*(6), 146–172.

Laurell, H., Achtenhagen, L., & Andersson, S. (2017). The changing role of network ties and critical capabilities in an international new venture's early development. *International Entrepreneurship and Management Journal, 13*(1), 113–140.

Lecerf, M.-A. (2012). Internationalization and innovation: The effects of a strategy mix on the economic performance of French SMEs. *International Business Research, 5*(6), 2–13.

Leonardi, P. M., & Vaast, E. (2017). Social media and their affordances for organizing: A review and agenda for research. *Academy of Management Annals, 11*(1), 150–188.

Mathews, S., Bianchi, C., Perks, K. J., Healy, M., & Wickramasekera, R. (2016). Internet marketing capabilities and international market growth. *International Business Review, 25*(4), 820–830.

McDougall, P. P., Shane, S., & Oviatt, B. M. (1994). Explaining the formation of international new ventures: The limits of theories from international business research. *Journal of Business Venturing, 9*(6), 469–487.

Michaelidou, N., Siamagka, N. T., & Christodoulides, G. (2011). Usage, barriers and measurement of social media marketing: An exploratory investigation of small and medium B2B brands. *Industrial Marketing Management, 40*(7), 1153–1159.

Miller, K. D., Fabian, F., & Lin, S. J. (2009). Strategies for online communities. *Strategic Management Journal, 30*(3), 305–322.

Monaghan, S., Tippmann, E., & Coviello, N. (2019). Born digitals: Thoughts on their internationalization and a research agenda. *Journal of International Business Studies, 5*(1), 1–12.

Muntinga, D. G., Moorman, M., & Smit, E. G. (2011). Introducing COBRAs: Exploring motivations for brand-related social media use. *International Journal of Advertising, 30*(1), 13–46.

Nakara, W. A., Benmoussa, F. Z., & Jaouen, A. (2012). Entrepreneurship and social media marketing: Evidence from French small business. *International Journal of Entrepreneurship and Small Business, 16*(4), 386–405.

Nambisan, S. (2017). Digital entrepreneurship: Toward a digital technology perspective of entrepreneurship. *Entrepreneurship Theory and Practice, 41*(6), 1029–1055.

Neti, S. (2011). Social media and its role in marketing. *International Journal of Enterprise Computing and Business Systems, 1*(2), 1–15.

Ojala, A., Evers, N., & Rialp, A. (2018). Extending the international new venture phenomenon to digital platform providers: A longitudinal case study. *Journal of World Business, 53*(5), 725–739.

Okazaki, S., & Taylor, C. R. (2013). Social media and international advertising: Theoretical challenges and future directions. *International Marketing Review, 30*(1), 56–71.

Oviatt, B. M., & McDougall, P. P. (1994). Toward a theory of international new ventures. *Journal of International Business Studies, 25*(1), 45–64.

Patton, M. Q. (2002). *Qualitative research and evaluation methods*. Thousand Oaks, CA: Sage.

Petersen, B., Welch, L. S., & Liesch, P. W. (2002). The Internet and foreign market expansion by firms. *Management International Review, 42*(2), 2–22.

Rapp, A., Beitelspacher, L. S., Grewal, D., & Hughes, D. E. (2013). Understanding social media effects across seller, retailer, and consumer interactions. *Journal of the Academy of Marketing Science, 41*(5), 547–566.

Shaheer, N. A., & Li, S. (2020). The CAGE around cyberspace? How digital innovations internationalize in a virtual world. *Journal of Business Venturing, 35*(1).

Shih, C. (2009). *The Facebook era: Tapping online social networks to build better products, reach new audiences, and sell more stuff*. Upper Saddle River, NJ: Prentice Hall.

Siamagka, N., Christodoulides, G., Michaelidou, N., & Valvi, A. (2015). Determinants of social media adoption by B2B organizations. *Industrial Marketing Management, 51*, 89–99.

Sigfusson, T., & Chetty, S. (2013). Building international entrepreneurial virtual networks in cyberspace. *Journal of World Business, 48*(2), 260–270.

Sinkovics, N., Sinkovics, R., & Jean, R. J. B. (2013). The Internet as an alternative path to internationalization? *International Marketing Review, 30*(2), 130–155.

Stallkamp, M., & Schotter, A. P. (2018). Platforms without borders? The international strategies of digital platform firms. *Global Strategy Journal*, 1–23. https://doi.org/10.1002/gsj.1336

Sussan, F., & Acs, Z. J. (2017). The digital entrepreneurial ecosystem. *Small Business Economics, 49*(1), 55–73.

Thackeray, R., Neiger, B. L., Hanson, C. L., & McKenzie, J. F. (2008). Enhancing promotional strategies within social marketing programs: Use of Web 2.0 social media. *Health Promotion Practice, 9*(4), 338–343.

Tsimonis, G., & Dimitriadis, S. (2014). Brand strategies in social media. *Marketing Intelligence & Planning, 32*(3), 328–344.

Vadana, I. I., Torkkeli, L., Kuivalainen, O., & Saarenketo, S. (2019). The internationalization of born-digital companies. In *The changing strategies of international business* (pp. 199–220). Cham, Switzerland: Palgrave Macmillan.

Wang, W. Y., Pauleen, D. J., & Zhang, T. (2016). How social media applications affect B2B communication and improve business performance in SMEs. *Industrial Marketing Management, 54*, 4–14.

Zahoor, S. Z., & Qureshi, I. H. (2017). Social media marketing and brand equity: A literature review. *IUP Journal of Marketing Management, 16*(1), 47.

Zolkepli, I. A., & Kamarulzaman, Y. (2015). Social media adoption: The role of media needs and innovation characteristics. *Computers in Human Behavior, 43*, 189–209.

Part IV
Social Media in Entrepreneurship Research: Where Could We Go?

Chapter 9
The Devil on the Entrepreneur's Shoulder: Analyzing the Relationship Between Moral Disengagement, Founders' Motives, and Unethical Behavior of Entrepreneurs on Social Media

Christian V. Baccarella, Christian W. Scheiner, and Felix Diehlmann

Abstract For quite some time now, research has discussed the importance of social media in the corporate context. Due to their simplicity and cost efficiency, social media applications are also particularly attractive for entrepreneurs. However, studies on social media have mainly concentrated on the benefits. Besides the many advocated advantages of social media, there are also many critical issues which can lead to negative consequences for users. Recent corporate social media–related scandals illustrate this and sparked a public discourse regarding ethically appropriate behavior of companies on social media. Using social media in an inappropriate way can have devastating consequences for a company, which can be especially fatal for young ventures. This chapter seeks to explore why especially entrepreneurs may lower their moral standards on social media and behave unethically. We find that the concept of moral disengagement can explain this negative behavior. We also find that entrepreneurs' attention to economic goals is positively related to moral disengagement, whereas entrepreneurs' attention to ethical responsibilities is negatively related to moral disengagement. We discuss implications for theory, practice, and future research.

Keywords Dark side · Entrepreneurial motives · Mediation · Moral disengagement · Social networking sites · Regression · Unethical behavior

C. V. Baccarella (✉)
Friedrich-Alexander-Universität Erlangen-Nürnberg, Nuremberg, Germany
e-mail: christian.baccarella@fau.de

C. W. Scheiner
Universität zu Lübeck, Lübeck, Germany

Christian-Albrechts-Universität zu Kiel, Kiel, Germany

F. Diehlmann
Oliver Wyman, Munich, Germany

L. Schjoedt et al. (eds.), *Understanding Social Media and Entrepreneurship*,
Exploring Diversity in Entrepreneurship,
https://doi.org/10.1007/978-3-030-43453-3_9

9.1 Introduction

The rise of social media has profoundly changed not only the way we as individuals communicate with each other but also how we live and work together as a society (Baccarella, Wagner, Kietzmann, & McCarthy, 2020). Next to the significant changes that social media has on our personal lives, they of course also mean a paradigm shift for the "business world". For quite some time now, research has therefore discussed the importance of social media in the corporate context (e.g., Scheiner, 2015; Wagner, Baccarella, & Voigt, 2017). Opportunities stemming from using social media include, for example, the potential to increase brand awareness as well as having a possibility to target specific customers/groups to promote products and services (Kumar, Bezawada, Rishika, Janakiraman, & Kannan, 2016). Social media applications are rather easy to use and they are relatively cost-efficient (Kaplan & Haenlein, 2010). The seeming simplicity and cost efficiency are compelling reasons that make social media applications also a particularly attractive choice for entrepreneurs, because capital and liquidity constraints are major obstacles for these young ventures (e.g., Blanchflower & Oswald, 1998; Evans & Jovanovic, 1989; Markman & Baron, 2003). Moreover, social media offers a variety of benefits for entrepreneurs that help them to better manage their business activities. Using social media applications can, for example, help entrepreneurs to directly and efficiently manage their network of corporate stakeholders (Smith & Brock Smith, 2019) or can help to gain legitimacy in the marketplace by reducing the uncertainty regarding their organization and their product offerings (Fischer & Reuber, 2014; Singh, Tucker, & House, 1986). Consequently, the utilization of social media applications has become an integral part in the management and communication repertoire of entrepreneurial firms (Olanrewaju, Hossain, Whiteside, & Mercieca, 2020).

The use of social media is, however, a double-edged sword. In addition to the many advantages that social media offer, research has increasingly started to highlight their "darker" side (Baccarella, Wagner, Kietzmann, & McCarthy, 2018). Recent corporate social media–related scandals have shown the downside of social media usage and sparked a public discourse regarding ethically appropriate behavior of companies on social media. For example, in order to engage their users, the popular video chat app Snapchat published an advertisement asking: "would you rather 'slap Rihanna' or 'punch Chris Brown'?" The advertisement was a reference to the case of domestic violence of Rihanna's former boyfriend Chris Brown in 2009 (Beaumont-Thomas, 2017). Not surprisingly, the advertisement caused a public outcry. Although Snapchat withdrew the advertising again shortly after it was published, the young company almost lost $800 million of its market value (Valinsky, 2018). This example shows clearly that using social media in an inappropriate way can have devastating consequences for a company, which can be particularly fatal for young ventures (Berthon, Pitt, Plangger, & Shapiro, 2012). In order to prevent these fatal consequences, entrepreneurs must be fully aware in which situation they can make the best use of social media and in which situations it is more advisable to think twice. The mentioned example (and several other examples of unethical or at least questionable behavior of entrepreneurs on social media) illustrates that entrepreneurs show behavior on social media that may not necessarily meet their moral standards. The question remains as to why this might be particularly relevant for and prevalent among entrepreneurs.

Similar to social media, entrepreneurship can also be understood as a social phenomenon (Smith & Brock Smith, 2019). Entrepreneurs' activities significantly impact both their personal and their corporate environment (Salaff & Greve, 2013). Moreover, due to the close bond between the founder and the company, entrepreneurs set the guidelines and the direction for a company's actions (Baum & Locke, 2004) and have thus an enormous effect on the company's culture. Subsequently, employees' behavior is determined by the example that entrepreneurs set for them each and every day (Barnard, 1962). One explanation why especially entrepreneurs might behave unethically on social media can therefore be found in the entrepreneurs' motives and goals that drive them to start, operate, and further grow their companies (Baron, Zhao, & Miao, 2014). These motives may also translate into the overall behavior and mindsets within their companies. It is thus not surprising that research argues that especially startups that demonstrate aggressive behavior are more likely to succeed in the market (Romanelli, 1989). Moreover, research has shown that entrepreneurs not necessarily consider honesty and having a good character as a prerequisite in order to be successful (McClelland, 1987). Similarly, there exists evidence that the perception of the attribution of responsibility seems to be distorted for some entrepreneurs. In that context, Baron (1998) showed that entrepreneurs relate success to internal causes, while negative outcomes are attributed to external causes. Thus, it is worthwhile to explore why especially entrepreneurs may lower their moral standards on social media. In that vein, it is crucial to find underlying mechanisms or theoretical lenses to look through that might help to explain such behavior.

One theoretical lens that might be particularly suited for understanding the underlying mechanisms of unethical behavior of entrepreneurs on social media is the concept of moral disengagement. Moral disengagement can explain why we disregard our own ethical standards in a particular context (Bandura, 1990). This concept has received increasing research attention in recent years (e.g., Baron et al., 2014; Detert, Treviño, & Sweitzer, 2008). Despite this growing research attention, little evidence exists which explores the relationship between managers (including entrepreneurs) and moral disengagement (Johnson & Ronald Buckley, 2014). Moreover, due to the influence of individual goals on the probability to morally disengage (Barsky, 2008), entrepreneurs' motives may play a critical role in this context. Therefore, this chapter seeks to explore how entrepreneurs' motives affect their moral disengagement and ultimately unethical behavior on social media. This chapter thus contributes to existing literature by providing first empirical evidence that explores the interplay of entrepreneurs' motives, moral disengagement, and unethical behavior on social media.

This chapter is organized as follows. First, we provide a theoretical background and derive our hypotheses. Afterward, we present the results of our analyses. Finally, we discuss our findings, highlight our limitations, and provide avenues for further research.

9.2 Theoretical Background

9.2.1 The Dark Side of Social Media

Social media has become an indispensable marketing tool for companies of all sizes (e.g., Danaher & Dagger, 2013; Maecker, Barrot, & Becker, 2016). Social media practices generally focus thereby on "creating, enhancing and sustaining ties among brand community members" (Schau, Muñiz, & Arnould, 2009, p. 34). According to Kietzmann, Hermkens, McCarthy, and Silvestre (2011), social media consist of seven functional building blocks: first of all users can decide how much of their *identity* they want to reveal. Social media applications also allow users to *communicate* and *share* content with each other. For example, companies can inform consumers about their current product offerings, prices, and promotions. Furthermore, social media applications help to inform users about the *presence* of others in the "real" as well as in the virtual world. Users are also able to establish online *relationships* and may create *groups and communities*. Finally, the *reputation* of users and brands can be measured by "likes" or "followers."

Research on social media has mainly highlighted the benefits, such as the possibility to increase positive brand evaluations (Kumar et al., 2016) or the possibility to leverage brand communities (Wagner et al., 2017). Due to the possibility of attracting a considerable amount of public attention with relatively little financial resources, social media applications are also particularly attractive for entrepreneurs. On various websites, founders can find help on how to give their company an extra edge with the help of "clever" social media strategies. One website, for example, offers support and claims to know "7 ways to build hype months before your business launches" (Eugenio, 2016).

Besides the many advocated advantages, there are, however, also many critical issues which can lead to negative consequences for social media users. Many of these issues are related to social media's inherent characteristics. For example, communication in the social media sphere is not one-directional like traditional marketing channels, leading to increased coordination effort. Hennig-Thurau et al. (2010, p. 313) even describe social media activities as a "chaotic and interactive game of pinball." Based on the already mentioned seven functional building blocks of social media, Baccarella et al. (2018) discuss the "dark side of social media." They emphasize social media's duality, which means that positive aspects of social media can backfire and turn into the opposite. For example, it is widely common that social media apps track the location of their users in order to provide their services. The popular app Uber also needs to track the location of their users and drivers in order to make sure that they can locate each other. In 2016, however, it became public that

Uber employees used this same location data of their customers to spy on ex-partners and celebrities without asking for their permission (Hern, 2016). This example illustrates that the "darkness" or "brightness" of social media usage depends largely on the specific context social media applications are used and on the concrete goals that social media users aim for. Or in other words, every social media app has a silver lining.

In order to further understand why individuals and especially entrepreneurs show "dark behavior" on social media, it is important to find a suitable theoretical lens to look through. Therefore, the next section introduces the concept of moral disengagement in order to understand and to further explore unethical behavior of entrepreneurs on social media.

9.2.2 Moral Disengagement and Unethical Decision-Making

Paulhus and Williams (2002) coined the term "dark trait" to highlight three prominent malevolent personalities: subclinical narcissism, subclinical psychopathy, and Machiavellianism. While subclinical narcissism delineates the degree to which a person shows grandiosity, superiority, entitlement, and dominance, subclinical psychopathy comprises character elements such as low levels of empathy and anxiety or thrill-seeking and impulsivity (Paulhus & Williams, 2002). Machiavellianism, as the third trait, generally describes a manipulative personality. Despite their inherent differences, Paulhus and Williams (2002) argue that all three traits share self-promotion, emotional coldness, duplicity, and aggressiveness. Although some voices claim that malevolent traits may be more common among entrepreneurs (Forbes, 2016), evidence is missing that entrepreneurs actually possess more frequently a dark personality than the average population. In addition to the fact that research on personality traits among entrepreneurs in general has yet failed to come to universal results, we decided to focus on the "why" in order to further understand the reasons why entrepreneurs may refrain from their moral standards when it comes to the usage of social media.

Following social cognitive theory, people continuously monitor and evaluate their conduct against their own (moral) standards and given situational ramifications (Bandura, 1986; Bandura, Barbaranelli, Caprara, & Pastorelli, 1996). When a behavior seems to be in contradiction to one's own moral standards, an anticipatory self-sanctioning occurs and motivates people to adjust their behavior accordingly. However, as self-reactive influences need to be activated, individuals can disengage from their self-regulatory system (Bandura et al., 1996). As a result, the combination of a selective activation and disengagement of the self-regulation enables individuals to perform ethical and unethical behavior without any feeling of guilt (Bandura et al., 1996). This deactivation process is called moral disengagement. Bandura (1990) emphasizes that moral disengagement is not restricted to extraordinary circumstances. These mechanisms can occur in "everyday situations in which regular people routinely perform activities that further their interests but have injurious human effects" (Bandura, 1990, p. 162).

Bandura (1986) distinguishes eight disengagement mechanisms which occur at different points in the process of self-regulation. *Moral justification*, *euphemistic language*, and *advantageous or palliative comparison* form the first set of mechanisms and focus on the reprehensible conduct itself. All three mechanisms allow people to justify their behavior in the service of moral ends (Bandura, 1986). Hence, the conduct is not evaluated as immoral (Bandura, 1999). In case of *moral justification*, inhumane actions are made socially and personally acceptable by regarding the social and moral purposes. Masking questionable activities is called *euphemistic language*. *Advantageous or palliative comparison* makes it possible to put own actions into a better light although they still remain inhumane (Bandura, 1986; Bandura & Jourden, 1991).

Displacement of responsibility and *diffusion of responsibility comprise the second set.* These mechanisms distort or obscure the relationship between actions and effects (Bandura, 1986). *Displacement of responsibility allows* individuals to not feel responsible for their actions, because they experience pressure or because their actions are dictated. *Diffusion of responsibility occurs* especially in group decision-making. Here, the exercise of moral control is weakened as people do not hold themselves personally accountable for their conduct.

Individuals are also able to morally disengage by *disregarding or distorting consequences* themselves. As a result, the third set includes the mechanisms that lead individuals to misinterpret or ignore the consequences of their actions (Bandura, 1986).

The last element in the process of self-regulation centers on the victim (Bandura, 1986). Through *dehumanization*, other persons are regarded as subhuman objects which allows for actions of inhumane conduct without self-censure. In case of *attribution of blame*, individuals regard themselves as innocent because they are driven to behave unethically through compulsive provocation.

In the following, we will argue how moral disengagement can explain unethical behavior of entrepreneurs on social media.

9.3 Development of Hypotheses

Based on the notion of moral disengagement, individuals perform actions that they normally would morally disapprove. Moral disengagement has already been linked to unethical decision-making in different contexts. Detert et al. (2008), for example, found that college students' moral disengagement leads to unethical behavior such as cheating. According to a study conducted by Moore, Detert, Treviño, Baker, and Mayer (2012), employees' unethical behavior depended on their individual level of moral disengagement.

In the context of entrepreneurship, Baron et al. (2014) linked Chinese entrepreneurs' moral disengagement to unethical decision-making. One explanation may be that entrepreneurs tend to identify strongly with their own companies (Cardon, Zietsma, Saparito, Matherne, & Davis, 2005), and this strong identification can drive individuals to behave unethically (Chen, Chen, & Sheldon, 2016; Umphress & Bingham, 2011). Moreover, entrepreneurs are under a lot of pressure to be successful (e.g., Evans & Jovanovic, 1989; Markman & Baron, 2003). The already mentioned mechanisms of moral disengagement can therefore increase the likelihood to lower their moral standards in certain situations.

This present chapter focuses on unethical behavior in the social media environment. Due to the anonymity and the de-linking of action and consequence on social media, entrepreneurs may underrate the severity of their actions. Thus, it may be likely that moral disengagement will be high in a social media context, because usual moral standards may not apply. This is also emphasized by a study of Naquin, Kurtzberg, and Belkin (2010) that found that individuals are more likely to engage unethically via email than via pen and paper. Moreover, entrepreneurs may "construct" their own reality that will help them legitimize and justify their own actions. This sense-making and justification process may be based on their expectations and motivations (Sonenshein, 2007). For example, it would be easier for entrepreneurs to justify unethical behavior on social media if they feared that their previously set goals were in danger or if their business was not developing as expected. In addition to this, entrepreneurs are often characterized as overoptimistic and goal-oriented (Cassar, 2010). Taken together, we assume that it is possible that entrepreneurs may construct their own reasoning when they find themselves in situations where their set goals compete with their ethical standards and that they might ultimately choose to reach the goals; although this might lead to unethical behavior. Thus, we hypothesize:

> H1: Entrepreneurs' moral disengagement is positively related to unethical behavior on social media.

Entrepreneurs start a business due to different reasons. Some entrepreneurs are driven by financial gains, a few want to serve their community, and others simply "want to make the world a better place" (Fauchart & Gruber, 2011). Generally, entrepreneurs can be clustered into two groups. First, entrepreneurs found new ventures for economic reasons (Fauchart & Gruber, 2011). Second, they may be driven by social reasons to create "social value for the public good" (Austin, Stevenson, & Wei-Skillern, 2006, p. 2) as their primary purpose. Thus, we focus on these two main motives that mainly guide entrepreneurs' behavior: attention to economic goals and attention to ethical responsibilities.

Entrepreneurs who are driven by economic success will mainly see the positive financial outcomes of their decisions, although they might be morally and ethically questionable. Barsky (2008) argues that organizational goal setting has an impact on unethical behavior. Difficult to reach and specific outcome performance goals increase the likelihood of unethical behavior and moral disengagement, especially if individuals are highly committed to achieving these goals. Moreover, entrepreneurs are under a lot of pressure to be financially successful since they have the responsibility for the whole business (Alstete, 2008). They thus need to be driven by concrete financial goals in order to secure the longtime survival of their firms. Therefore, attention to economic goals could be a reason why entrepreneurs might lower their moral standards in particular contexts and behave unethically.

On the contrary, entrepreneurs who want to contribute to society may pay closer attention to their ethical responsibilities. These entrepreneurs will not focus on maximizing their profit but rather want to "give something back" and want to be perceived positively by their peers (Fauchart & Gruber, 2011). In that case, it is very likely that their generally higher moral awareness may lead to lower levels of moral disengagement (Moore, 2008) and ultimately to a lower likelihood to behave unethically. Thus, we hypothesize:

> H2: Entrepreneurs' attention to economic goals is positively related to moral disengagement.

> H3: Entrepreneurs' attention to ethical responsibilities is negatively related to moral disengagement.

It has been argued that moral disengagement meditates the relationship between founders' motives and unethical decision-making in the context of social media (Scheiner, Krämer, & Baccarella, 2016). Entrepreneurs' motives will affect moral disengagement which will in turn affect their behavior on social media. Greater attention to economic goals will thus lead to unethical behavior on and through social media. On the contrary, a higher degree of attention to ethical responsibility will decrease the probability of unethical behavior in social media through moral disengagement.

In accordance with the previous hypotheses, we therefore state:

> H4a: Moral disengagement mediates the positive relationship between entrepreneurs' attention to economic goals and the tendency for unethical behavior on social media.

> H4b: Moral disengagement mediates the negative relationship between entrepreneurs' attention to ethical responsibilities and the tendency for unethical behavior on social media.

Figure 9.1 summarizes the proposed hypotheses in our conceptual model.

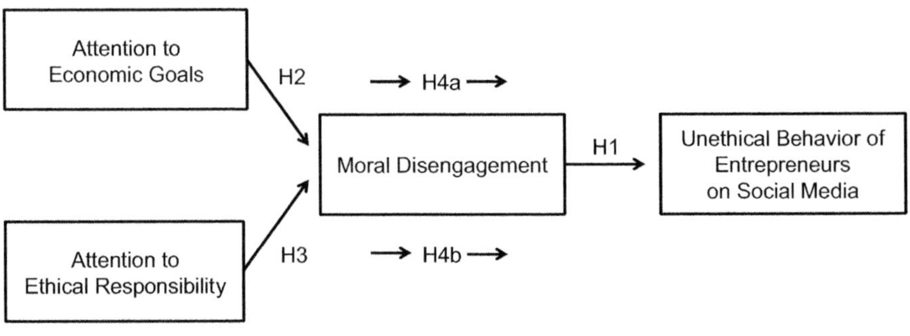

Fig. 9.1 Conceptual model

9.4 Method

9.4.1 *Data Collection and Sample*

In order to answer our hypotheses, we created a database of German startups that were founded after 2010 and which served as the basis for this chapter. In total, the database included 580 young ventures. After creating the database, most startups were directly contacted by phone. The goal thereby was to get a personal email address and to establish a personal relationship to increase the likelihood of participation of the respective entrepreneurs in the survey. After receiving an email address, a personalized link to the online questionnaire was sent out. Additionally, a non-personalized link to the questionnaire was placed on social media pages such as the German career-oriented social networking site XING (www.xing.de). Moreover, the questionnaire was sent to a German university's entrepreneurship center that distributed the link among its members.

Of the 580 entrepreneurs we reached out to, 191 started the online questionnaire and 106 completed it. In addition, 25 entrepreneurs completed the survey via the non-personalized link. After eliminating surveys with missing data, responses from 108 participants were used for our analysis. In line with previous research on entrepreneurship, most participants are male (74%) (Parker & Belghitar, 2006), and 72% have a university degree. The average firm age was 2.5 years and 74% of the startups employed less than ten employees. Eighty-seven of the 108 companies reported revenues of less than 2 million Euros in the last fiscal year.

9.4.2 *Measures*

9.4.2.1 Unethical Behavior of Entrepreneurs on Social Media

Due to the fact that there is no existing scale that measures unethical behavior on social media, we developed an index to capture unethical conduct on social media. Respondents had to evaluate on a 7-point Likert scale how likely their company would engage in 21 different "dark" social media behavioral activities. Each of these activities was discussed with several social media experts to guarantee a realistic setting. All items can be found in Appendix A. In order to analyze the tendency of unethical behavior on social media platforms, an average score of the 21 items was created. The items loaded between 0.48 and 0.84, and the alpha coefficient for this measure was with 0.95 very high (Cortina, 1993).

9.4.2.2 Moral Disengagement

Moral disengagement was captured by using Moore et al.'s (2012) widely used measure. The 8-item scale captures an entrepreneurs' propensity to morally disengage. Answers of the 7-point Likert scale ranged from 1 (strongly agree) to 7 (strongly disagree). Sample items are "It is okay to spread rumors to defend those you care about" and "Taking something without the owner's permission is okay as long as you're just borrowing it." In order to make the analysis easier to understand, all items were reverse-coded afterwards. Subsequently, the value 7 shows a high likelihood to morally disengage. As already proposed by Bandura et al. (1996), moral disengagement should be measured as a single higher-order concept. Therefore, responses of the eight items were averaged in order to create an overall measure of moral disengagement (see also Detert et al., 2008). All items loaded sufficiently with the lowest value being 0.48 (Costello & Osborne, 2005). The alpha reliability coefficient for this measure was 0.84 and therefore above the desired value of 0.7 (Cortina, 1993).

9.4.2.3 Attention to Economic Goals and Attention to Ethical Responsibilities

Carroll (1979) divided the responsibilities of a company into four major aspects: discretionary, ethical, legal, and economic responsibilities. Six years later, Aupperle et al. (1985, p. 455) used this model to develop a measure to "assess orientations toward social responsibility of corporate executives." Since then, the measure has been applied in various studies (e.g., Agle & Mitchell, 1999; Ibrahim & Angelidis, 1995) and was therefore used for the empirical part of this chapter as well. The purpose of our measure is to capture the attention entrepreneurs pay to economic goals and to ethical responsibilities. Respondents allocated ten points according to their economic and ethical responsibilities. This measure uses an ipsative scale. Ipsative scales have several advantages: they reduce common method bias and socially desirable answers, and in comparison to Likert scales, respondents have to prioritize their answers (Stevens, Moray, & Bruneel, 2015). Moreover, ipsative scales are especially suitable for the comparison of "intraindividual differences" (Baron, 1996). Cronbach's alpha for the economic dimension ($\alpha = 0.55$) is fairly low but is still acceptable for ipsative scales (Cortina, 1993). The reliability of the ethical dimension was with a value of $\alpha = 0.17$ very low. However, ipsative scales require respondents to allocate a certain amount of points to different statements, which means that some statements get very low scores. Therefore, it is not surprising that internal consistency values are generally very low for ipsative scales.

9.4.2.4 Control Variables

In order to make sure that no other factors would influence the variance of our dependent variables, we additionally captured four control variables. The control variables are gender, hierarchy level, startup size, and founding year. Gender was measured as a dichotomous variable (0 = female and 1 = male). Since not all respondents were the founders, a dichotomous control variable (0 = non-founder and 1 = founder) was introduced. One mechanism through which moral disengagement occurs is displacement of responsibilities (Bandura et al., 1996). Subsequently, the probability to morally disengage might increase with the number of employees. Therefore, a dichotomous variable was entered which separates companies with 9 or less employees (1) and companies with 10 or more employees (0). Moore (2008) pointed out that moral disengagement manifests itself over time in organizations. Subsequently, the founding year was entered into each regression model as a control variable. Companies which were founded in 2013 or earlier were assigned a "0," while the startups which were founded between 2014 and 2016 were coded as "1."

9.5 Results

First, standard deviations and correlations of our variables were analyzed. The results are shown in Table 9.1. The bivariate correlations between the founders' motives, moral disengagement, and unethical behavior on social media are all in the predicted direction.

In order to check our first three hypotheses, regression analyses were conducted. For that purpose, five models were calculated. The first model included the relationship between the control variables and unethical behavior of entrepreneurs on social media. Model 2 tests the first hypothesis: the relationship between moral disengagement and unethical behavior on social media. Model 3 again included our control variables with moral disengagement as our dependent variable. In model 4 and 5, we analyzed the effects of attention to economic goals and attention to ethical responsibilities on moral disengagement. Finally, the mediation effects stated in hypotheses 4a and 4b were tested by using the SPSS macro PROCESS by Hayes (2013). This macro uses bootstrapping analysis and is considered to be more accurate than, for example, the Sobel (1982) test (Zhao, Lynch Jr., & Chen, 2010).

Models 1 and 2 are shown in Table 9.2. The control variables do not affect unethical behavior on social media. The highly significant positive effect of moral disengagement on unethical behavior is shown in model 2 ($B = 0.26$; SE = 0.08; $p = 0.00$). Therefore, hypothesis 1 is supported.

Table 9.3 includes models 3, 4, and 5. Model 3 shows that all control variables are not significant (dependent variable, moral disengagement). As predicted, the attention to economic goals is significantly positively related to moral disengagement ($B = 0.19$; SE = 0.08; $p = 0.02$). The results of model 5 show a significant negative relationship between attention to ethical responsibilities and moral

Table 9.1 Means, standard deviations, and bivariate correlations

	Mean	SD	1	2	3	4	5	6	7
1. Gender	0.74	0.44	–						
2. Founder	0.69	0.46	0.53**	–					
3. Startup size	0.74	0.44	0.37**	0.62**	–				
4. Founding year	0.64	0.48	0.26**	0.34**	0.48**	–			
5. Attention to economic goals	3.32	1.30	0.23*	0.08	0.14	0.17	–		
6. Attention to ethical responsibilities	2.24	0.79	−0.18	0.09	−0.04	−0.13	−0.58**	–	
7. Moral disengagement	2.16	1.03	0.10	0.06	−0.01	0.02	0.24*	−0.29**	–
8. Unethical behavior on social media	1.72	0.88	0.03	0.09	0.13	0.08	0.24*	−0.14	0.30**

$n = 108$
SD standard deviation
$^{*}p < 0.05$, $^{**}p < 0.01$

disengagement ($B = -0.40$; SE = 0.13; $p = 0.00$). Thus, the results provide evidence for our hypotheses 2 and 3.

The results of the mediation analyses are shown in Table 9.4. Attention to economic goals has a direct effect on unethical behavior on social media, and the bootstrapped 95% confidence interval of the indirect effect does not include zero (LLCI = 0.01, ULCI = 0.10). Subsequently, moral disengagement partially mediates the relationship.

In case of the attention to ethical responsibilities, there is no direct effect on unethical behavior on social media. However, as in the previous analysis, the bootstrapped 95% confidence interval does not include zero (LLCI = −0.19, ULCI = −0.03). As a result, there is a full mediation effect between attention to ethical responsibilities and unethical behavior on social media through moral disengagement. Thus, hypotheses 4a and 4b are supported by the results mentioned above.

9.5.1 Additional Analyses

Research increasingly focuses on the role of gender in entrepreneurship (e.g., Marlow & Patton, 2005). For example, Wilson et al. (2004) found evidence for gender-related differences regarding entrepreneurial self-efficacy and entrepreneurial intentions. Similarly, a study by Humbert and Drew (2010) found that male and female entrepreneurs significantly differ in regard to the factors that motivate them to found a business. More specifically, they reveal that generating greater income is significantly more important for male entrepreneurs than for female entrepreneurs. Therefore and despite the fact that gender differences

Table 9.2 Test of H1

	DV = Unethical behavior on social media			
	Model 1		Model 2	
	B	SE	*B*	SE
Gender	−0.06	0.23	−0.12	0.22
Founder	0.05	0.26	0.02	0.25
Startup size	0.22	0.27	0.28	0.26
Founding year	0.04	0.20	0.03	0.20
Moral disengagement			0.26**	0.08
R^2	0.02		0.11	
Adj. R^2	−0.02		0.07	
F	0.44		2.51*	

$n = 108$
DV dependent variable, *B* regression coefficient, *SE* standard error
*$p < 0.05$, **$p < 0.01$

Table 9.3 Test of H2 and H3

	DV = Moral disengagement					
	Model 3		Model 4		Model 5	
	B	SE	*B*	SE	*B*	SE
Gender	0.21	0.27	0.07	0.27	0.01	0.27
Founder	0.14	0.30	0.21	0.30	0.37	0.30
Startup size	−0.23	0.31	−0.26	0.31	−0.28	0.30
Founding year	0.05	0.24	−0.01	0.23	−0.04	0.23
Attention to economic goals			0.19*	0.08		
Attention to ethical responsibilities					−0.40**	0.13
R^2	0.01		0.07		0.10	
Adj. R^2	−0.02		0.02		0.06	
F	0.36		1.51		2.24	

$n = 108$
DV dependent variable, *B* regression coefficient, *SE* standard error
*$p < 0.05$, **$p < 0.01$

were not the initial motivation for our chapter – we additionally ran two mediation analyses with gender as the independent variable, attention to economic goals and attention to ethical responsibilities as mediators, and unethical behavior of entrepreneurs on social media as the dependent variable. Table 9.5 shows the outcomes of our analyses. It is interesting to note that our results support existing findings that male entrepreneurs consider financial goals significantly more important than female entrepreneurs. Although gender has no direct effect on unethical behavior of entrepreneurs on social media, we find a significant indirect effect of gender on unethical behavior through attention to economic goals. However, we could not find an indirect effect of gender on unethical behavior through attention to ethical responsibilities.

Table 9.4 Test of H4a and H4b

DV = Unethical behavior on social media				
MV = Moral disengagement				
	Effect	SE	LLCI	ULCI
Attention to economic goals	0.04	0.02	0.01	0.10
Attention to ethical responsibilities	−0.09	0.04	−0.19	−0.03

Bootstrapping with 5000 iterations
DV dependent variable, *MV* mediating variable, *SE* standard error, *LLCI* lower-level confidence interval, *ULCI* upper level confidence interval

Table 9.5 Results of additional mediation analyses

Mediator model I	*B*	SE	*t*	R^2
DV: Attention to economic goals				0.05
Gender	0.69	0.28	2.46*	
DV: Unethical behavior on social media				0.06
Gender	−0.05	0.19	−0.28	
Attention to economic goals	0.17	0.07	2.56*	
Mediator model II				
DV: Attention to ethical responsibilities				0.03
Gender	−0.32	0.17	−1.84	
DV: Unethical behavior on social media				0.02
Gender	0.01	0.20	0.06	
Attention to ethical responsibilities	−0.16	0.11	−1.44	
Indirect effects	Effect	SE		95% CI
Gender → economic goals → unethical behavior	0.12	0.06		0.01, 0.26
Gender → ethical responsibilities → unethical behavior	0.05	0.05		−0.02, 0.16

Bootstrapping with 5000 iterations, $*p < 0.05$
DV dependent variable, *SE* standard error, *CI* confidence interval

9.6 Discussion

9.6.1 Theoretical Contributions

Our chapter has several theoretical implications that contribute to existing research. First, this is the first study which analyzes the relationship between entrepreneurial motives, moral disengagement, and unethical behavior of entrepreneurs in the context of social media. Due to the still growing importance of social media marketing not only for entrepreneurs, this chapter contributes to existing literature in this field. Because of financial constraints and a limited visibility in the market (Markman & Baron, 2003), entrepreneurs might be particularly tempted to behave unethically on social media. We were able to show that moral disengagement is a suitable perspective that can explain entrepreneurs' unethical behavior on social media.

Second, we further help to uncover the mechanisms that help to explain unethical behavior on social media. The tendency to engage in unethical conduct largely depends on the context we find ourselves in. A central reason why unethical behavior might be especially present in the context of social media may be due to social media's inherent characteristics. For example, the perceived anonymity in the social media sphere may lead individuals to feel safe from potential prosecution (Naquin et al., 2010). The concept of moral disengagement includes a similar explanation for why individuals lower their moral standards in certain situations. Moreover and as already suggested by Baron et al. (2014), we show that founders' motives can explain why entrepreneurs behave unethically also in the context of social media.

Third, we contribute to existing literature by linking entrepreneurs' motives to unethical behavior on social media. Entrepreneurs seek to satisfy intrinsic as well as extrinsic goals. On the one hand, they are motivated by generally achieving superior financial success. However, they are also driven by providing security and autonomy for themselves and their families (Kuratko, Hornshy, & Naffziger, 1997). Our chapter shows that their motives can explain why they behave unethically on social media. This relationship is mediated by moral disengagement.

Finally, we shed further light on the role of gender in the context of the dark side of social media in entrepreneurship. Although we did not intend to focus on gender-related differences in this regard, our additional analyses offer interesting insights that might be especially suitable for future research projects. In line with the study by Humbert and Drew (2010), we find evidence that male entrepreneurs are especially motivated by financial goals. More interestingly, we find that this mediates the relationship between gender and unethical behavior on social media. Thus, this finding could motivate future work regarding the relationship between gender, the darks side of social media, and entrepreneurship.

9.6.2 Practical Implications

Social media is increasingly important for the success of new ventures. A sound social media strategy can increase a firm's sales and profits. For example, adequately integrating social networking sites such as Facebook or Instagram in the marketing strategy of a company can increase brand awareness and can help to promote products and services (Kumar et al., 2016). However, unethical behavior on social media can be a major threat for the whole company and can negatively influence the company–consumer relationship if unethical conduct is found.

Therefore, companies should set up a clear set of rules and guidelines for the use of social media (Shu, Gino, & Bazerman, 2011). Entrepreneurs need to know which behavior on social media is acceptable and ethically justifiable. Such guidelines should be developed in an inclusive rule-forming process. Entrepreneurs as well as their employees should be sensitized regarding the concrete consequences of their behavior on social media (Baccarella et al., 2019). Although shown behavior on social media may be based on well-intended objectives, it is necessary to make aware the potential negative consequences of such actions for other social media users. Even the discussions about ethical behavior on social media can increase moral awareness (Butterfield, Trevin, & Weaver, 2000). Thus, entrepreneurial firms need to set up control mechanisms and need to actively integrate discussions about "good" behavior on social media into their everyday activities to minimize the risks of engaging in unethical conduct on social media platforms.

9.6.3 Limitations and Further Research

Our chapter has two main limitations that, however, offer avenues for further research. First, we looked through the lens of moral disengagement to explore unethical behavior on social media. However, there might be other explanations. For example, a lot of research has focused on entrepreneurial passion, i.e., an "entrepreneur's intense affective state accompanied by cognitive and behavioral manifestations of high personal value" (Chen, Yao, & Kotha, 2009, p. 201). The concept of entrepreneurial passion explains the deep identification of founders with their own ventures (Cardon et al., 2005). On the one hand, entrepreneurial passion will guarantee persistence during tough times. On the other hand, this passion can also have detrimental effects. For example, it may cloud entrepreneurs' judgments, which could in turn lead to the underestimation of the probability or the impact of negative outcomes (Cardon et al., 2005; Cardon, Wincent, Singh, & Drnovsek, 2009). Thus, future studies could focus on entrepreneurial orientation to explain unethical behavior on social media.

Second, this chapter has some limitations regarding its empirical part. Unethical behavior greatly depends on the respective context. The items for the measurement of unethical behavior on social media were developed by the authors of this chapter. Although the construct showed very high loadings and sufficient overall reliability, our results need to be replicated and further validated in future studies. Moreover, social desirability might be an issue in our empirical part (Randall & Fernandes, 1991). Participants may answer the way they think they are supposed to answer. Thus, future studies should try to rule out this bias by using other survey forms that do not depend on self-reports. A further limitation of the empirical part is the self-selection bias. This bias occurs when "observed differences in groups are the result of self-selection" (James, 2006, p. 561). Although potential participants were directly contacted to avoid this specific bias, individuals who are less prone to moral disengagement might generally be more willing to participate in such studies. Furthermore, our empirical part might contain a survival bias. Although we contacted mainly startups which were founded less than 3 years ago to reduce this effect, we only reached out to ventures that still exist. In order to generate a non-biased sample, future studies should also include entrepreneurs that stopped being active in the market. Future research could moreover use a longitudinal survey design to find out how the tendency to morally disengage influences the long-term development of young ventures. It would be interesting to explore whether founders with primarily higher levels of moral disengagement will be more successful in the long term.

9.6.4 Concluding Remarks

Research on the dark side of social media is still in its infancy. We are only just beginning to understand the impact that social media has on us as individuals and on our society as a whole. Therefore, more research is necessary that uncovers underlying mechanisms and that explores concrete effects of "dark" social media usage. This chapter focused on the dark side of social media in the field of entrepreneurship. We believe that entrepreneurs are a particularly interesting population to study dark behavior on social media. We were able to show that factors that motivate entrepreneurs ultimately may lead to unethical behavior on social media. In particular, being driven by financial goals may lead entrepreneurs to lower their moral standards and engage in unethical behavior. On the flipside, we could also show that entrepreneurs that cherish ethical responsibilities seem to be less likely to lower their moral standards and behave unethically on social media. Practically as a side result, we also found that male entrepreneurs are more likely to engage in unethical behavior on social media through their attention to economic goals. In sum, we hope that this chapter will serve as a basis for further research at the fascinating intersection of social media and entrepreneurship.

Appendix A

Items used to assess unethical behavior on social media.

How likely is it that you would:

1. Deliberately disseminate misleading information on social media?
2. Put others in a bad light on social media?
3. Compromise others on social media?
4. Engage someone to negatively portray a competitor under false identity on social media (e.g., through negative ratings)?
5. Try to provoke other social media users with negative information about competitors (e.g., to trigger an online firestorm)?
6. Manipulate information about competitors on social media (e.g., on Wikipedia)?
7. Misuse private content of employees on social media sites for corporate purposes?
8. Use data from customers without their consent (e.g., crawling and passing on e-mail addresses)?
9. Disturb competitors' social media sites in a targeted manner (e.g., with false posts)?

10. Pretend ideas from others are your own ideas?
11. Monitor private social media sites of employees without their consent?
12. Use private content from competitors on social media sites for corporate purposes?
13. Use private content from customers on social media sites for corporate purposes?
14. Hire someone to positively promote your company under a false identity on social media?
15. Promote your own company under a false identity (e.g., through positive reviews)?
16. Exploit lack of knowledge of social media users for your own purposes?
17. Insult competitors on social media sites?
18. Disseminate untrue information via social media sites because they have not been previously verified?
19. Exploit customers for own purposes without their knowledge (e.g., use statements for advertising purposes without asking)?
20. Tolerate misconduct by suppliers on social media sites against other companies?
21. Tolerate misconduct by own employees on social media sites against other companies?

References

Agle, B. R., & Mitchell, R. K. (1999). Who matters to CEOs? An investigation of stakeholder attributes and salience, corporate performance, and CEO values. *Academy of Management Journal, 42*(5), 507–525.

Alstete, J. W. (2008). Aspects of entrepreneurial success. *Journal of Small Business and Enterprise Development, 15*(3), 584–594.

Aupperle, K. E., Carroll, A. B., & Hatfield, J. D. (1985). An empirical examination of the relationship between corporate social responsibility and profitability. *The Academy of Managment Journal, 28*(2), 446–463.

Austin, J., Stevenson, H., & Wei-Skillern, J. (2006). Social and commercial entrepreneurship: Same, different, or both? *Entrepreneurship Theory and Practice, 30*(1), 1–22.

Baccarella, C. V., Wagner, T. F., Kietzmann, J. H., & McCarthy, I. P. (2018). Social media? It's serious! Understanding the dark side of social media. *European Management Journal, 36*(4), 431–438.

Baccarella, C. V., Wagner, T. F., Kietzmann, J. H., & McCarthy, I. P. (2020). Averting the rise of the dark side of social media: The role of sensitization and regulation. *European Management Journal, 38*, 3–6. https://doi.org/10.1016/j.emj.2019.12.011

Bandura, A. (1986). *Social foundations of thought & action: A social cognitive theory*. Englewood Cliffs, NJ: Prentice Hall.

Bandura, A. (1990). Mechanisms of moral disengagement. In W. Reich (Ed.), *Origins of terrorism: Psychologies, ideologies, theologies, states of mind* (pp. 161–191). Cambridge, UK: Cambridge University Press.

Bandura, A. (1999). Moral disengagement in the perpetration of inhumanities. *Personality and Social Psychology Review, 3*(3), 193–209.

Bandura, A., Barbaranelli, C., Caprara, G. V., & Pastorelli, C. (1996). Mechanisms of moral disengagement in the exercise of moral agency. *Journal of Personality and Social Psychology, 71*(2), 364–374.

Bandura, A., & Jourden, F. J. (1991). Self-regulatory mechanisms governing the impact of social comparison on complex decision making. *Journal of Personality and Social Psychology, 60*(6), 941–951.

Barnard, C. I. (1962). *The functions of the executive* (15th ed.). Cambridge, MA: Harvard University Press.

Baron, H. (1996). Strengths and limitations of ipsative measurement. *Journal of Occupational and Organizational Psychology, 69*(1), 49–56.

Baron, R., Zhao, H., & Miao, Q. (2014). Personal motives, moral disengagement, and unethical decisions by entrepreneurs: Cognitive mechanisms on the "slippery slope". *Journal of Business Ethics, 128*(1), 1–12.

Baron, R. A. (1998). Cognitive mechanisms in entrepreneurship: Why and when entrepreneurs think differently than other people. *Journal of Business Venturing, 13*(4), 275–294.

Barsky, A. (2008). Understanding the ethical cost of organizational goal-setting: A review and theory development. *Journal of Business Ethics, 81*(1), 63–81.

Baum, J. R., & Locke, E. A. (2004). The relationship of entrepreneurial traits, skill, and motivation to subsequent venture growth. *Journal of Applied Psychology, 89*(4), 587–598.

Beaumont-Thomas, B. (2017, August 17). Chris Brown discusses abuse of Rihanna: "I felt like a monster". *The Guardian*. https://www.theguardian.com/music/2017/aug/17/chris-brown-discusses-abuse-of-rihanna-i-felt-like-a-monster. Accessed 24 November 2019.

Berthon, P. R., Pitt, L. F., Plangger, K., & Shapiro, D. (2012). Marketing meets Web 2.0, social media, and creative consumers: Implications for international marketing strategy. *Business Horizons, 55*(3), 261–271.

Blanchflower, D. G., & Oswald, A. J. (1998). What makes an entrepreneur? *Journal of Labor Economics, 16*(1), 26–60.

Butterfield, K. D., Trevin, L. K., & Weaver, G. R. (2000). Moral awareness in business organizations: Influences of issue-related and social context factors. *Human Relations, 53*(7), 981–1018.

Cardon, M. S., Wincent, J., Singh, J., & Drnovsek, M. (2009). The nature and experience of entrepreneurial passion. *The Academy of Management Review, 34*(3), 511–532.

Cardon, M. S., Zietsma, C., Saparito, P., Matherne, B. P., & Davis, C. (2005). A tale of passion: New insights into entrepreneurship from a parenthood metaphor. *Journal of Business Venturing, 20*(1), 23–45.

Carroll, A. B. (1979). Three-dimensional conceptual model of corporate performance. *Academy of Management Journal, 4*(4), 497–505.

Cassar, G. (2010). Are individuals entering self-employment overly optimistic? An empirical test of plans and projections on nascent entrepreneur expectations. *Strategic Management Journal, 51*(2), 822–840.

Chen, M., Chen, C. C., & Sheldon, O. J. (2016). Relaxing moral reasoning to win: How organizational identification relates to unethical pro-organizational behavior. *Journal of Applied Psychology, 7*(11), 1–30.

Chen, X. P., Yao, X., & Kotha, S. (2009). Entrepreneur passion and preparedness in business plan presentations: A persuasion analysis of venture capitalists' funding decisions. *Academy of Management Journal, 52*(1), 199–214.

Cortina, J. M. (1993). What is coefficient alpha? An examination of theory and applications. *Journal of Applied Psychology, 78*(1), 98–104.

Costello, A. B., & Osborne, J. W. (2005). Best practices in exploratory factor analysis: Four recommendations for getting the most from your analysis. *Practical Assessment, Research & Evaluation, 10*(7), 1–9.

Danaher, P. J., & Dagger, T. S. (2013). Comparing the relative effectiveness of advertising channels: A case study of a multimedia blitz campaign. *Journal of Marketing Research, 50*(4), 517–534.

Detert, J. R., Treviño, L. K., & Sweitzer, V. L. (2008). Moral disengagement in ethical decision making: A study of antecedents and outcomes. *The Journal of Applied Psychology, 93*(2), 374–391.

Eugenio, S. (2016, September 2). 7 ways to build hype months before your business launches. *Entrepeneur*. https://www.entrepreneur.com/article/280830. Accessed 2 October 2019.

Evans, D. S., & Jovanovic, B. (1989). An estimated model of entrepreneurial choice under liquidity constraints. *Journal of Political Economy, 97*(4), 808–827.

Fauchart, E., & Gruber, M. (2011). Darwinians, communitarians, and missionaries: The role of founder identity in entrepreneurship. *Academy of Management Journal, 54*(5), 935–957.

Fischer, E., & Reuber, A. R. (2014). Online entrepreneurial communication: Mitigating uncertainty and increasing differentiation via Twitter. *Journal of Business Venturing, 29*(4), 565–583.

Forbes. (2016, August 30). The world's most successful entrepreneurs definitely have psychopathic tendencies. *Forbes*. https://www.forbes.com/sites/quora/2016/08/30/the-worlds-most-successful-entrepreneurs-definitely-have-psychopathic-tendencies/#a5d5f63753d4t. Accessed 15 August 2019.

Hayes, A. F. (2013). *Introduction to mediation, moderation, and conditional process analysis: A regression-based approach*. New York: Guilford.

Hennig-Thurau, T., Malthouse, E. C., Friege, C., Gensler, S., Lobschat, L., Rangaswamy, A., et al. (2010). The impact of new media on customer relationships. *Journal of Service Research, 13*(3), 311–330.

Hern, A. (2016, December 13). Uber employees "spied on ex-partners, politicians and Beyoncé". *The Guardian*. https://www.theguardian.com/technology/2016/dec/13/uber-employees-spying-ex-partners-politicians-beyonce. Accessed 4 September 2019.

Humbert, A. L., & Drew, E. (2010). Gender, entrepreneurship and motivational factors in an Irish context. *International Journal of Gender and Entrepreneurship, 2*(2), 173–196.

Ibrahim, N. A., & Angelidis, J. P. (1995). The corporate social responsiveness orientation of board members: Are there differences between inside and outside directors? *Journal of Business Ethics, 14*(5), 405–410.

James, H. S. (2006). Self-selection bias in business ethics research. *Business Ethics Quarterly, 16*(4), 559–577.

Johnson, J. F., & Ronald Buckley, M. (2014). Multi-level organizational moral disengagement: Directions for future investigation. *Journal of Business Ethics, 130*(2), 291–300.

Kaplan, A. M., & Haenlein, M. (2010). Users of the world, unite! The challenges and opportunities of social media. *Business Horizons, 53*(1), 59–68.

Kietzmann, J. H., Hermkens, K., McCarthy, I. P., & Silvestre, B. S. (2011). Social media? Get serious! Understanding the functional building blocks of social media. *Business Horizons, 54*(3), 241–251.

Kumar, A., Bezawada, R., Rishika, R., Janakiraman, R., & Kannan, P. K. (2016). From social to sale: The effects of firm generated content in social media on customer behavior. *Journal of Marketing, 80*(1), 7–25.

Kuratko, D. F., Hornshy, J. S., & Naffziger, D. W. (1997). An examination of owner's goals in sustaining entrepreneurship. *Journal of Small Business Management, 35*(1), 24–33.

Maecker, O., Barrot, C., & Becker, J. (2016). The effect of social media interactions on customer relationship management. *Business Research, 9*(1), 133–155.

Markman, G. D., & Baron, R. A. (2003). Person-entrepreneurship fit: Why some people are more successful as entrepreneurs than others. *Human Resource Management Review, 13*(2), 281–301.

Marlow, S., & Patton, D. (2005). All credit to men? Entrepreneurship, finance, and gender. *Entrepreneurship Theory and Practice, 29*(6), 717–735.

McClelland, D. C. (1987). Characteristics of successful entrepreneurs. *The Journal of Creative Behavior, 21*(3), 219–233.

Moore, C. (2008). Moral disengagement in processes of organizational corruption. *Journal of Business Ethics, 80*(1), 129–139

Moore, C., Detert, J. R., Treviño, L. K., Baker, V. L., & Mayer, D. M. (2012). Why employees do bad things: Moral disengagement and unethical organizational behavior. *Personnel Psychology, 65*(1), 1–48.

Naquin, C. E., Kurtzberg, T. R., & Belkin, L. Y. (2010). The finer points of lying online: e-mail versus pen and paper. *The Journal of Applied Psychology, 95*(2), 387–394.

Olanrewaju, A.-S. T., Hossain, M. A., Whiteside, N., & Mercieca, P. (2020). Social media and entrepreneurship research: A literature review. *International Journal of Information Management, 50*, 90–110.

Parker, S. C., & Belghitar, Y. (2006). What happens to nascent entrepreneurs? An econometric analysis of the PSED. *Small Business Economics, 27*(1), 81–101.

Paulhus, D., & Williams, K. (2002). The dark triad of personality: narcissism, machiavellianism, and psychopathy. *Journal of Research in Personality, 36*(6), 556–563.

Randall, D. M., & Fernandes, M. F. (1991). The social desirability response bias in ethics research. *Journal of Business Ethics, 10*(11), 805–817.

Romanelli, E. (1989). Environments and strategies of organization start-up: Effects on early survival. *Administrative Science Quarterly, 34*(3), 369–387.

Salaff, J. W., & Greve, A. (2013). Social networks and family relations in return migration. In C. Kwok-bun (Ed.), *International handbook of Chinese families* (pp. 77–90). New York: Springer.

Schau, H. J., Muñiz, A. M., & Arnould, E. J. (2009). How brand community practices create value. *Journal of Marketing, 73*(September), 30–51.

Scheiner, C. W. (2015). The importance of social media as source of information in the technology identification in dependence of external and internal factors. In G. Meiselwitz (Ed.), *Social computing and social media. SCSM 2014* (Lecture Notes in Computer Science) (Vol. 8531). Cham: Springer.

Scheiner, C. W., Krämer, K., & Baccarella, C. V. (2016). Cruel intentions? – The role of moral awareness, moral disengagement, and regulatory focus in the unethical use of social media by entrepreneurs. In G. Meiselwitz (Ed.), *Social computing and social media. SCSM 2016* (Lecture Notes in Computer Science) (Vol. 9742). Cham: Springer.

Shu, L. L., Gino, F., & Bazerman, M. H. (2011). Dishonest deed, clear conscience: When cheating leads to moral disengagement and motivated forgetting. *Personality & Social Psychology Bulletin, 37*(3), 330–349.

Singh, J., Tucker, D., & House, R. (1986). Organizational legitimacy and the liability of newness. *Administrative Science Quarterly, 31*(2), 171–193.

Smith, C. G., & Brock Smith, J. (2019). Founders' uses of digital networks for resource acquisition: Extending network theory online. *Journal of Business Research*. https://doi.org/10.1016/j.jbusres.2019.07.032

Sobel, M. E. (1982). Asymptotic confidence intervals for indirect effects in structural equation models. *Sociological Methodology, 13*(1982), 290–312.

Sonenshein, S. (2007). The role of construction, intuition, and justification in responding to ethical issues at work: The sensemaking-intuition model. *Academy of Management Review, 32*(4), 1022–1040.

Stevens, R., Moray, N., & Bruneel, J. (2015). The social and economic mission of social enterprises: Dimensions, measurement, validation, and relation. *Entrepreneurship: Theory and Practice, 39*(5), 1051–1082.

Umphress, E. E., & Bingham, J. B. (2011). When employees do bad things for good reasons: Examining unethical pro-organizational behaviors. *Organization Science, 22*(3), 621–640.

Valinsky, J. (2018, March 16). Snapchat stock loses $800 million after Rihanna responds to offensive ad. *CNN*. https://money.cnn.com/2018/03/16/technology/snapchat-stock-rihanna/index.html. Accessed 1 November 2019.

Wagner, T. F., Baccarella, C. V., & Voigt, K.-I. (2017). Framing social media communication: Investigating the effects of brand post appeals on user interaction. *European Management Journal, 35*(5), 606–616.

Wilson, F., Marlino, D., & Kickul, J. (2004). Our entrepreneurial future: Examining the diverse attitudes and motivations of teens across gender and ethnic identity. *Journal of Developmental Entrepreneurship, 9*(3), 177–197.

Zhao, X., Lynch Jr., J. G., & Chen, Q. (2010). Reconsidering Baron and Kenny: Myths and truths about mediation analysis. *Journal of Consumer Research, 37*(2), 197–206.

Chapter 10
In Pursuit of Socioemotional Wealth: The Affordances of Social Media in Family Firms

Shainaz Firfiray and Luis R. Gomez-Mejia

Abstract Social media which is characterized by easily accessible information technology applications has become ubiquitous in a range of organizations. It simultaneously presents both opportunities and challenges for organizations. Social media has influenced many aspects of organizing and has generated new ways of connecting with employees, customers, suppliers, and other stakeholders. Despite the pervasiveness of social media, there is limited understanding on the impact of social media on family firms. In this chapter, we attempt to remedy the absence of theory on the organizational effects of social media use in a family business context. We utilize an affordance lens to explain how social media can offer four types of affordances to family firms that pursue socioemotional objectives – visibility, persistence, editability, and association. Overall, this chapter yields several theoretical contributions to the family business literature and to our understanding of social media affordances in family firms.

Keywords Affordance lens · Amoral familism · Socioemotional wealth · Stakeholder engagement · Transgenerational succession

S. Firfiray (✉)
University of Warwick, Organisation & HRM Group, Warwick Business School, Coventry, UK
e-mail: shainaz.firfiray@wbs.ac.uk

L. R. Gomez-Mejia
Arizona State University, Department of Management, Tempe, AZ, USA
e-mail: luis.gomez-mejia@asu.edu

L. Schjoedt et al. (eds.), *Understanding Social Media and Entrepreneurship*, Exploring Diversity in Entrepreneurship,
https://doi.org/10.1007/978-3-030-43453-3_10

10.1 Introduction

The prevalence of social media across organizations is on the rise as managers are making greater effort to tap into the power of their firms' informal information economies. Social media refers to a relatively new generation of computer-mediated communication tools which offer new capabilities that facilitate broader knowledge sharing within an organization. The term social media refers to "a group of internet-based technologies that allow users to easily create, edit, evaluate, and/ or link to content or to other creators of content" (Majchrzak et al. 2013, p. 38). As of 2019, there were 3.5 billion active social media users worldwide representing approximately 46 percent of the world's population (Datareportal, 2019). Given its reach and influence, the opportunities offered to family businesses by social media are receiving a lot of attention. It is being increasingly recognized that knowing how to exploit the strengths of social media can play a pivotal role in helping a family firm build its unique capabilities.

Several commentators have argued that social media technologies may facilitate communication practices in organizations in ways that contrast with other computer-mediated communication technologies such as email, teleconferencing, and intranets (Grundin, 2006; McAfee, 2006; Steinhuser, Smolnik, & Hoppe, 2011). However, despite the increased diffusion of social media, there is limited understanding within the literature on the implications of these technologies for family firms. It is generally acknowledged that organizational adoption of social media is surpassing theoretical understanding of their use and how they might alter various organizational processes (Raeth, Smolnik, Urbach, & Zimmer, 2009). In this chapter, we utilize an affordance perspective to explain how family firms draw on material features of social media to enhance their socioemotional wealth (SEW). Affordance is defined as the "potential for action that new technologies provide to users" (Leonardi & Vaast, 2017, p. 152). We argue that the affordances of social media can enable family firms to preserve their SEW which is defined as the stock of affect-related value embedded in the family firm that induces family owners to protect and pursue family-centered noneconomic objectives (Gómez-Mejía, Haynes, Nuñez-Nickel, Jacobson, & Moyano-Fuentes, 2007).

10.2 The Use of Social Media in Pursuit of Socioemotional Wealth

To begin with, we need to reflect on the differences between social media technologies and other forms of computer-mediated communication used in organizations. Social media possesses a number of material features that make it dissimilar to other communication technologies that are used in organizations. In contrast to other technologies that are used for organizational communication, social media offers a channel for visible communication about user-generated content (DiMicco, Geyer,

Millen, Dugan, & Brownholtz, 2009; Leonardi & Vaast, 2017; McAfee, 2009). Given that social media offers a unique avenue for communication in organizations, there is growing interest on the ways in which social media within organizations impacts firms and actors within them (Colbert, Yee, & George, 2016). Indeed, social media offers affordances that engender several new phenomena in organizations that can transform the way people work and how organizations organize (Leonardi & Vaast, 2017).

Some studies on social media have attempted to develop frameworks about the consequences of social media use for organizing (Ellison, Gibbs, & Weber, 2015; Leonardi & Barley, 2010; Treem & Leonardi, 2012). There are several reasons it is important for organizational scholars to study the impact of social media technologies. First, the content that is shared on social media is often user-generated which implies that employees are more than ever before gaining a voice within their organizations and have access to platforms where they might share their thoughts, concerns and perceptions. Second, the content shared on social media gains a lot of visibility and can be seen by many people within and beyond the organization. Thus, individuals can now post content and transmit messages in ways that were simply not possible prior to the introduction of social media in organizations.

To date, however, there is little understanding on the implications of social media use for family businesses. In particular, we still know little about how the use of social media within family firms will impact the quality of relationships between people working in the firm in terms of their levels of trust, identification and mutual commitment. Family firms offer a unique contextual setting in which to study use of social media given their focus on family-centered noneconomic objectives in addition to economic goals. It is the pursuance of these family-centered goals referred to as socioemotional wealth that scholars think is the distinguishing feature of family firms (Chua, Chrisman, & De Massis, 2015; Gomez-Mejia, Cruz, Berrone, & De Castro, 2011). Socioemotional wealth (SEW) refers to the nonfinancial endowment of the firm that meets the family's desire to exercise control and influence, fulfills their social and affective needs, addresses the desire for belonging and identity and perpetuates family values and dynasty (Berrone, Cruz, & Gomez-Mejia, 2012; Gómez-Mejía et al., 2007). We argue that social media possesses certain features which can offer affordances to family firms that can help them in pursuing socioemotional objectives.

10.3 An Affordance Lens on the Use of Social Media to Achieve Socioemotional Objectives

Within family businesses, strategic decisions are often based on socioemotional reference points (Berrone, Cruz, Gomez-Mejia, & Larraza-Kintana, 2010; Gomez-Mejia, Cruz, & Imperatore, 2014; Gomez-Mejia, Larraza-Kintana, & Makri, 2003; Gomez-Mejia, Makri, & Kintana, 2010; Gomez-Mejia, Nunez-Nickel, & Gutierrez,

2001) which aim to maximize the family's affective value through the preservation and pursuit of SEW. SEW refers to a range of family-oriented goals that involve meeting the family's affective needs such as identity, family control of the firm and the intention to pass the firm to the next generation (Berrone et al., 2012; Gomez-Mejia, Campbell, Martin, Hoskisson, & Sirmon, 2014). The unique features of social media can offer novel opportunities to family firms in pursuit of their socio-emotional goals. When individuals perceive that certain features of technology can enable them to perform specific actions, the technology is said to provide an "affordance". The affordance perspective is based on the work of ecological psychologist James Gibson (1986) and refers to the opportunity for action that new technologies provide to users (Leonardi & Vaast, 2017). The affordance perspective on use of technology examines the match between people's goals and a technology's material features. Although the materiality of an object is shared by the people who come into contact with it, people's perceptions of affordances of that technology are characteristic of the way they perceive materiality. Therefore, the affordance perspective on technology posits that affordances are not solely in the possession of people or of objects but are present in the relationships between people and the materiality of the objects they encounter. This implies that while the characteristics of social media are relatively stable, the affordances are socially constructed and may differ according to the context (Leonardi & Barley, 2010; Vaast & Kaganer, 2013).

An affordance lens is useful in the context of family firms as it helps us understand how, why and when new technologies such as social media affect organizational action (Faraj & Azad, 2012). Therefore, in adopting an affordance perspective, we could examine how the affordance or opportunities for action offered by social media can be utilized for the attainment of socioemotional goals. Under the affordance lens, technologies such as social media that afford the achievement of socio-emotional goals may be seen as facilitating conditions. Following the framework proposed on social media use by Treem and Leonardi (2012), we discuss the four affordances of social media to explain how family firms engage in creation of SEW: visibility, persistence, editability and association.

10.3.1 Visibility

Visibility is referred to as "the means, methods, and opportunities for presentation" (Bregman & Haythornwaite, 2001, p. 5). Social media provides users the opportunity to make their behaviors, knowledge, and communication networks which were once very hard to see visible to others in the organization. Visibility reflects the amount of effort people must make to locate information. Empirical evidence suggests that if people perceive that information is difficult to access or if they are unaware of the information that exists for them to access, they will likely not seek it out (Brown & Duguid, 2001). There are three types of information or actions that can be made visible through the use of social media in organizations: (1) work behaviors, (2) metaknowledge, and (3) organizational activity streams (Treem &

Leonardi, 2012). Below, we will outline how each of these actions may be used in family firms to pursue SEW goals.

10.3.1.1 Work Behaviors as a Means of Building a Family Identity and Renewing Family Bonds

Social media enables communal sharing of content, allowing contributions to be easily located and viewed by employees (Treem & Leonardi, 2012). Prior studies on the use of internal blogs, wikis, social tagging, and social networking sites at IBM have concluded that social media has helped people to communicate and share ideas across organizational boundaries and noted how comments on blogs could lead to extensive organizational conversations (Farrell, Kellogg, & Thomas, 2008; Treem & Leonardi, 2012).

We argue that sustained organizational communications by employees through social media can help in pursuing SEW goals for the following reasons. First, the visibility of work behaviors through social media can allow employees in family businesses to develop a sense of family identity. Through the use of social media, the founders or earlier generations involved in a family business can share celebrated anecdotes from the firm's history which contributed to their success and sustainability. Discussion of these success stories and the visibility of these behaviors can lead to greater family identification as employees become more aware of the family firm's history, learn to value it, and become more emotionally invested in it (Deephouse & Jaskiewicz, 2013). Second, this type of storytelling can also help in renewal of the family business through succession as younger generations of the owning family can draw inspiration from the accomplishments of previous generations. This can be particularly useful in ensuring transgenerational sustainability as members of the younger generation might be reluctant to query the previous generations about the evolution of their business or have few opportunities to discuss such matters with them. Therefore, work behaviors facilitated by social media can contribute to the perpetuation of family values and strengthen its ability to pass the business to subsequent generations.

10.3.1.2 Metaknowledge as a Mode of Facilitating Opportunity Recognition and Firm Longevity

The visibility of social media also provides metaknowledge about the characteristics of the people working in an organization and gives unique insight into the knowledge they possess (Treem & Leonardi, 2012). Typically, people's metaknowledge is limited to those individuals with whom they are in direct communication (Hollingshead, 1998; Leonardi, 2015). As social media enables people to observe communications of a large group of people and not just those in their close physical proximity (e.g., teammates or people within their informal network), the vicarious learning about who knows what is derived from examination of transparent messages which enable the building of more accurate metaknowledge (Leonardi, 2015).

We argue that this greater accuracy about metaknowledge can facilitate better opportunity recognition through the building of social ties and active knowledge networks. One of the major barriers to knowledge contribution is an individual's belief that their own knowledge is not useful to others at the organization (Leonardi, 2017). This is often referred to as the "curse of knowledge" as when people begin to think that individuals understand something well, they fail to recognize that everyone might not possess this knowledge (Heath & Staudenmayer, 2000) and what they know is unique and different from what others know. Sharing knowledge through social media allows individuals to confirm or disconfirm whether the knowledge they possess is different from the knowledge possessed by others through active feedback seeking. This kind of feedback can also strengthen existing social ties among members of the family and nonfamily system and enable them to recognize opportunities that would have otherwise gone unnoticed. Prior empirical evidence also shows that when metaknowledge is characterized by both correctness (identifying what and whom a co-worker knows) and breadth (the ability to correctly identify not just a few but many workers), it is often related to better team performance on routine tasks (Ren, Carley, & Argote, 2006), higher ability to merge existing ideas into new innovations (Majchrzak, Cooper, & Neece, 2004), reduction in duplication of work across the organization, and several other valuable outcomes. Thus, when users of social media in family firms develop an awareness of the information being exchanged by other users, they will use this information to make inferences that will improve the accuracy of their metaknowledge and will ultimately promote the building of new capabilities. This will also enhance opportunity recognition, business growth, and firm longevity.

10.3.1.3 Organizational Activity Streams as a Means of Exercising Family Influence

Social media offers individuals access to information which enables them to keep track of ongoing organizational activities (Treem & Leonardi, 2012). For instance, one study on the use of social media at HP described a tool that used contributions to blogs, wikis, and social tagging tools to identify popular organizational content, and employees saw this content as a means of orienting themselves to the organization (Brzozowski, 2009). Another study by Yardi, Golder, and Brzozowski (2009) has examined log data on an internal blog for a period of 1 year and found that posting information on social media helped in increasing social recognition within the organization, and lack of recognition diminished subsequent participation.

Likewise, we argue that within a family firm context, keeping informed about the material being posted on social media can enable the owning family to exercise influence by gaining an understanding of the issues that are pivotal to employees working for the firm. Exercising influence through formal authority and control is frequently a challenge in family businesses as it can cause rifts between family and nonfamily employees. Occasionally, such an approach can result in amoral familism (Banfield, 1958) which refers to a reluctance to accept nonfamily employees as legitimate and equal contributors to the success of the family firm. This inability to accept manifests itself in damaged relationships between family and nonfamily employees (Verbeke & Kano, 2012). A more effective way of exercising influence may be achieved by developing an accurate understanding of the cognitive social structure or the network of relationships that prevails in organizations (Krackhardt, 1990). The effective monitoring of social networks is crucial for the success of organizations (Brands, 2013), but even the most perceptive social observers face challenges in accurately discerning their organizational networks given the complexity and dynamism of human relationships that develop in organizations (Janicik & Larrick, 2005; Krackhardt & Kilduff, 1999).

Until the advent of social media and social networking sites, it was very difficult to have oversight of who people were communicating with or how often they were communicating with specific individuals. The use of social media has afforded people the ability to make communication networks public and visible to third parties (Boyd & Ellison, 2007). This allows family firm managers to gain an insight into the issues that are considered important by both family and nonfamily employees as well as how advice and information networks are configured within the organization.

Understanding the issues that are important to family and nonfamily employees through social media can enhance knowledge on how individual outcomes are affected by their surrounding social networks. This is closely intertwined with the social capital perspective which suggests that individuals working together can achieve far more than individuals acting alone (Field, 2008; Putnam, 2000). Relatedly, research utilizing a social network lens has examined how the structure of ties at the network level can influence the success or failure of collective action (Marwell, Oliver, & Prahl, 1988) and people's involvement in collective action (Passy, 2002).This knowledge can help family firms determine expectations about the nature of relationships between individuals, the aspects of social interactions that individuals will pay attention to, and the attributes of others that are meaningful within those interactions (Baldwin, 1992). Hence, obtaining a view of the organization's cognitive social structure, especially its advice networks (Krackhardt, 1990), and keeping track of significant organizational issues can be a source of influence for the owning family and thereby increase its stock of SEW.

10.3.2 Persistence

The persistence of communication is determined by the extent to which information remains in its original form after an individual has concluded his presentation (Bregman & Haythornwaite, 2001; Donath, Karahalios, & Viegas, 1999; Treem & Leonardi, 2012). Social media allows conversations to remain accessible beyond the time they are initially posted, and hence such communication can have consequences long after the messages have been posted. Therefore, persistence of communications paves the way for a variety of new uses and practices. For instance, conversations can be searched, browsed, replayed, reorganized, and recontextualized (Erickson & Kellogg, 2000). This arguably assists in the transmission of complex ideas (Clark & Brennan, 1991) given that a record of prior conversations can allow people to correctly contextualize the information and develop a clearer understanding of the conversations. Treem and Leonardi (2012) have identified three different ways to explain how the affordance of persistence affects organizational action: (1) sustaining knowledge over time, (2) creating robust forms of communication, and (3) growth of content. We argue that these processes will influence the preservation of SEW in family firms through the building of social capital, facilitating better knowledge management, and building legitimacy.

10.3.2.1 Sustaining Knowledge Over Time to Build Binding Social Ties

The persistence of information created and shared on social media allows it to develop and remain accessible at a later point in time (Treem & Leonardi, 2012). For instance, a study by Kolari et al. (2007) on internal blog use at IBM over a 3-year period found that a minority of contributors attracted the majority of attention. However, a major implication of this study was that even if a moderate number of bloggers were no longer active in the network, it would not significantly alter their ability to connect to information of interest on other users' blogs. Similarly, Jackson, Yates, and Orlikowski (2007) also examined internal blog use and participation within the context of a global IT firm and found that greater blog use was not necessary for organizational members to perceive value from the information available. Furthermore, the availability of content on social media can enable individuals to collaborate over a long period of time (Holtzblatt, Damianos, & Weiss, 2010) and can be especially effective in the context of an organizational crisis (Wagner, 2004).

In family firms, this persistence of information on social media can improve collaboration and help in building social capital which can support their longevity. However, few family firms are effectively able to develop their social capital beyond the context of their affective family and kinship networks (Ciravegna, Kano, Rattalino, & Verbeke, 2019). Despite this, family firm scholars have acknowledged the ability to manage stakeholder relationships by using the family firm's social capital as one of the main factors leading to the long-term survival of some family firms (Miller & Le Breton-Miller, 2005; Sharma, 2008). Although family businesses have some unique governance advantages, they are also extremely vulnerable to the effects of "social closure" or a situation in which the family firm gets entrenched in a network of trusted individuals and organizations (Berrone et al., 2010; Stadler, Mayer, Hautz, & Matzler, 2018) at the exclusion of other relevant partners.

The retrievability of information on social media can allow family firms to develop an understanding of the characteristics of a range of stakeholders beyond those who are linked to the family through existing social ties. Family firm owners and managers can identify relevant actors in the evolving environment with whom reciprocal relationships might be established (Kano, 2018) and also assess the relevance of existing linkages in order to determine whether these linkages are helping or hindering the firm's adaptation to its external environment (Seigal, 2007). These efforts are critical for building social capital and enable the intergenerational transmission of governance mechanisms which can potentially help in improving the longevity of family firms.

10.3.2.2 Robustness of Communication as a Means of Facilitating Knowledge Sharing and Strategic Renewal

Robustness of communication refers to "how difficult it is to destroy, compromise, or abandon content" (Treem & Leonardi, 2012, p. 157). It is argued that keeping track of information exchange on social media and recording these interactions can lead to higher social resilience in organizations (Farrell et al., 2008; Treem & Leonardi, 2012), reuse of organizational content (Mejova, Schepper, Bergman, & Lu, 2011), and formation of communities of practice (Muller, 2007). We argue that the robustness of communication on social media can strengthen familiness and knowledge sharing, improve innovation outcomes, and ensure strategic renewal of the family firm.

Familiness is defined as a bundle of unique, inseparable, and synergistic resources and capabilities arising from family involvement in the firm (Habbershon & Williams, 1999). Despite the unique capabilities offered by familiness, the promotion of effective knowledge sharing among employees is a challenging activity for many family firms. While some family firms possess ideal settings for driving innovation, risk-taking and entrepreneurship (Rogoff & Heck, 2003; Zahra, Neubaum, & Larrañeta, 2007), others might stifle such activities (Caberera-Suarez, de Saa-Perez, & Garcia-Almedia, 2001; Schulze, Lubatkin, Dino, & Buchholtz, 2001). For instance, in some family firms, members might intentionally or unintentionally withhold information and knowledge from other members (Zahra et al., 2007) which might lead such firms to overlook alternative views and perspectives (Kellermanns & Eddleston, 2004). Nepotism and amoral familism may also prevent family firms from giving credence to the new or divergent perspectives of nonfamily members (Cruz, Gomez-Mejia, & Becerra, 2010). Furthermore, the unique social structures within family businesses may inhibit open exchange of knowledge. Due to the close kinship ties between family business employees, the exchange of knowledge and decision-making might occur outside normal business hours and make it difficult to capitalize on the knowledge of nonfamily employees.

Social media can overcome these barriers and help family firms develop open and decentralized structures facilitating sharing of knowledge. Although familiness offers valuable, rare, and inimitable resources and capabilities (Ensley & Pearson, 2005; Habbershon, Williams, & MacMillan, 2003), the informal knowledge sharing practices of family firms can occasionally hinder effective information exchange. Nevertheless, the robust nature of communication on social media can strengthen familiness or the structural coupling of the family and business systems in a way that yields an inimitable set of resources that potentially position a family firm for growth and survival (Frank, Lueger, Nosé, & Suchy, 2010; Kraus, Harms, & Fink, 2011). More specifically, in line with the social capital perspective, the ability to keep track of information and prevent it from being compromised can allow family firms to build the structural, relational, and cognitive dimensions of familiness. The structural dimension of familiness allows members of the owning family to build on existing network ties and leverage the value of these ties (Arregle, Hitt, Sirmon, & Very, 2007). The relational dimension refers to the trust, norms, obligations, and the presence of a family identity (Carr, Cole, Ring, & Blettner, 2011). Finally, the cognitive dimension of familiness refers to enduring social understandings which are hard to replicate (Lansberg, 1999). Together, the different dimensions of familiness enhance the efficacy of internal information exchange (Pearson, Carr, & Shaw, 2008). Furthermore, enhanced information exchange facilitates better knowledge sharing which can improve the family firm's capability to transform and exploit knowledge which is critical to enhanced innovation outcomes (Daspit, Long, & Pearson, 2019) and strategic renewal (Augier & Teece, 2009).

10.3.2.3 Content Growth as a Means of Building Legitimacy

The inexhaustible space provided by social media can facilitate the growth of content as information shared can be readily stored, indexed, and utilized for future use. Although one consequence of this boundless storage space is that information may become cumbersome (Treem & Leonardi, 2012), it can also be a useful tool for managing and finding content through filters and search tools. This allows previously created and published content to remain discoverable and accessible for an unlimited period of time (Wagner & Majchrzak, 2006). Thus, social media possesses material capabilities to help distribute positive information widely and durably to a large audience (Vaast & Kaganer, 2013).

The growth of content on social media offers a variety of opportunities to promote a desired image to external audiences and stakeholders. It serves as a dynamic platform for spreading information about a family firm to a large audience, while also allowing for a bidirectional interaction between firms and stakeholders where they can generate, share, recommend, like, or comment on company or user-generated content (Zanon, Scholl-Grissemann, Kallmuenzer, Kleinhansl, & Peters, 2019). Social media sites like Twitter and LinkedIn offer free platforms that let the world know more about family businesses and their key areas of activity. Moreover, if owners or managers of small family businesses want to establish business alliances, it can offer an excellent way of introducing their business and expanding their network. These sites also allow companies to recommend someone as a potential client, visibly build their online reputation, increase transparency, and make it easier to build trust among potential business partners.

The increased space for information afforded by social media can propel a family firm to consider more than its bottom line and extend its objectives to consider its wider impact and legacy. Leveraging themselves on social media can also allow family firms to publicize their involvement in socially responsible causes and help bolster their corporate reputation. Since family owners have a strong sense of emotional attachment to their firm (Berrone et al., 2012), they are usually very concerned about their image and reputation. The importance of preserving a positive image among external stakeholders will arguably lead family firms to exploit the space offered by social media to broadcast their involvement in social practices that improve their legitimacy in the external environment (Cennamo, Berrone, Cruz, & Gomez-Mejia, 2012).

10.3.3 Editability

Editability refers to individual ability to spend time and effort crafting and recrafting content to be posted on social media before it is visible to others (Walther, 1993) or the ability to revise content that has already been communicated (Rice, 1987). Therefore, the individual posting the content maintains some control over the content after it has been posted. This can allow for more focused communication that may enable better comprehension of the material. Thus, editability allows communicators to reflect on the context in which the message is likely to be seen and customize their content accordingly. In line with Treem and Leonardi's (2012) framework, we argue that there are three ways in which editability of content on social media can shape a family firm's pursuit of SEW: a) regulating personal expressions, b) targeting content, and c) the improvement of information quality.

10.3.3.1 Regulating Personal Expressions for Building a Favorable Corporate Image

The editability of content on social media allows users to purposefully control the ways that personal information is shared with others. This is particularly important for family firms because they need to get the message right if they wish to engage effectively with relevant stakeholders. People who are involved in posting information and adding updates on the family business need to be equipped with the right skills not just in using the social media platforms but also what to say, how to present a message, and the values that should be conveyed.

The possibility of editing the content posted on social media sites complements the family firm's ability to ensure the right message is getting across to a range of stakeholders. Since "a positive reputation in the minds of key stakeholders may serve as a form of social insurance, protecting the firm's (and family's) assets in times of crisis" (Dyer & Whetten, 2006, p. 785), it is in the interest of firms to create and maintain a favorable reputation in the marketplace. Maintaining a favorable reputation is a significant concern for family business owners since family firms are cautious not to engage in any activity that might tarnish the good name of the family or reflect on them poorly (Dyer & Whetten, 2006). The editability of content on social media can offer many advantages to family firms that are keen to sustain and project a favorable image such as generating competitiveness, attracting better job applicants, and providing better access to capital markets.

Regulation of personal expressions also enhances a family firm's ability to preserve its SEW as it offers them the opportunity to present themselves in a more favorable light on social media over time. Getting the message right is important to minimize the risk of an undesirable corporate image being conveyed. To ensure that a family firm is able to build a favorable reputation, every post must be planned accordingly and backed with the right information such as the history and values that underpin the family firm and have defined its trajectory. This can facilitate reciprocity between family owners and a wide set of constituencies that form part of their networks. These reciprocal relationships can enhance the family firm's sense of belonging to a community and offer stability to the firm (Miller & Le Breton-Miller, 2005). Therefore, the editability of social media can allow family firms to pursue socioemotional objectives as this places them in a better position to reflect on the content posted and ensure the right values and objectives are communicated.

10.3.3.2 Targeting Content to Improve Social Ties and Ensure Continuity of the Family Firm

Social media users often customize their messages for specific groups of people. Given the degree of editorial control, it is possible for individuals posting content on social media to time when they post information and revise messages based on the feedback received from their audience. Empirical evidence shows that technology is often used to monitor how and when certain groups of people are given access to content posted on social media (Grudin & Poole, 2010; Holtzblatt et al., 2010) so as to ensure greater control on how the content is viewed by others (Treem & Leonardi, 2012). The ability to differentiate content to target specific constituencies can allow family firms to proactively engage with stakeholders and hence forge better social ties.

Family owners exert a lot of influence over a firm's management, and hence their views might be given a lot of credence within a firm (Cennamo et al., 2012; Gomez-Mejia, Larraza-Kintana, Moyano, & Firfiray, 2017; Gomez-Mejia, Neacsu, & Martin, 2019; Gomez-Mejia, Patel, & Zellweger, 2018). However, the owning family often has to tread very cautiously, while trying to convince other influential stakeholders who have a direct financial interest in the firm such as institutional investors, pension fund owners, or banking institutions (La Porta, Lopez-de-Silanes, & Shleifer, 1999). The family business literature acknowledges that proactive stakeholder engagement activities oriented towards these stakeholders can assist controlling family principals to execute strategies aligned with their objectives in a more unconstrained fashion (Cennamo, Berrone, & Gomez-Mejia, 2009). For many family principals, perpetuating the family owner's influence over the firm is the primary method of preserving their SEW. Therefore, efforts directed towards stakeholder management will be underpinned by instrumental motives and target primarily those stakeholder groups that are critical for the continuance and survival of the firm including shareholders, employees, and suppliers (Clarkson, 1995). While this does not imply that family firms will overlook other stakeholders such as the environment, the local community, and the media, they may adopt a different approach in responding to their demands. Therefore, the ability to customize social media content can enable differentiation of family firms' strategies for engaging with key stakeholders and thus help in ensuring the continuity of the firm.

10.3.3.3 Improving Information Quality to Enable New Knowledge Creation and Long-Term Sustainability

Social media enables individuals to edit, modify, and amend organizational content long after it is first posted. The ability to review and alter content is considered valuable by social media users who think it improves collaboration (Danis & Singer, 2008). Editability also enhances a family firm's ability to preserve its SEW as it offers them the opportunity to correct and improve their contributions to social media over time (Vaast & Kaganer, 2013). Furthermore, as individuals continue to amend content, they can collaborate towards new knowledge creation and improve their ability to innovate (Mejova et al., 2011; Ransbotham & Kane, 2011).

The enhanced information quality stemming from social media usage can ensure continuity of the family business through the process of recombinant innovation (Hargadon, 2002). Recombinant innovation is defined as the innovation that arises when knowledge which already exists in organizations is reutilized in novel ways that result in useful changes in products, processes, or services (Majchrzak et al., 2004). More specifically, it involves use of methods through which old ideas can be reconfigured in new ways to craft new ideas (Weitzman, 1998). It has several benefits which include shortening the learning curve by combining known ideas in novel ways, reinterpreting existing ideas in different contexts, sharing of previous experiences beyond organizational boundaries, and ensuring better competitiveness.

Recombinant innovation requires individuals to be cognizant of the existing knowledge within organizations and how it can be combined with other knowledge (Leonardi, 2014). Nevertheless, managing knowledge and ensuring that the right people have access to the right information at the right time is challenging. At a minimum, it involves encouraging people who develop knowledge to share it with others so that people who need it can find it and make use of it (Leonardi, 2017). Despite the value involved in knowledge sharing, the number of people who contribute knowledge to communal systems that might benefit others remains low (Cress, Kimmerle, & Hesse, 2006). However, the effective use of social media can help organizations surmount these barriers to enable the free flow of information. Social media usage can improve the quality of information available to organizations, foster better awareness of the knowledge already possessed by the firm, enable innovation through the recombination of knowledge, promote superior growth, and ensure the long-term sustainability of a family business.

10.3.4 Association

Association refers to "the established connections between individuals, between individuals and content, or between an actor and a presentation" (Treem & Leonardi, 2012, p. 162). There are two main forms of associations in social media. The first type of association refers to a connection between two individuals and is referred to as a social tie. This type of an association implies an explicit relationship of no discernible strength that exists between two individuals. The second form of association refers to the connection between individuals and a piece of information which they may have either created, revised, or recognized.

The social media linkages that tie people to other people, people to content, or content to content can have a significant impact on both users and potential audiences. Prior research has shown that relationships formed through computer-mediated communications can allow individuals to build social capital and support networks (Blanchard & Horan, 1998; DiMaggio, Hargittai, Neuman, & Robinson, 2001; Wellman, Haase, Witte, & Hampton, 2001). Treem and Leonardi (2012) have argued that three different outcomes arise when social media helps in creating an association with other individuals or content: (a) supporting social connections, (b) accessing relevant information, and (c) enabling emergent connections. Below, we discuss how these outcomes might unfold in the context of family businesses.

10.3.4.1 Supporting Social Connections to Facilitate Family Identification and Emotional Attachment

Social media allows individuals a means of making their associations with others more explicit. Often this explicitness is achieved through a signalling of relationships with other people. Prior research has shown that this ability to develop new connections with people has contributed to the development of social capital in organizations, creation of support networks, and a stronger sense of attachment to the organization (Jackson et al., 2007; Steinfield, DiMicco, Ellison, & Lampe, 2009; Treem & Leonardi, 2012). We argue that within a family business context, the connections afforded by social media can contribute to a sense of identification and emotional attachment with the family business.

The affordance of making social connections more explicit allows for the development of a sense of identification within the family firm. Social identity theory posits that the self-concept of a person encompasses not only a personal identity (e.g., one's traits and characteristics) but also a social identity (e.g., the group one belongs to) (Ashforth, Harrison, & Corley, 2008; van Dick et al., 2004). Social identification develops when individuals categorize themselves and others into social categories (e.g., a member of the marketing department in a company). The social identification process enables individuals to make sense of their environment and leads to a sense of belongingness to some social group (Ashforth & Mael, 1989). According to Tajfel (1982), social identification with a group requires people to become more aware of their group membership and learn to value it. The connections afforded by social media that link an individual to other individuals can help both family and nonfamily employees become more aware of their membership within a family firm. By engaging in identity expression through the signalling of relationships, family and nonfamily employees will exchange information that should lead them to value their membership in the family firm and develop a strong sense of identification with the firm. Furthermore, we argue that family and nonfamily employees will over time also become more emotionally attached to the firm. As individuals begin to explicitly indicate their relationships and develop an understanding of the family firm's history and shared experiences, they begin to develop emotional attachment to the firm which can "facilitate self-continuity by connecting a person with a desirable past self (e.g., memories), a present self (me now), or a future self (who I am becoming)" (Kleine, Kleine III, & Allen, 1995, p. 328).

10.3.4.2 Access to Relevant Information to Foster Adaptation and Sustainability

Beyond the creation of individual social ties, ties can also be established between individuals and the content found on social media. Prior research has shown that the linkages between individuals and content can serve as a way for users to determine relationships between content. By establishing linkages between the original source and quality and utility of information, social media may enable better use of content in organizations. We argue that the establishment of ties between individuals and content in family firms will allow for better use of information and organizational adaptation and thus ensure longevity of the firm.

Organizational adaptation is "the ability of an organization to change itself, or the way in which it behaves, in order to survive in the face of external changes which were not predicted in any precise way when the organization was designed" (Tomlinson, 1976, p. 533). Recognizing enablers of dynamic organizational adaptation is essential to business sustainability. This is very relevant in the context of family firms where specific threats to transgenerational succession and survival have long been acknowledged. It is argued that the speed of change in competitive environments can drive firms to develop processes that are geared towards transforming existing capabilities, increasing their strategic adaptiveness, and strengthening their competitive advantage (Eisenhardt & Martin, 2000; Teece, Pisano, & Shuen, 1997). Nevertheless, family influence can occasionally hamper the development of effective processes and knowledge integration. The disagreements which arise due to unrestricted power of family owners and weak systems for addressing conflict (Harvey & Evans, 1994) may make family firms inconducive to knowledge integration and change (Beckhard & Gibb Dyer, 1983; Eddleston & Kellermanns,

2007; Zahra et al., 2007). Such conflicts can be unproductive and undermine the efficiency of an organization, thus reducing the value derived from collaborative efforts (Jehn, 1995). If left unaddressed, relationship conflicts in family firms can decrease mutual understanding, inhibit knowledge exchange, and prevent change even when needed (Kellermanns & Eddleston, 2004). These conflicts can manifest themselves in an unwillingness on the part of family members to share business information with others, which can limit a family firm's growth potential.

For an organization to adapt rapidly to environmental changes, it needs to be flexible. In other words, organizations need to possess a repertoire of organizational and managerial capabilities which enable them to adapt quickly to environmental shifts (Teece et al., 1997). If an organization wishes to adapt to its environment and compete successfully, it should have access to superior information about the environment in which it is operating (Duncan, 1972; Pfeffer & Salancik, 1978). The ability to establish connections between individuals and content on social media can improve access to relevant information and allow for more effective knowledge sharing. Therefore, establishing ties between individuals and content and improving access to relevant information can help family firms overcome barriers to knowledge integration, enhance the family firm's core capabilities, and foster organizational adaptation. Hence, access to relevant information (as well as knowledge of the source and utility of that information) can lead to better decision-making, adaptiveness, greater competitiveness, and long-term sustainability of the family firm.

10.3.4.3 Enabling Emergent Connections to Ensure Survivability

Some features of social media such as rankings and recommendations also facilitate emergent forms of associations. Such features of social media can match users with relevant content and increase opportunities for interaction among users (Dugan, Geyer, & Millen, 2010). For instance, a study by Shami, Ehrlich, Gay, and Hancock (2009) in IBM found that people were more likely to approach those who were active in social media at the company because in their view these users not only signalled expertise but were also more likely to respond to questions. Prior research has shown that the implementation of four different recommender systems in IBM expanded friend networks in different ways (Chen, Geyer, Dugan, Muller, & Guy, 2009), and hence organizations could rely upon different algorithms to support certain connections or find a way to support desired associations (Daly, Geyer, & Millen, 2010). Furthermore, a study by Green, Contractor, and Yao (2006) showed how a social networking application that made emergent associations between individuals and user-generated content triggered cross-functional interactions and knowledge sharing. This increased collaboration took place because once users learned that others were interested in similar topics, they were more willing to work collaboratively to overcome disciplinary differences, even if they did not share common domain knowledge.

Given the prevalence of bifurcation bias or preferential treatment of assets that have affective value for the family firm (Jennings, Dempsey, & James, 2018; Kano

& Verbeke, 2018), ensuring easier access to relevant information and reducing bounded rationality biases are critical for ensuring survivability of the family firm. The SEW perspective on family firms suggests that family firms may be better placed at surviving in the long-term than nonfamily firms given the family members' willingness to steward the firm in the long run (Corbetta & Salvato, 2004; Davis, Schoorman, & Donaldson, 1997) and the desire for transgenerational continuity (Memili, Chrisman, & Chua, 2011; Miller & Le Breton-Miller, 2005). However, the desire for dynastic succession if prioritized indiscriminately can also pose a threat to the survival of a family business (Ciravegna et al., 2019; Kano & Verbeke, 2018). Even if family managers decide to act as stewards of the firm, their inherent bounded rationality and biases in processing information may prevent them from achieving intended pro-organizational outcomes, unless there are mechanisms in place to address information asymmetries. The presence of large amounts of information coupled with affective biases may cloud the judgment of family managers leading to poorer decision-making and lower rates of business survival.

For family firms, these emergent associations supported by social media may allow for better processing of information which can improve the family firm's performance and survivability. Research suggests that one of the main reasons people do not actively seek knowledge within the organization is that they are overloaded with information and they do not have the capacity to process more information (Dabbish & Kraut, 2006). One solution to this problem would be to connect people with relevant information rather than all kinds of information. People will take a look at new information even when they feel overwhelmed, if they think it is valuable for their work (Haas, 2006). The affordances of social media may prove useful in this context. Prior research has shown that user-generated social tags to classify information can assist people in identifying relevant information. For example, when conducting search for information, a study found that employees at IBM reused social tags already in the system and referred to other employees' lists of tags because doing so provided faster access to relevant information than doing a regular search (Millen & Feinberg, 2006). When individuals understand how others tag content and begin to tag content in a similar manner, they can find relevant information a lot faster (Leonardi, 2017). Given the importance of relevant information for organizational adaptation, the emergent connections supported by social media can enable quicker responses to the evolving environment and ensure the survivability of the family firm.

10.4 Conclusion

This chapter has utilized an affordance perspective to explore how family firms can pursue SEW. We have integrated the evidence from the disparate streams of family business and information systems research to show how the four affordances of social media (visibility, persistence, editability, and association) can expand our understanding of the processes through which family firms increase their stock of

SEW. Following Treem and Leonardi's (2012) affordance lens, our analysis suggests that together the different affordances of social media can enable achievement of several socioemotional objectives including identification with the family firm, exercising family influence, transgenerational succession and longevity, creation of strong social ties, and building a favorable reputation among others.

To conclude, empirical research will need to analyze the dynamic interplay between the material features of social media and the family firm context to understand how family firms can continue to preserve their SEW. We also think that an in-depth understanding of the association between use of social media and pursuit of socioemotional goals will help us identify the strategies that can improve the image of family businesses and foster competitiveness, growth, and business sustainability. Although social media has been around for over two decades, it has not found widespread adoption in family businesses. There are certain obvious benefits of social media use to family businesses such as building a favorable reputation, social capital, and strategic alliances. However, the downside of social media cannot be ignored as it requires proactive engagement and constant monitoring to ensure that the identity and competitiveness of the family business continues to thrive.

References

Arregle, J. L., Hitt, M. A., Sirmon, D. G., & Very, P. (2007). The development of organizational social capital: Attributes of family firms. *Journal of Management Studies, 44*, 73–95.

Ashforth, B. E., Harrison, S. H., & Corley, K. G. (2008). Identification in organizations: An examination of four fundamental questions. *Journal of Management, 34*, 325–374.

Ashforth, B. E., & Mael, F. (1989). Social identity theory and the organization. *Academy of Management Review, 14*, 20–39.

Augier, M., & Teece, D. J. (2009). Dynamic capabilities and the role of managers in business strategy and economic performance. *Organization Science, 20*, 410–421.

Baldwin, M. W. (1992). Relational schemas and the processing of social information. *Psychological Bulletin, 112*, 461–484.

Banfield, E. C. (1958). *The moral basis of a backward society*. New York: Free Press.

Beckhard, R., & Gibb Dyer, W. (1983). Managing continuity in the family-owned business. *Organizational Dynamics, 12*, 5–12.

Berrone, P., Cruz, C., & Gomez-Mejia, L. R. (2012). Socioemotional wealth in family firms: Theoretical dimensions, assessment approaches, and agenda for future research. *Family Business Review, 25*, 258–279.

Berrone, P., Cruz, C., Gomez-Mejia, L. R., & Larraza-Kintana, M. (2010). Socioemotional wealth and corporate responses to institutional pressures: Do family-controlled firms pollute less? *Administrative Science Quarterly, 55*, 82–113.

Blanchard, A., & Horan, T. (1998). Virtual communities and social capital. *Social Science Computer Review, 16*, 293–307. https://doi.org/10.1177/089443939801600306

Boyd, D., & Ellison, N. (2007). Social network sites: The role of networked publics in teenage social life. *Journal of Computer-Mediated Communication, 13*, 210–230.

Brands, R. A. (2013). Cognitive social structures in social network research: A review. *Journal of Organizational Behavior, 34*(S1), S82–S103.

Bregman, A., & Haythornwaite, C. (2001). Radicals of presentation in persistent conversation. In *Proceedings of the 34th Annual Hawaii International Conference on System Sciences*. Los Alamitos, CA: IEEE Computer Society Press. https://doi.org/10.1109/HICSS.2001.926499

Brown, J. S., & Duguid, P. (2001). Knowledge and organization: A social-practice perspective. *Organization Science, 12*, 198–213.

Brzozowski, M. J. (2009). WaterCooler: Exploring an organization through enterprise social media. In *Proceedings of the 2009 International Conference on Supporting Group Work* (pp. 219–228). New York: ACM. https://doi.org/10.1145/1531674.1531706

Caberera-Suarez, K., de Saa-Perez, P., & Garcia-Almedia, D. (2001). The succession process from a resource- and knowledge-based view of the family firm. *Family Business Review, 14*, 37–49.

Carr, J. C., Cole, M. S., Ring, J. K., & Blettner, D. P. (2011). A measure of variations in internal social capital among family firms. *Entrepreneurship Theory and Practice, 35*, 1207–1227.

Cennamo, C., Berrone, P., Cruz, C., & Gomez-Mejia, L. R. (2012). Socioemotional wealth and proactive stakeholder engagement: Why family–controlled firms care more about their stakeholders. *Entrepreneurship Theory and Practice, 36*, 1153–1173.

Cennamo, C., Berrone, P., & Gomez-Mejia, L. (2009). Does stakeholder management have a dark side? *Journal of Business Ethics, 89*, 491–507.

Chen, J., Geyer, W., Dugan, C., Muller, M., & Guy, I. (2009). Make new friends, but keep the old: Recommending people on social networking sites. In *Proceedings of the 27th International Conference on Human Factors in Computing Systems* (pp. 201–210). New York: ACM. https://doi.org/10.1145/1518701.1518735

Chua, J. H., Chrisman, J. J., & De Massis, A. (2015). A closer look at socioemotional wealth: Its flows, stocks, and prospects for moving forward. *Entrepreneurship Theory and Practice, 39*, 173–182.

Ciravegna, L., Kano, L., Rattalino, F., & Verbeke, A. (2019). Corporate diplomacy and family firm longevity. *Entrepreneurship Theory and Practice*. https://doi.org/10.1177/1042258719838477

Clark, H. H., & Brennan, S. E. (1991). Grounding in communication. In L. B. Resnick, J. M. Levine, & S. D. Teasley (Eds.), *Perspectives on socially shared cognition* (pp. 127–149). Washington, DC: American Psychological Association.

Clarkson, M. E. (1995). A stakeholder framework for analyzing and evaluating corporate social performance. *Academy of Management Review, 20*, 92–117.

Colbert, A., Yee, N., & George, G. (2016). The digital workforce and the workplace of the future. *Academy of Management Journal, 59*, 731–739.

Corbetta, G., & Salvato, C. (2004). Self-serving or self-actualizing? Models of man and agency costs in different types of family firms: A commentary on "comparing the agency costs of family and non-family firms: Conceptual issues and exploratory evidence". *Entrepreneurship Theory and Practice, 28*, 355–362.

Cress, U., Kimmerle, J., & Hesse, F. W. (2006). Information exchange with shared databases as a social dilemma: The effect of metaknowledge, bonus systems, and costs. *Communication Research, 33*, 370–390.

Cruz, C., Gomez-Mejia, L. R., & Becerra, M. (2010). Perceptions of benevolence and the design of agency contracts: CEO-TMT relations in family firms. *Academy of Management Journal, 53*(1), 69–89.

Dabbish, L. A., & Kraut, R. E. (2006, November). Email overload at work: an analysis of factors associated with email strain. In *Proceedings of the 2006 20th Anniversary Conference on Computer Supported Cooperative Work* (pp. 431–440). ACM.

Daly, E. M., Geyer, W., & Millen, D. R. (2010). The network effects of recommending social connections. In *Proceedings of the Fourth Conference on Recommender Systems* (pp. 301–304). New York: ACM. https://doi.org/10.1145/1864708.1864772

Danis, C., & Singer, D. (2008). A wiki instance in the enterprise: Opportunities, concerns and reality. In *Proceedings of the 2008 Conference on Computer Supported Cooperative Work* (pp. 495–504). New York: ACM. https://doi.org/10.1145/1460563.1460642

Daspit, J. J., Long, R. G., & Pearson, A. W. (2019). How familiness affects innovation outcomes via absorptive capacity: A dynamic capability perspective of the family firm. *Journal of Family Business Strategy, 10*, 133–143.

Datareportal (2019). Digital 2019: Global Digital Overview (https://datareportal.com/reports/digital-2019-global-digital-overview)

Davis, J. H., Schoorman, F. D., & Donaldson, L. (1997). Toward a stewardship theory of management. *Academy of Management Review, 22*, 20–47.

Deephouse, D. L., & Jaskiewicz, P. (2013). Do family firms have better reputations than non-family firms? An integration of socioemotional wealth and social identity theories. *Journal of Management Studies, 50*, 337–360.

DiMaggio, P., Hargittai, E., Neuman, W. R., & Robinson, J. P. (2001). Social implications of the Internet. *Annual Review of Sociology, 27*, 307–336. https://doi.org/10.1146/annurev.soc.27.1.307

DiMicco, J. M., Geyer, W., Millen, D. R., Dugan, C., & Brownholtz, B. (2009). People sensemaking and relationship building on an enterprise social networking site. In *Proceedings of the 42nd Hawaii International Conference on System Sciences*. Los Alamitos, CA: IEEE Computer Society Press. https://doi.org/10.1109/HICSS.2009.343

Donath, J., Karahalios, K., & Viegas, F. (1999). Visualizing conversation. *Journal of Computer-Mediated Communication, 4*(4). Retrieved 19th November, 2019, from https://academic.oup.com/jcmc/article/4/4/JCMC442/4584411

Dugan, C., Geyer, W., & Millen, D. R. (2010). Lessons learned from blog muse: Audience-based inspiration for bloggers. In *Proceedings of the 28th International Conference on Human Factors in Computing Systems* (pp. 1965–1974). New York: ACM. https://doi.org/10.1145/1753326.1753623

Duncan, R. B. (1972). Characteristics of organizational environments and perceived environmental uncertainty. *Administrative Science Quarterly, 17*, 313–327.

Dyer, W., & Whetten, D. (2006). Family firms and social responsibility: Preliminary evidence from the S&P 500. *Entrepreneurship Theory and Practice, 30*, 785–802.

Eddleston, K., & Kellermanns, F. (2007). Destructive and productive family relationships: A stewardship theory perspective. *Journal of Business Venturing, 22*, 545–565.

Eisenhardt, K. M., & Martin, J. A. (2000). Dynamic capabilities: What are they? *Strategic Management Journal, 21*, 1105–1121.

Ellison, N. B., Gibbs, J. L., & Weber, M. S. (2015). The use of enterprise social network sites for knowledge sharing in distributed organizations: The role of organizational affordances. *American Behavioral Scientist, 59*, 103–123.

Ensley, M. D., & Pearson, A. W. (2005). An exploratory comparison of the behavioral dynamics of top management teams in family and nonfamily new ventures: Cohesion, conflict, potency, and consensus. *Entrepreneurship Theory and Practice, 29*, 267–284.

Erickson, T., & Kellogg, W. (2000). Social translucence: An approach to designing systems that support social processes. *ACM Transactions on Computer–Human Interaction, 7*, 59–83. https://doi.org/10.1145/344949.345004

Faraj, S., & Azad, B. (2012). The materiality of technology: An affordance perspective. In P. M. Leonardi, B. A. Nardi, & J. Kalalinkos (Eds.), *Materiality and organizing: Social interaction in a technological world* (pp. 237–258). Oxford: Oxford University Press.

Farrell, R. G., Kellogg, W., & Thomas, J. C. (2008, November). The participatory web and the socially resilient enterprise. Paper presented at the What to Expect from Enterprise 3.0: Adapting Web 2.0 to Corporate Reality workshop at the *2008 Conference on Computer Supported Cooperative Work*, San Diego, CA.

Field, J. (2008). *Social capital* (2nd ed.). New York: Routledge.

Frank, H., Lueger, M., Nosé, L., & Suchy, D. (2010). The concept of "Familiness": Literature review and systems theory-based reflections. *Journal of Family Business Strategy, 1*, 119–130.

Gibson, J. J. (1986). *The ecological approach to visual perception*. Hillsdale, NJ: Lawrence Erlbaum.

Gomez-Mejia, L. R., Campbell, J., Martin, G., Hoskisson, R., & Sirmon, D. (2014). Socioemotional wealth as a mixed gamble: Revisiting family R & D with the behavioural agency model. *Entrepreneurship Theory and Practice, 38*(6), 1351–1374.

Gomez-Mejia, L. R., Cruz, C., Berrone, P., & De Castro, J. (2011). The bind that ties: Socioemotional wealth preservation in family firms. *Academy of Management Annals, 5*, 653–707.

Gomez-Mejia, L. R., Cruz, C., & Imperatore, C. (2014). Financial reporting and the protection of socioemotional wealth in family-controlled firms. *European Accounting Review, 23*(3), 387–403.

Gómez-Mejía, L. R., Haynes, K., Nuñez-Nickel, M., Jacobson, K., & Moyano-Fuentes, J. (2007). Socioemotional wealth and business risks in family-controlled firms: Evidence from Spanish olive oil mills. *Administrative Science Quarterly, 52*, 106–137.

Gomez-Mejia, L. R., Larraza-Kintana, M., & Makri, M. (2003). The determinants of executive compensation in family controlled firms. *Academy of Management Journal, 46*, 226–238.

Gomez-Mejia, L. R., Larraza-Kintana, M., Moyano, J., & Firfiray, S. (2017). Managerial family ties and employee risk bearing: Evidence from Spanish car dealers. *Human Resource Management, 16*(3), 439–453.

Gomez-Mejia, L. R., Makri, M., & Kintana, M. L. (2010). Diversification decisions in family-controlled firms. *Journal of Management Studies, 47*, 223–252.

Gomez-Mejia, L. R., Neacsu, I., & Martin, G. (2019). CEO risk taking and socioemotional wealth: The behavioural agency model, family control and CEO option wealth. *Journal of Management, 44*(3), 972–1000.

Gomez-Mejia, L. R., Nunez-Nickel, M., & Gutierrez, I. (2001). The role of family ties in agency contracts. *Academy of Management Journal, 44*(1), 21–45.

Gomez-Mejia, L. R., Patel, P. C., & Zellweger, T. (2018). In the horns of the dilemma: Socioemotional wealth, financial wealth and acquisitions in family firms. *Journal of Management, 44*(4), 1369–1397.

Green, H. D., Contractor, N., & Yao, Y. (2006, December). C-IKNOW: Cyberinfrastructure knowledge networks on the web: A social network enabled recommender system for locating resources in cyberinfrastructures. Paper presented at the *American Geophysical Union*, San Francisco, CA.

Grudin, J., & Poole, E. S. (2010). Wikis at work: Success factors and challenges for sustainability of enterprise Wikis. In *Proceedings of the 6th International Symposium on Wikis and Open Collaboration*. New York: ACM. https://doi.org/10.1145/1832772.1832780

Grundin, J. (2006). Enterprise knowledge management and emerging technologies. In *Proceedings of the 39th Annual Hawaii International Conference on System Sciences*. Los Alamitos, CA: IEEE Computer Society Press. https://doi.org/10.1109/HICSS.2006.156

Haas, L. (2006). Beauty and the beast: The theory and practice of information integration. In *International Conference on Database Theory* (pp. 28–43). Berlin, Heidelberg: Springer.

Habbershon, T., & Williams, M. (1999). A resource-based framework for assessing the strategic advantages of family firms. *Family Business Review, 12*, 1–22.

Habbershon, T. G., Williams, M., & MacMillan, I. C. (2003). A unified systems perspective of family firm performance. *Journal of Business Venturing, 18*, 451–465.

Hargadon, A. B. (2002). Brokering knowledge: Linking learning and innovation. *Research in Organizational Behavior, 24*, 41–85.

Harvey, M., & Evans, R. (1994). Family business and multiple levels of conflict. *Family Business Review, 7*, 331–348.

Heath, C., & Staudenmayer, N. (2000). Coordination neglect: How lay theories of organizing complicate coordination in organizations. *Research in Organizational Behavior, 22*, 153–191.

Hollingshead, A. B. (1998). Communication, learning, and retrieval in transactive memory systems. *Journal of Experimental Social Psychology, 34*, 423–442.

Holtzblatt, L. J., Damianos, L. E., & Weiss, D. (2010). Factors impeding wiki use in the enterprise: A case study. In *Proceedings of the 28th International Conference Extended Abstracts on Human Factors in Computing Systems* (pp. 4661–4676). New York: ACM. https://doi.org/10.1145/1753846.1754208

Jackson, A., Yates, J., & Orlikowski, W. (2007). Corporate blogging: Building community through persistent digital talk. In *Proceedings of the 40th Annual Hawaii International Conference on System Sciences*. Los Alamitos, CA: IEEE Computer Society Press. https://doi.org/10.1109/HICSS.2007.155

Janicik, G. A., & Larrick, R. P. (2005). Social network schemas and the learning of incomplete networks. *Journal of Personality and Social Psychology, 88*, 348–364.

Jehn, K. A. (1995). A multimethod examination of the benefits and detriments of intragroup conflict. Administrative science quarterly, 256–282.

Jennings, J. E., Dempsey, D., & James, A. E. (2018). Bifurcated HR practices in family firms: Insights from the normative-adaptive approach to stepfamilies. *Human Resource Management Review, 28*, 68–82.

Kano, L. (2018). Global value chain governance: A relational perspective. *Journal of International Business Studies, 49*, 684–705.

Kano, L., & Verbeke, A. (2018). Family firm internationalization: Heritage assets and the impact of bifurcation bias. *Global Strategy Journal, 8*, 158–183.

Kellermanns, F. W., & Eddleston, K. A. (2004). Feuding families: When conflict does a family firm good. *Entrepreneurship Theory and Practice, 28*, 209–228.

Kleine, S. S., Kleine III, R. E., & Allen, C. T. (1995). How is a possession "me" or "not me"? Characterizing types and an antecedent of material possession attachment. *Journal of Consumer Research, 22*, 327–343.

Kolari, P., Finin, T., Lyons, K., Yesha, Y., Yesha, Y., Perelgut, S., et al. (2007). On the structure, properties and utility of internal corporate blogs. In *Proceedings of the International Conference on Weblogs and Social Media*. Menlo Park, CA: AAAI Press.

Krackhardt, D. (1990). Assessing the political landscape: Structure, cognition, and power in organizations. *Administrative Science Quarterly, 35*, 342–369.

Krackhardt, D., & Kilduff, M. (1999). Whether close or far: Social distance effects on perceived balance in friendship networks. *Journal of Personality and Social Psychology, 76*, 770–782.

Kraus, S., Harms, R., & Fink, M. (2011). Family firm research: Sketching a research field. *International Journal of Entrepreneurship & Innovation Management, 13*, 32–47.

Lansberg, I. (1999). *Succeeding generations: Realizing the dream of families in business*. Cambridge, Massachusetts: Harvard University Press.

La Porta, R., Lopez-de-Silanes, F., & Shleifer, A. (1999). Corporate ownership around the world. *Journal of Finance, 54*, 471–517.

Leonardi, P. M. (2014). Social media, knowledge sharing, and innovation: Toward a theory of communication visibility. *Information Systems Research, 25*, 796–816.

Leonardi, P. M. (2015). Ambient awareness and knowledge acquisition: Using social media to learn 'who knows what'and 'who knows whom'. *MIS Quarterly, 39*, 747–762.

Leonardi, P. M. (2017). The social media revolution: Sharing and learning in the age of leaky knowledge. *Information and Organization, 27*, 47–59.

Leonardi, P. M., & Barley, S. R. (2010). What's under construction here? Social action, materiality, and power in constructivist studies of technology and organizing. *Academy of Management Annals, 4*, 1–51.

Leonardi, P. M., & Vaast, E. (2017). Social media and their affordances for organizing: A review and agenda for research. *Academy of Management Annals, 11*, 150–188.

Majchrzak, A., Cooper, L. P., & Neece, O. E. (2004). Knowledge reuse for innovation. *Management Science, 50*, 174–188.

Majchrzak, A., Faraj, S., Kane, G. C., & Azad, B. (2013). The contradictory influence of social media affordances on online communal knowledge sharing. *Journal of Computer-Mediated Communication, 19*, 38–55.

Marwell, G., Oliver, P. E., & Prahl, R. (1988). Social networks and collective action: A theory of the critical mass, III. *American Journal of Sociology, 94*, 502–534.

McAfee, A. (2006). Enterprise 2.0: The dawn of emergent collaboration. *MIT Sloan Management Review, 47*, 19–28.
McAfee, A. (2009). *Enterprise 2.0: New collaborative tools for your organization's toughest challenges*. Boston: Harvard Business School Press.
Mejova, Y., Schepper, K. D., Bergman, L., & Lu, J. (2011). Reuse in the wild: An empirical and ethnographic study of organizational content reuse. In *Proceedings of the 2011 Annual Conference on Human Factors in Computing Systems* (pp. 2877–2886). New York: ACM. https://doi.org/10.1145/1978942.1979370
Memili, E., Chrisman, J. J., & Chua, J. H. (2011). Transaction costs and outsourcing decisions in small-and medium-sized family firms. *Family Business Review, 24*, 47–61.
Millen, D. R., & Feinberg, J. (2006). Using social tagging to improve social navigation. *Proceedings of the Workshop on the Social Navigation and Community-Based Adaption Technologies*. Dublin, Ireland: Springer. Retrieved from http://www.sis.pitt.edu/~paws/SNC_BAT06/proceedings.html
Miller, D., & Le Breton-Miller, I. (2005). *Managing for the long run: Lessons in competitive advantage from great family businesses*. Boston: Harvard Business Press.
Muller, M. (2007). Comparing tagging vocabularies among four enterprise tag-based services. In *Proceedings of the 2007 International Conference on Supporting Group Work* (pp. 341–350). New York: ACM. https://doi.org/10.1145/1316624.1316676
Passy, F. (2002). Social networks matter. But how? In M. Diani & D. McAdam (Eds.), *Social movement analysis: The network perspective*. Oxford: Oxford University Press.
Pearson, A. W., Carr, J. C., & Shaw, J. C. (2008). Toward a theory of familiness: A social capital perspective. *Entrepreneurship Theory and Practice, 32*, 949–969.
Pfeffer, J., & Salancik, G. R. (1978). *The external control of organizations: A resource dependence perspective*. New York: Harper & Row.
Putnam, R. (2000). *Bowling alone: The collapse and revival of American community*. New York: Simon and Schuster.
Raeth, P., Smolnik, S., Urbach, N., & Zimmer, C. (2009). Towards assessing the success of social software in corporate environments. *AMCIS 2009 Proceedings*. Retrieved from http://aisel.aisnet.org/amcis2009/662
Ransbotham, S., & Kane, G. C. (2011). Membership turnover and collaboration success in online communities: Explaining rises and falls from grace in Wikipedia. *MIS Quarterly, 35*, 613–627.
Ren, Y., Carley, K. M., & Argote, L. (2006). The contingent effects of transactive memory: When is it more beneficial to know what others know? *Management Science, 52*, 671–682.
Rice, R. E. (1987). Computer-mediated communication and organizational innovation. *Journal of Communication, 37*, 65–94. https://doi.org/10.1111/j.1460-2466.1987.tb01009.x
Rogoff, E. G., & Heck, R. K. Z. (2003). Evolving research in entrepreneurship and family business: Recognizing family as the oxygen that feeds the fire of entrepreneurship. *Journal of Business Venturing, 18*, 559–566.
Schulze, W. S., Lubatkin, M. H., Dino, R. N., & Buchholtz, A. K. (2001). Agency relationships in family firms: Theory and evidence. *Organization Science, 12*, 99–116.
Seigal, J. (2007). Contingent political capital and international alliances: Evidence from South Korea. *Administrative Science Quarterly, 52*, 621–666.
Shami, N. S., Ehrlich, K., Gay, G., & Hancock, J. T. (2009). Making sense of strangers' expertise from signals in digital artifacts. In *Proceedings of the 27th International Conference on Human Factors in Computing Systems* (pp. 69–78). New York: ACM. https://doi.org/10.1145/1518701.1518713
Sharma, P. (2008). Commentary: Familiness: Capital stocks and flows between family and business. *Entrepreneurship Theory and Practice, 32*, 971–977.
Stadler, C., Mayer, M. C., Hautz, J., & Matzler, K. (2018). International and product diversification: Which strategy suits family managers? *Global Strategy Journal, 8*, 184–207.
Steinfield, C., DiMicco, J. M., Ellison, N. B., & Lampe, C. (2009). Bowling online: Social networking and social capital within the organization. In *Proceedings of the Fourth International Conference on Communities and Technologies* (pp. 245–254). New York: ACM. https://doi.org/10.1145/1556460.1556496

Steinhuser, M., Smolnik, S., & Hoppe, U. (2011). Towards a measurement model of corporate social software success- evidences from an exploratory multiple case study. In *Proceedings of the 44th Hawaii International Conference on System Sciences*. Los Alamitos, CA: IEEE Computer Society Press. https://doi.org/10.1109/hicss.2011.447

Tajfel, H. (1982). Social psychology of intergroup relations. *Annual Review of Psychology, 33*, 1–39.

Teece, D. J., Pisano, G., & Shuen, A. (1997). Dynamic capabilities and strategic management. *Strategic Management Journal, 18*, 509–533.

Tomlinson, R. C. (1976). Organizational design and adaptivity. *Omega, 4*, 527–537.

Treem, J. W., & Leonardi, P. M. (2012). Social media use in organizations: Exploring the affordances of visibility, editability, persistence, and association. *Communication Yearbook, 36*, 143–189.

Vaast, E., & Kaganer, E. (2013). Social media affordances and governance in the workplace: An examination of organizational policies. *Journal of Computer-Mediated Communication, 19*, 78–101.

van Dick, R., Christ, O., Stellmacher, J., Wagner, U., Ahlswede, O., Grubba, C., et al. (2004). Should I stay or should I go? Explaining turnover intentions with organizational identification and job satisfaction. *British Journal of Management, 15*, 351–360.

Verbeke, A., & Kano, L. (2012). The transaction cost economics theory of the family firm: Family–based human asset specificity and the bifurcation bias. *Entrepreneurship Theory and Practice, 36*, 1183–1205.

Wagner, C. (2004). Wiki: A technology for conversational knowledge management and group collaboration. *Communications of the Association for Information Systems, 13*, 265–289. Retrieved from http://aisel.aisnet.org/cais/vol13/iss1/19

Wagner, C., & Majchrzak, A. (2006). Enabling customer-centricity using wikis and the wiki way. *Journal of Management Information Systems, 23*, 17–43.

Walther, J. B. (1993). Impression development in computer-mediated interaction. *Western Journal of Communication, 57*, 381–398. https://doi.org/10.1080/10570319309374463

Weitzman, M. L. (1998). Recombinant growth. *Quarterly Journal of Economics, 113*, 331–360.

Wellman, B., Haase, A. Q., Witte, J., & Hampton, K. (2001). Does the internet increase, decrease, or supplement social capital? Social networks, participation, and community commitment. *American Behavioral Scientist, 45*, 436–455. https://doi.org/10.1177/00027640121957286

Yardi, S., Golder, S. A., & Brzozowski, M. (2009). Blogging at work and the corporate attention economy. In *Proceedings of the 27th International Conference on Human Factor in Computing Systems* (pp. 2071–2080). New York: ACM. https://doi.org/10.1145/1518701.1519016

Zahra, S. A., Neubaum, D. O., & Larrañeta, B. (2007). Knowledge sharing and technological capabilities: The moderating role of family involvement. *Journal of Business Research, 60*, 1070–1079.

Zanon, J., Scholl-Grissemann, U., Kallmuenzer, A., Kleinhansl, N., & Peters, M. (2019). How promoting a family firm image affects customer perception in the age of social media. *Journal of Family Business Strategy, 10*, 28–37.

Index

L. Schjoedt et al. (eds.), *Understanding Social Media and Entrepreneurship*, Exploring Diversity in Entrepreneurship,
https://doi.org/10.1007/978-3-030-43453-3

Printed by Printforce, the Netherlands